Fro...

P O R T A B L E

Aruba

2nd Edition

by Ken Lindley

Here's what critics say about Frommer's:

"Amazingly easy to use. Very portable, very complete."

—*Booklist*

"Detailed, accurate, and easy-to-read information for all price ranges."

—*Glamour Magazine*

Wiley Publishing, Inc.

Published by:

WILEY PUBLISHING, INC.

111 River St.
Hoboken, NJ 07030

ISBN: 0-7645-3876-4
ISSN: 1534-9101

Editor: Marie Morris
Production Editor: Suzanna R. Thompson
Photo Editor: Richard Fox
Cartographer: Elizabeth Puhl
Production by Wiley Indianapolis Composition Services

For information on our other products and services or to obtain technical
support, please contact our Customer Care Department within the U.S. at
800-762-2974, outside the U.S. at 317-572-3993 or fax 317-572-4002.

Wiley also publishes its books in a variety of electronic formats. Some con-
tent that appears in print may not be available in electronic formats.

Manufactured in the United States of America

5 4 3 2

Contents

List of Maps

ABOUT THE AUTHOR

Before finishing graduate school, **Ken Lindley** had lived in Asia and Europe and around the United States. He's spent more than half of his life in New York, but call before dropping by—he's frequently out of town, traipsing the globe from India to Peru to China to Turkey. He's never been anywhere that wasn't interesting in some way (although he does keep a list of extremely dreadful destinations). When he's not on a travel assignment, there's a good chance he'll be on Wall Street, where he writes and edits financial reports for hotshot financial firms. His travel writings have appeared in *Frommer's Caribbean Cruises & Ports of Call,* in *Out & About,* and online at Expedia Travels (ETravels.net).

AN INVITATION TO THE READER

In researching this book, we discovered many wonderful places—hotels, restaurants, shops, and more. We're sure you'll find others. Please tell us about them, so we can share the information with your fellow travelers in upcoming editions. If you were disappointed with a recommendation, we'd love to know that, too. Please write to:

Frommer's Portable Aruba, 2nd Edition
Wiley Publishing, Inc. • 111 River St. • Hoboken, NJ 07030

FROMMER'S STAR RATINGS, ICONS & ABBREVIATIONS

Every hotel, restaurant, and attraction listing in this guide has been ranked for quality, value, service, amenities, and special features using a **star-rating system.** In country, state, and regional guides, we also rate towns and regions to help you narrow down your choices and budget your time accordingly. Hotels and restaurants are rated on a scale of zero (recommended) to three stars (exceptional). Attractions, shopping, nightlife, towns, and regions are rated according to the following scale: zero stars (recommended), one star (highly recommended), two stars (very highly recommended), and three stars (must-see).

In addition to the star-rating system, we also use **seven feature icons** that point you to the great deals, in-the-know advice, and unique experiences that separate travelers from tourists. Throughout the book, look for:

Finds	Special finds—those places only insiders know about
Fun Fact	Fun facts—details that make travelers more informed and their trips more fun
Kids	Best bets for kids and advice for the whole family
Moments	Special moments—those experiences that memories are made of
Overrated	Places or experiences not worth your time or money
Tips	Insider tips—great ways to save time and money
Value	Great values—where to get the best deals

The following **abbreviations** are used for credit cards:

AE	American Express	DISC	Discover	V	Visa
DC	Diners Club	MC	MasterCard		

FROMMERS.COM

Now that you have the guidebook to a great trip, visit our website at **www.frommers.com** for travel information on more than 3,000 destinations. With features updated regularly, we give you instant access to the most current trip-planning information available. At Frommers.com, you'll also find the best prices on airfares, accommodations, and car rentals—and you can even book travel online through our travel booking partners. At Frommers.com, you'll also find the following:

- Online updates to our most popular guidebooks
- Vacation sweepstakes and contest giveaways
- Newsletter highlighting the hottest travel trends
- Online travel message boards with featured travel discussions

Planning Your Trip to Aruba

So many islands, so little time. With all the tropical paradises you could visit, why would you pick Aruba for your Caribbean vacation?

Well, there's the reliably near-perfect weather. If you have only a week away from the job, why not guarantee yourself 7 days of ideal tanning conditions—unwaveringly sunny skies, warm temperatures, and cooling breezes. And because the island's more of a desert than a rainforest, the humidity's low and it hardly ever rains. Hurricanes? Schmurricanes. There's never one within hundreds of miles. Aruba is far south of the tropical-storm belt.

You like beaches? Aruba's got beaches, some of the best in the Caribbean . . . in the world, for that matter. The photos only look as if they've been doctored. What you see is what you get: miles of white, sugary sand; warm, gentle surf; turquoise and aqua seas; and plenty of space.

When you tire of lolling on the beach, there's scuba diving, snorkeling, great windsurfing, and all the other watersports you expect from a sun-and-sea vacation. On land, you can golf, ride a horse, hike, or drive an all-terrain vehicle over the island's wild and woolly outback. Away from the beach, Aruba is a desert island full of cacti, iguanas, and strange boulder formations. Contrasting sharply with the resort area's serene beaches, the north coast features craggy limestone cliffs, sand dunes, and crashing breakers.

And such nice places to stay. You can choose from luxury resorts, all-inclusives, cozy boutique hotels, and modest budget spots. They're all well maintained and chock-full of bells and whistles to meet the whims of most travelers. With all the package tours available, they can be surprisingly affordable, too.

If you're a foodie, you may be surprised at how well you can eat in Aruba. Unlike the generally standard fare in most of the Caribbean, Aruba's culinary offerings are diverse, inventive, and often very good.

Once the sun sets, there's plenty to do besides eat. You can try your luck at one of the island's dozen casinos or take in a live Vegas-style show. Bars, clubs, booze cruises, you name it—if you're looking for a party, you'll find it.

You'll find the overwhelming majority of Arubans to be genuinely friendly and welcoming. Sure, the island's totally dependent on tourism, but nobody learns to be this nice. With little history of racial or cultural conflicts, the island has no cause for animosity. As the license plates say, it's One Happy Island. And though Dutch is the official language, almost everyone speaks English. You'll also hear Spanish and Papiamento, the local tongue (a mix of several European, African, and Native American languages).

If you're concerned about safety, you can relax. Aruba's low crime rate is the envy of nearly every other island in the region. With unemployment over the past few years next to nil, people are too busy working to look for trouble. Where else would you see tourists over 60 and women in their 20s hitchhiking without a qualm? Aruba's boomed in the past couple of decades, and the rapid changes and influx of new people have disturbed the way of life a bit, to the dismay of some locals. But you may find that you feel safer in Aruba than at home.

Enough of the good points. What's the downside? Well, if you're looking to stay in an old, converted, family-run sugar mill or immerse yourself in rich colonial history or pre-Columbian culture, you could do better elsewhere. From day one, Aruba's been pretty much of a backwater. It's still part of the Netherlands, so there's a Dutch influence, which adds a slight European flavor. There are a few small museums that highlight the island's past, and some centuries-old indigenous rock glyphs and paintings. But nobody visits Aruba for culture or history.

The people who do visit, though, come back. Aruba has the highest repeat-visitor rate in the Caribbean; the highest hotel-occupancy figures, too. Honeymooners, families, and couples of all ages and types fill the resorts during the winter high season . . . and in the traditionally quieter summer months as well. More than 60% come from the United States, and a fair number hail from Canada. Others come from Holland and South America, especially nearby Venezuela and Colombia.

The bottom line? Aruba's determined to make sure you have a good time. It's a great place to unwind, and few islands work as hard to make you feel as special and pampered. You'll learn your first Papiamento phrase when you arrive—*bon bini* (welcome!). The last words from your lips as you board your plane back home will probably be in the local dialect too—*masha danki, Aruba* (thank you, Aruba).

Aruba is a tiny island. Only 20 miles long and 6 miles across at its widest point, it's slightly larger than Washington, D.C. It's the westernmost of the Dutch ABC islands—Aruba, Bonaire, and Curaçao—and less than 20 miles north of Venezuela.

On a place as small as Aruba, it's easy to get your bearings, especially since just about everything for tourists centers around the two biggest beaches. Remember Mercury, the messenger god from Roman mythology? Aruba's shaped like his winged foot: toes to the east, heel to the west. Aruba's capital and largest city, **Oranjestad** (pronounced oh-*rahn*-juh-stahd or oh-*rahn*-yay-stahd), is on the island's southern coast, pretty far to the west, where Mercury's heel would be. The island's hotels stretch along the back-to-back shores of **Eagle Beach** and **Palm Beach,** a couple of miles west of Oranjestad, or up the god's Achilles' tendon. One of the island's landmarks, the **California Lighthouse,** stands at the wing on Mercury's foot, while **San Nicolas,** once Aruba's largest city and home of the island's oil refinery, steps on his toes. Between Oranjestad and San Nicolas on the south coast, Savaneta is Aruba's oldest town and major fishing center.

If you're like most visitors, you'll be staying in one of three areas: in Oranjestad, in the Low-Rise hotel area along Eagle Beach, or a little farther from town in the High-Rise hotel area on Palm Beach. The three locations have distinct atmospheres, so where you stay will determine the tone of your vacation. Would you rather be in the city or at the seaside? Are casinos and nightclubs important, or do you prefer quiet strolls along the beach? Are you looking for a casual beach town or a glamorous resort strip?

Let's start in the thick of the action. **Oranjestad** is Aruba's only town of any size or sophistication. If you want an "urban" environment with a variety of restaurants, nightclubs, and casinos, this is the place for you. The whole island has fewer than 90,000 residents, but most seem to live or work around the capital. Its waterfront bustles with cruise ships, yachts, fishing boats, and cargo carriers. Fueled by the boutiques, restaurants, bars, and casinos radiating from the docks, vehicular and pedestrian traffic in town is heavy much of the day and night. Contributing to the congestion, Arubans cruise the main boulevard to see and be seen, giving the strip an *American Graffiti* flavor. Much of the architecture combines Dutch gables and baroque ornamentation with Caribbean colors like pistachio, ochre, pink, and aqua. The result is a sun-drenched gingerbread confection with a touch of theme-park squeaky cleanliness. Walk 5 or 6 blocks away from the waterfront, though, and Oranjestad becomes a nondescript, workaday town with neighborhoods ranging from tony to

Frommer's Favorite Aruba Experiences

Bake on the Beach. This is why you came: powdery white sand, turquoise water, and soothingly monotonous waves. Whether basking at Palm, Eagle, Manchebo, or Druif Beach, close your eyes and feel the stress evaporate. You're a beach potato; use sunscreen or you'll be a fried potato.

Pretend You're Neil Armstrong. Alien boulders and stark terrain mark Aruba's northern coast. The roads are unpaved but easy to navigate in an all-terrain vehicle. You can stop at a lighthouse or an old chapel, but Nature supplies the major attractions.

Get Dirty. If you love the Discovery Channel, spend the better part of a day driving and hiking through expansive Arikok National Park to marvel at Aruba's diverse ecosystems and rural past. Ramble over hills strewn with boulders and cacti, visit old farms (known as *cunucus*), spelunk through caves in search of Indian rock glyphs, and slide down sand dunes. Along the way, you'll meet hummingbirds, hawks, iguanas, goats, and donkeys.

Watch the Sun Rise. Stroll along the beach as the sun rubs its eyes. You and your love will be pretty much by yourselves, except for a few other romantics and the breakfasting pelicans. For an equally serene morning, visit the 80-odd bird species at the Bubali Bird Sanctuary or fall under the trance of the hundreds of flitter-fluttering butterflies at the Butterfly Farm. They're early risers, too.

Try Your Luck at a Casino. Gambling was once Aruba's major draw; now it's just another form of entertainment. Evenings are especially frenetic.

shabby. Staying in town doesn't necessarily mean sacrificing beach time: The best beaches are only minutes away, and one hotel even has its own nearby island replete with private beaches, a restaurant and bar, a gym, a spa, and a tennis court.

In sharp contrast to Oranjestad but only a 20-minute walk west, the **Low-Rise** hotel area feels like a laid-back summer beach town. This district stretches over several contiguous strands with names like Bushiri, Druif, Manchebo, and Eagle, but it's hard to see where one

Take in a Show. The island's current hottest ticket, a Latin extravaganza, sizzles with sexy singers and dancers in entertaining costumes. The budgets of the other shows in town are more modest, but the performers are still talented and entertaining.

Play Jacques Cousteau. Aruba's sister island to the east, Bonaire, has better diving and snorkeling, but Aruba's no slouch. Dive sites include reefs, shipwrecks, and a sunken airplane. If you'd rather not get wet, you can still descend 45m (150 ft.) below the surface to make friends with a variety of marine critters from the comfort of a tiptop submarine.

Get Lost. Rent a car or Jeep, take your trusty guidebook along, and see the real Aruba. You can pass through teeny hamlets (don't blink), discover a new beach, stop for a roadside snack, and rove the aisles of a Chinese supermarket that carries everything from aloe leaves to Dutch chocolate. Be forewarned, though: Roaming gangs of goats yield to no one. Because directional signs are practically nonexistent, expect to get lost. No sweat. This is one small island, and the divi divi trees always point west.

Shop Till You Drop. When it comes to bargains, the Caribbean ain't what it used to be. But who said you needed a legitimate excuse to shop?

Fight the Wind Traps Like Tiger Woods. Forget the towering cacti and the emerald putting greens. And don't let the picturesque lighthouse looming over the front nine distract you. Focus on those winds: They're the challenge at this 18-hole championship golf course Tierra del Sol, one of the Caribbean's best.

ends and another begins, and most people refer to the whole area as Eagle Beach. As the Low-Rise name implies, the dozen or so complexes here seldom climb above three or four stories. Some are directly on the beach; others are located across a relatively sleepy road. The small boutique hotels, quiet timeshares, and sprawling resorts (including several all-inclusives) attract a diverse group of people. A couple of the smaller hotels cater to couples, while the timeshares have a generally quieter, older clientele (with kids and grandkids appearing at certain times of the year). The all-inclusives and larger hotels boast all kinds of guests with an especially large number of families and children. Many apartment-style accommodations feature full kitchens, living rooms, and guest rooms, facilities attractive to families and groups of friends who want to save a bit by eating in from time to time (large supermarkets are a $6 taxi ride or 15-min. walk away). But there are plenty of restaurants in the area, and a couple of large casinos too. Low-Risers are quick to point out that Eagle Beach is wider, quieter, and less crowded than that other beach up the road, and they prefer the comfortable, casual ambience.

On the flip side, the **High-Rise** area begins about a quarter of a mile after Eagle Beach ends. Stretching along Palm Beach (aka that *other* beach), this strip of glitzy high-rise resorts is Aruba's Waikiki. The 13 hotels here tend to be swanky, self-contained resorts that ramble over acres of lushly landscaped grounds. Most boast splashy casinos, numerous restaurants and bars, and endless amenities and services. Some hotels here are definitely upscale, and others are perfectly middle-class: Whether you're a big cheese or small potato, there's a place here to suit your budget. These hotels, unlike the Low-Risers, are full-fledged glamour destinations. And if you're totally focused on sun time, you'll appreciate that all but a couple of the resorts are directly on the beach (the others are just across the street). The area also offers more places to eat, drink, and gamble, and its piers are a hubbub of dive boats and motorized watersports. However, with the increased number of amenities and giant resorts, Palm Beach doesn't offer the Low-Rise area's beach-town simplicity, and it's comparatively more crowded.

Aside from the big three, you have a couple of other options when deciding where to stay. Next to the island's championship golf course, **Tierra del Sol,** condominiums and freestanding villas appeal to vacationers who prefer time on the links to hours on the beach. This complex looks and feels like a desert resort in Arizona, and short-term rentals are available.

For the serious budget option, a handful of **motels** can be found a 10- to 20-minute walk inland from the beaches. They lack the glamour of the larger resorts, but they make Aruba affordable for almost everyone.

Away from the hotels and the capital, Aruba features splendid, if modest, natural wonders, more great beaches, and a handful of authentically native towns. But more about exploring the island later in the book.

1 Visitor Information

For information about visiting Aruba, contact the **Aruba Tourism Authority** (© **800/TO-ARUBA;** www.aruba.com) or its regional offices: 1000 Harbor Blvd., Weehawken, NJ 07087 (© **201/330-0800;** fax 201/330-8757; ata.newjersey@aruba.com); One Financial Plaza, Suite 136, Fort Lauderdale, FL 33394 (© **954/767-6477;** fax 954/767-0432; ata.florida@aruba.com); 1001 Garden View Dr. NE, Suite 418, Atlanta, GA 30319 (© **404/89-ARUBA;** fax 404/873-2193; ata.atlanta@aruba.com); 5901 N. Cicero, Suite 301, Chicago, IL 60646 (© **773/467-8170;** fax 773/202-9293; ata.chicago@aruba.com); 10655 Six Pines Dr., Suite 145, The Woodlands, TX 77380 (© **281/362-1616;** fax 281/362-1644; ata.houston @aruba.com); 5875 Hwy. 7, Suite 201, Woodbridge, Ontario L4L 1 T9 (© **800/268-3042** in Ontario and Quebec or 905/264-3434 in other provinces; fax 905/264-3437; ata.canada@aruba.com).

You also can gather tons of information from other Internet sources. A couple of Aruba's greatest fans compile **Aruba Bound!** (**www.arubabound.com**), an impressive, noncommercial collection of hard facts, informed opinions, and numerous links. **Visit Aruba** (**www.visitaruba.com**) has commercial links, practical information, news items, and a snappy gossip column—search for "Bati Bleki"—with the up-to-date scoop on what's happening on the island. For a lively exchange of information and opinion, visit **Aruba Bulletin Board** (**www.aruba-bb.com**), where you can post questions to seasoned Aruba-vacation veterans and search for great timeshare rental deals.

Once you're on the island, go to the **Aruba Tourism Authority** at L. G. Smith Blvd. 172, Oranjestad (© **297/582-3777**), or pick up the free local magazines *Island Temptations, Aruba Nights, Aruba Experience, Aruba Events,* and *Menu.* Two English-language dailies—*Aruba Today* and *The News*—provide entertainment listings, as does *K-Pasa,* a weekly brochure.

Tips Travel Agent Tip

Here's a great service courtesy of the Aruba Tourism Authority. Go to **http://news.aruba.com/AceFrame.html**, type in your zip code, and in an instant, you'll have a list of travel agents in your neck of the woods who know the ins and outs of Aruba, and have a certificate to prove it.

TRAVEL AGENTS   Travel agents can save you time and money by uncovering the best package deals, airfare, and rental car rates. Most are professional, but the occasional unscrupulous agent may push deals that bag the juiciest commissions, so shop around and ask hard questions. Arm yourself with the information in this book, and don't let anyone pressure you into a vacation that's not right for you.

If you enlist a travel agent, use a member of the **American Society of Travel Agents** (ASTA), 1101 King St., Suite 200, Alexandria, VA 22314 (© **703/739-2782;** www.astanet.com). Call ASTA or visit its website for a list of members in your area.

2 Entry Requirements & Customs

ENTRY REQUIREMENTS

Americans, Canadians, Australians, New Zealanders, and nationals of EU countries can stay in Aruba for up to 3 months without a visa. If you plan to stay longer, get a visa application from the Department of Foreign Affairs in Aruba (© **297/583-4705;** fax 297/583-8108) or at a Dutch embassy or consulate.

U.S. citizens need a valid passport or original birth certificate (with a raised seal), plus a government-issued photo ID. Canadians should have either a valid passport or a Canadian citizenship card with picture. Citizens of a member country of the European Union need a passport and an EU Travel Card. A valid passport is required of all other nationalities. When you arrive in Aruba, be prepared to show an onward or return ticket or proof of sufficient funds for your stay.

Americans and Canadians: If you have a passport, bring it. You'll need identification at some point, and a passport is the best form of ID for speeding through Customs and immigration.

Before leaving home, make two copies of your passport, driver's license, airline ticket, and hotel vouchers. Leave one copy with someone at home; carry the other with you separately from your passport. If you lose your papers, you'll be glad you took the trouble.

CUSTOMS

U.S. Customs regulations allow $600 worth of duty-free imports per person every 30 days. The next $1,000 worth of items is taxed at a rate of 3%. Members of a family traveling together can make joint Customs declarations, so if you're a couple with two children, you can bring back purchases worth up to $2,400 without paying any duty.

You also can send packages home duty-free—up to $600 worth per person for personal use—but the procedure is cumbersome.

Customs Form CF-255 (Declaration of Unaccompanied Articles) must accompany all packages sent to you at home. You can sometimes get this form from Aruban shopkeepers; if you can't, you'll have to get one when you return home. You then have to send the completed form to the store where you made your purchase, and have the store affix the completed form to the package and ship the package to you.

If you'd like to send friends or relatives back home a little something, mark the package "Unsolicited Gift." The limit is one package per addressee per day, and the value of the contents must not exceed $100.

Returning U.S. citizens at least 21 years old are allowed to bring in 1 liter of alcohol duty-free. Regardless of age, you can bring back 200 cigarettes and 200 cigars (no Cubans).

Collect receipts for all purchases made abroad. You're also required to declare on your Customs form the nature and value of all gifts received during your stay abroad. It's prudent to carry proof that you purchased expensive cameras or jewelry in the U.S. if you did. If you purchased them during an earlier trip abroad, carry proof that you previously paid Customs duty on them.

If you use any medication that contains controlled substances or requires injection, carry the original prescription or a note from your doctor.

For more specifics, contact the **U.S. Bureau of Customs and Border Security** (the post–Homeland Security name for the old Customs Service), 1300 Pennsylvania Ave. NW, Washington, DC 20229 (© **202/354-1000**), and request the free pamphlet *Know Before You Go*. It's also available on the Web at www.customs.gov (click on "Publications.").

Canadian Customs regulations allow $500 worth of duty-free imports if you've been out of the country for 7 days or more; the limit is $200 after a 2- to 6-day absence. A written declaration may be required. Anyone age 16 or over can bring back up to 200 cigarettes and 50 cigars. If you're old enough to possess alcohol in the province through which you re-enter Canada, you may include up to 1.14 liters (40 oz.) of wine or liquor or 24 12-ounce containers of beer or ale. You can send an unlimited number of gifts valued at less than $60 back to Canada duty-free if you mark the packages "Unsolicited Gift—Value Under $60." Not alcohol or tobacco, though.

For a summary of Canadian rules, call © **800/461-9999** or click the **Canada Customs and Revenue Agency** at **www.ccra-adrc.gc.ca**.

United Kingdom subjects can receive detailed regulations by contacting **HM Customs & Excise** (✆ **0845/010-9000**) or by visiting **www.hmce.gov.uk**.

Australians should request the helpful brochure *Travelling from Australia—Know Before You Go,* available from the **Australian Customs Service** (✆ **1-300/363-263** from within Australia, or 61-2/6275-6666 from abroad). For additional information, go to **www.customs.gov.au**.

For **New Zealand** customs information, contact the **Customs Service** at ✆ **0800 4 CUSTOMS,** or visit **www.customs.govt.nz**.

Aruba Customs regulations allow incoming visitors to bring articles for personal use. Persons over age 18 can also bring in 2.25 liters of wine, 3 liters of beer or 1 liter of liquor, and 200 cigarettes, 25 cigars, and 250 grams of tobacco.

3 Money

CASH/CURRENCY   U.S. dollars are as widely accepted as the **Aruba florin (AFl),** and most items and services are priced in both currencies. Traveler's checks and major credit cards are almost universally accepted.

The florin is divided into 100 cents. Silver coins come in denominations of 5¢, 10¢, 25¢, and 50¢ and 1, 2½, and 5 florins. The 50-cent piece, the square *yotin,* is Aruba's best-known coin. Paper currency comes in denominations of 5, 10, 25, 50, and 100 florins. The florin fluctuates with the dollar on the world market. At press time, the (fairly stable) exchange rate was 1.79 AFl to US$1 (1 AFl is worth about U.S. 56¢). Hotels, restaurants, and stores accept dollars at rates of between 1.75 and 1.80 AFl; supermarkets and gas stations use a conversion rate of 1.75 AFl to the dollar.

The currency used in the neighboring Dutch islands of Curaçao and Bonaire, the Netherlands Antillean florin (Naf), is not accepted in Aruba.

Note: Prices are quoted in U.S. dollars throughout this book.

TRAVELER'S CHECKS   Traveler's checks are becoming a bit of a relic now that ATMs make cash accessible at any time. If you want to avoid ATM service charges, though, or if you just want the security of knowing you can get a refund if your wallet's stolen, go ahead and get traveler's checks. Of course, you'll have to show identification every time you cash one. Most banks sell them, and most Aruban businesses accept them. If you carry traveler's checks, be sure to keep a record of the serial numbers (separate from the checks, of course). You'll need the numbers to get a refund if your checks are lost or stolen.

You can get **American Express** traveler's checks by calling ✆ **800/221-7282** or at **www.americanexpress.com**. American Express has an Aruban office at S. E. L. Maduro & Sons, Rockefellerstraat 1, Oranjestad (✆ **297/582-3888**). It's open Monday through Friday from 8am to noon and 1 to 5pm. **Visa** offers traveler's checks at financial institutions nationwide; call ✆ **800/227-6811** to find a location near you. **MasterCard** offers traveler's checks through **Thomas Cook Currency Services;** call ✆ **800/223-9920** for a location near you.

ATMS   Aruba has plenty of cash machines—at the airport, in Oranjestad, in Noord, at the Allegro, Holiday Inn, and Playa Linda in the High-Rise area, and at La Cabana in the Low-Rises. Your hotel can steer you in the right direction, and an ATM's never far away. Most dispense both florins and dollars. Expect to pay a fee of about $3 per transaction.

CREDIT CARDS   Does anyone travel without a credit card? They're safer than cash, and you get a detailed record of your expenses. With most cards, you can also get cash advances from banks or ATMs. Plastic hasn't completely replaced cash, though. You'll still need good old paper money for small purchases, cabs, and the occasional restaurant or small shop that doesn't honor cards.

Major credit-card companies have emergency toll-free numbers to call if your card is lost or stolen. Usually, the office will wire you a cash advance immediately, and deliver an emergency card in a day or two. **Citicorp Visa**'s U.S. emergency number is ✆ **800/336-8472.** **American Express** cardholders and traveler's check holders should call ✆ **800/221-7282** for all money emergencies (or go to S. E. L. Maduro & Sons, Rockefellerstraat 1, Oranjestad; ✆ **297/582-3888** for assistance). **MasterCard** holders should call ✆ **800/307-7309.** Both MasterCard and Visa cardholders can visit branches of Aruba Bank, Caribbean MercantileBank, or Interbank for cash advances or to report a lost or stolen card. In the U.S., **Discover Card** holders can get assistance by calling ✆ **800/DISCOVER;** in Aruba, call ✆ 801/902-3100.

If you lose your card, chances are slim that the police will find it. Notify them anyway: Lots of credit-card companies and insurers require a police report number.

TAXES, SERVICE CHARGES & TIPPING   Aruba has no sales tax, but hotels charge an 11% government tax on rooms, and most routinely add 5% to 7% for "service." In addition, a few resorts charge an energy surcharge, usually $4 to $8 per unit per night.

Most, but not all, restaurants charge 10% to 15% for service. The charge is distributed among all restaurant personnel, so if you think your server deserves extra, leave cash on the table, too. If no charge is included in your tab, leave 15% to 20%.

Taxi drivers expect 15%, and porters should get about $2 per bag. Some of the hotel service charge should trickle down to the chambermaids, but if you're staying in a nice place, leave $2 per day for the housekeeper anyway. For spa treatments and such, see if a service charge is included. If it's not, leave 15%.

4 When to Go

THE WEATHER

Almost invariably, the weather is wonderful—warm, sunny, dry, and breezy. There's no monsoon season and no threat of tropical storms—the island is far outside the hurricane belt. The average annual temperature is 82°F (28°C), and no month of the year has an average high temperature lower than 85°F (29°C) or higher than 89°F (32°C). Lows range from 76°F (24°C) to 80°F (27°C).

The sun can be hot, and its reflection off the white sandy beaches is blinding. Fortunately, the almost-constant trade winds make it easy to forget just how warm it is. Usually a godsend, these pleasant, gentle breezes can occasionally escalate to surprising gusts or sustained winds, so hold onto your hat. In September, though, you'll wish they were back. Tropical storms plaguing less fortunate islands far to the north suck away the trade winds during that back-to-school month, making Aruba as hot as any other spot in the Caribbean. Unless you fancy relentless heat with no relieving breezes, avoid visiting in September.

The wind provides a collateral perk, too. It blows away annoying mosquitoes and other flying pests. When the breezes wane, it's time to bring out the insect repellent. Aruba's dry, though, so you'll never encounter the number of bugs that infest lusher islands.

Rainfall averages about 18 inches a year, with most precipitation falling from October through January. Even then rains tend to be erratic and brief; it's rare for the sun not to shine most of the day.

Another plus: The humidity is less oppressive in Aruba than in most of the Caribbean. Although not exactly Arizona, the island's more dusty than sultry.

Tips **Take It on the Chin**

The warm trade winds that blow across Aruba will hit you as soon as you leave the airport terminal. Usually dry and steady, these breezes offset the strong sun and make for very pleasant conditions. They're generally gentler in the morning, gaining momentum through the course of the day. When they gather some fury, watch out. You'll never see so many people holding onto their headgear. Hats with chinstraps are a must; in fact, in Aruba, chinstraps are practically shorthand for "in the know."

HURRICANES   The curse of much of the Caribbean, hurricanes are something you can gleefully ignore if you're vacationing in Aruba. The island is miles and miles from the storms that wreak havoc on much of the region from June to November. On rare occasions, storm activity far to the north is so violent it causes wave action to ripple in Aruba. Some damage has occurred over the years, but it's relatively negligible.

THE HIGH SEASON & THE OFF SEASON

Because the weather is consistently nice year-round, Aruba's high and low seasons reflect climates in the United States and Canada rather than weather on the island. When it's cold and wintry in North America, demand for Aruba's warmth and sunshine peaks. Roughly speaking, the island's high season runs from mid-December to mid-April. During this period, hotels charge their highest prices, and you'll need to reserve a room well in advance—months in advance if you want to bask on the beach over Christmas or in the depths of February. Guests during the high season tend to be older and wealthier, although there are plenty of families. The national mix weighs heavily toward Americans and Canadians.

The off season—roughly from mid-April to mid-December (although it varies from hotel to hotel)—is one big summer sale. All resorts routinely slash their room rates, which means you can get the same accommodations in the low season for 20% to 50% less than you would in darkest winter.

But if you think Aruba's a ghost town in the summer, think again. The deals are so attractive, and the season dovetails so nicely with Europe's traditional vacation time and South America's winter, that the island's resorts are still pretty full. The mix of visitors in the summer shifts toward families, Europeans (especially Dutch), South Americans, and the more budget-conscious from everywhere. Americans still make up the largest national group.

Some activities and attractions scale back a bit in the summer, but not much. For example, instead of six excursions a day, a tour operator may offer only three; restaurants might close an hour earlier; and hotels may use the "downtime" for new construction or renovation (ask if work is scheduled; if it's potentially disturbing, request a room far away from the noise).

If you're single and want crowds, don't worry. Lots of potential playmates are around in the summer, too.

Because the difference in high-season and low-season rates at most hotels is drastic, I've included both in chapter 3. See for yourself how much you can save if you wait a bit for your fun in the sun.

Since September 11, 2001, the travel industry worldwide has suffered from political developments (such as the war in Iraq) and the reluctance of people to venture far from home. Aruba's tourist-based economy has at times been hit hard. It may sound predatory, but in uncertain times, fearless, opportunistic travelers can find significant bargains.

HOLIDAYS

Most stores and restaurants close on official holidays. If you stay near the resort areas, however, you may not be affected at all. Here's a list of Aruba's holidays: January 1 (New Year's Day); January 25 (Birthday of Betico Croes, the father of Aruba's semi-independence); February 23, 2004, and February 7, 2005 (Carnival Monday); March 18 (National Anthem and Flag Day); April 9, 2004, and March 25, 2005 (Good Friday); April 12, 2004, and March 28, 2005 (Easter Monday); April 30 (Queen's Birthday); May 1 (Labor Day); May 20, 2004, and May 5, 2005 (Ascension Day); December 25 (Christmas Day); December 26 (Boxing Day).

ARUBA CALENDAR OF EVENTS

For an updated list of events, and specific dates, times, and locations, call the **Aruba Tourism Authority** at ℂ **800/TO-ARUBA** or visit **www.aruba.com/ calendar/index.html**.

JANUARY

Dande. For almost 200 years, roaming troubadours have marked the end of the old year and the beginning of the new in Aruba. As the clock strikes 12, groups of musicians go from house to house serenading each family with good wishes for the coming year. Although the tune and refrain are constant, lyrics are improvised for individual families, leading to innuendo and light-hearted hilarity. If the dande group misses your home, you'll have nothing but bad luck in the coming year. Some families set off fireworks after they've been serenaded, and the mother of the house often sweeps out the "old spirit." January 1.

Betico Croes Day. G. F. "Betico" Croes, Aruba's seminal political leader, was instrumental in the island's fight for "Status Aparte"—semi-independence from Holland and autonomy from the other Dutch islands in the Caribbean. Low-key patriotic observances mark the holiday. January 25.

FEBRUARY

Carnival. Highlights of Aruba's version of pre-Lenten revelry include the Children's Parade (toddlers, dwarfed by their elaborate costumes, dance down the street) and the Grand Carnival Parades in Oranjestad and San Nicolas (calypso, marching, and drumming contests). During the Tivoli Lighting Parade, thousands of miniature lights blanket the costumes and floats. Representatives of the island's various districts vie for the title of Carnival queen, and unsuspecting tourists, whisked off their planes, help decide the winner. Many hotels get into the spirit by hosting their own parties and queen elections. The parties, dancing, and music begin in January, culminating on the weekend before Ash Wednesday. February 25 in 2004, February 9 in 2005.

MARCH

National Anthem and Flag Day. In celebration of Aruba's flag, anthem, and autonomy, nationalistic exhibits, folkloric presentations, and fireworks displays take place island-wide. Children sing the national anthem—on the streets, television, and radio— *ad infinitum* and off-key. March 18.

APRIL

Queen's Birthday. To celebrate the birthday of Queen Beatrix of the Netherlands, kite contests, sporting events, and cultural programs are held around the island. April 30.

JUNE

Hi-Winds World Challenge. Windsurfers from 30 countries gather at Hadicurari, or Fishermen's Huts, just north of the High-Rise hotels, for one of the most popular competitions in the Caribbean. For information, call © **297/582-3777.** End of June through early July.

Dera Gai (St. John's Day). Centuries ago, after harvesting crops, the island's indigenous people built bonfires, then challenged one another to jump over them. Storytelling, music, dancing, and food and drink fueled the merriment. Later a rooster was buried up to its neck and covered with a calabash gourd. Blindfolded men with sticks had three chances to "find" the rooster; the winner kept the fowl for dinner. Spanish Catholic influence later tied the celebration to the feast day of John the Baptist. Today a dummy rooster is used, but the music and dancing persist. Crop remnants and other disposable items are buried in a symbolic soul cleansing. June 24.

Aruba Jazz & Latin Music Festival. International and local artists perform in a weekend celebration of two of the hemisphere's great musical traditions. Call ℂ **297/582-3777** for information. End of June.

JULY

Heineken Music Festival, Oranjestad. Bands from around the Caribbean perform in a free concert. Call ℂ **297/582-3777** for information. First week of July.

Aruba Perrier Reef Care Project. Joining forces to raise awareness of the marine environment, certified divers, snorkelers, and topsiders clean up beaches and underwater sites. For details, call ℂ **297/582-3777.** First weekend in July.

AUGUST

Aruba International Pro-Am Golf Tournament. Professional and amateur golfers team up in this 2-day, 36-hole tournament that features prizes, special events, and parties. Call ℂ **297/582-3777** for details. Late August.

OCTOBER

Festival de Las Américas. Musical groups from far and wide perform rhythms from around the Americas. Call ℂ **297/582-3777** for information. Early October.

Deep Sea Fishing Tournament. The Aruba Nautical Club hosts yachts from the United States, Venezuela, Puerto Rico, Curaçao, Bonaire, and Aruba. Call ℂ **297/585-3022** for information. End of October.

NOVEMBER

Aruba Super Nationals, San Nicolas. This international drag racing event takes place at International Raceway Palo Marga in San Nicolas and draws competitors from the U.S., Puerto Rico, Venezuela, Curaçao, Bonaire, and St. Maarten. Early November.

Aruba International Catamaran Regatta. Catamarans from Europe and North and South America compete. For details, call © **297/582-3777.** Mid- to late November.

DECEMBER

Sint Nicolaas Day, Oranjestad. Sint Nicolaas arrives at Paardenbaai Harbor in Oranjestad to greet Aruba's children and reward them with gifts for their good behavior during the year. December 5.

5 Health & Insurance

STAYING HEALTHY

Keep the following suggestions in mind.

- You can relax about water. Aruba's tap water is completely safe to drink and tastes fine.
- Aruba's sun can be brutal. Wear sunglasses and a hat (with a strap—remember the wind) and use sunscreen liberally. The best sunscreens contain zinc oxide, titanium dioxide, or avobenzone (check "active ingredients" on the label). Limit your time on the beach the first day or two. If you get burned, stay out of the sun until you recover.
- The wind is usually strong enough to blow mosquitoes away, but the pests can sometimes be a nuisance anyway. Malaria's not a concern, but bring insect repellent for your own comfort.
- Food is generally safe. Be careful, though, about street vendors. Make sure that what you get is hot and that it hasn't been sitting out for any length of time.
- The **United States Centers for Disease Control and Prevention** (© **404/332-4559;** www.cdc.gov/travel) provides up-to-date information on necessary vaccines and health hazards by region or country. Unfortunately, its information on Aruba is lumped with the other Caribbean islands, most of which lack Aruba's generally modern and sanitary conditions.
- Pack prescription medications in your carry-on luggage. Carry written prescriptions in generic, not brand-name form, and dispense all prescription medications from their original labeled vials.
- If you wear contact lenses, pack an extra pair in case you lose or tear one.

WHAT TO DO IF YOU GET SICK

Finding a good doctor in Aruba is not a problem, and all speak English. Hotels have physicians on call, and the modern **Horacio**

Oduber Hospital, L. G. Smith Boulevard z/n, near Eagle Beach (© **297/587-4300,** also the number to call in case of a medical emergency; www.arubahospital.com), has excellent medical facilities. If you have an emergency while you're on the eastern end of the island, San Nicolas has a medical center, the **Centro Médico,** Bernardstraat 75 (© **297/584-8833**). Consulting hours are limited, but emergency assistance is available 24 hours a day, 7 days a week. The **Posada Clinic Aruba,** L. G. Smith Blvd. 14 (© **297/582-0840**), has modern hemodialysis equipment, but reservations must be made 3 months in advance. **Labco Medical and Homecare Service NV,** Cabuyastraat 6A, Ponton (© **297/582-6651**), rents wheelchairs, walkers, crutches, bedpans, and other medical equipment. Service is available 24 hours a day, and delivery is free. If your emergency cannot be handled locally, **Air Ambulance** (© **297/582-9197**) service is available to Curaçao and Venezuela. The island's dental facilities are good; make appointments through your hotel.

If you worry about getting sick away from home, consider medical travel insurance (see the section on travel insurance, below). In most cases, though, your existing health plan will provide the coverage you need. Be sure to carry your identification card with you.

If you suffer from a chronic illness, consult your doctor before you depart. For conditions like epilepsy, diabetes, or heart problems, wear a **Medic Alert Identification Tag** (© **888/633-4298,** or 209/668-3333 outside the U.S.; www.medicalert.org), which immediately alerts doctors to your condition and gives them access to your records through Medic Alert's 24-hour hot line.

Contact the **International Association for Medical Assistance to Travelers** (© **716/754-4883** or 416/652-0137 in Canada; www.iamat.org) for tips on travel and health concerns in Aruba, as well as a list of local doctors.

INSURANCE

There are three kinds of travel insurance: trip-cancellation, medical, and lost-luggage coverage. Check your existing medical and homeowner's policies before you buy additional coverage.

Trip-cancellation insurance is a good idea if you've paid most of your vacation expenses upfront, say, by purchasing a package or a cruise. It protects you if you have to cancel your trip because of sickness or a death in the family.

Medical contingencies may be covered by your existing health policy, but emergency evacuation sometimes isn't, and Medicare often doesn't cover all medical expenses overseas. If you need hospital treatment, most health insurance plans cover out-of-country hospital visits and procedures, at least to some extent. Most make you pay the bills upfront, however, and reimburse you only after all the paperwork's been processed.

The differences between travel assistance and insurance are often blurred, but the former generally offers on-the-spot assistance and 24-hour hot lines, while the latter reimburses you for travel problems after you've complied with the filing requirements.

Homeowner's insurance often covers stolen luggage. On international flights, airlines are responsible for approximately $9.07 per pound ($20 per kg) for checked baggage and $400 per passenger for unchecked baggage unless a higher value is declared in advance and additional charges are paid. Liability is for a maximum of 70 pounds ($640) per checked bag. If you're carrying anything more valuable than that, keep it in your carry-on bag.

Reputable issuers of travel insurance include **Access America** (© 866/807-3982; www.accessamerica.com); **Travel Guard International** (© 800/826-4919; www.travelguard.com); and **Travelex Insurance Services** (© 888/457-4602; www.travelex-insurance.com). For medical coverage, try **MEDEX International** (© 800/537-2029 or 410/453-6300; www.medexassist.com); or **Travel Assistance International** (Worldwide Assistance Services, Inc.; © 800/821-2828 or 202/828-5894). Scuba divers can obtain dive-accident insurance through the **Divers Alert Network** (© 800/446-2671; www.diversalertnetwork.org).

6 Tips for Travelers with Special Needs

FOR TRAVELERS WITH DISABILITIES

Traveling with a disability is seldom a piece of cake, and like most places, Aruba could do more to welcome vacationers with disabilities. Queen Beatrix International Airport was renovated in 2000, yet facilities compliant with the Americans with Disabilities Act (ADA) weren't part of the overhaul. Instead, the facility has a truck to transfer wheelchair passengers from the plane to the terminal using a special ramp and door.

A few resorts boast ADA-compliant facilities, including the Marriott, Holiday Inn, Hyatt Regency, Marriott's Aruba Ocean Club, Radisson, and Divi Phoenix. The Costa Linda even has a beach wheelchair. Many other hotels are equipped for wheelchairs, including the Aruba Grand, Wyndham, Renaissance, Allegro, Costa Linda, and Tamarijn.

If you need special equipment while you're on the island, **Labco Medical and Home Heathcare Services** specializes in oxygen-delivery systems, but it also sells and rents medical and home health-care products like oxygen concentrators, tanks, commodes, scooters, crutches, wheelchairs, walkers, shower chairs, and lifts. Call (✆ **297/ 582-6651** or send a fax to 297/582-6567.

For more general information, a number of organizations and websites assist travelers with disabilities. **Moss Rehab ResourceNet (www.mossresourcenet.org)** has great information, tips, and resources about accessible travel and travel agents who specialize in planning trips for disabled travelers. So does **Access-Able Travel Source (www.access-able.com)**. Its user-friendly site lists relay and voice numbers for hotels, airlines, and car-rental companies, as well as links to accessible accommodations, attractions, transportation, tours, local medical resources, and equipment repairers.

When you become a member of the **Society for Accessible Travel & Hospitality,** 347 Fifth Ave., Suite 610, New York, NY 10016 (✆ 212/447-7284; www.sath.org), you gain access to a vast network of travel industry connections. The group provides desti-nation information sheets and referrals to tour operators with a spe-cial expertise in disabled travel.

A World of Options, a 600-plus-page resource book for travelers with disabilities, gives the low-down on everything from biking trips to scuba outfitters. Available from **Mobility International USA** (✆ **541/343-1284** voice and TTY; www.miusa.org), the book costs $35 (10% discount for members).

Vision-impaired travelers should contact the **American Founda-tion for the Blind,** 11 Penn Plaza, Suite 300, New York, NY 10001 (✆ **800/232-5463**), for information on traveling with Seeing Eye dogs.

FOR GAY & LESBIAN TRAVELERS

Arubans seem genuinely confounded when asked about homopho-bia on the island. People here pride themselves on Aruba's diversity, and most are gentle and remarkably nonjudgmental, certainly of tourists, but also of their gay and lesbian neighbors. Compared to notoriously homophobic Jamaica and Grand Cayman Island, Aruba is truly gay-friendly. Homosexuality is a non-issue here.

But Aruba's not a big destination on the gay travel itinerary. You're not going to see thousands of other friends of Dorothy, and straight couples and families are legion. Nonetheless, it's a welcoming place regardless of your sexuality, and couples of all stripes can relax and feel comfortable. It's not gay paradise, but given the anti-gay prejudice of some Americans, you're likely to find Aruba less threatening than small-town U.S.A.

Some Arubans are out, especially those under age 40; others aren't. Those who are live pretty much like their straight friends and family. Gay visibility, especially in the hotel, restaurant, and entertainment industries, is undeniable. The influx of no-apologies gay Latinos over the past few years has increased gay visibility significantly. And if it's any indication, the island's top show for almost a decade was a drag-queen extravaganza.

If you want help planning your trip, the **International Gay & Lesbian Travel Association** (© 800/448-8550 or 954/776-2626; www.iglta.org) can link you up with gay-friendly tour specialists. **Out & About** (© 800/929-2268; www.outandabout.com) offers a monthly newsletter packed with good information on the global gay and lesbian travel scene, with specific information about Aruba. The website also features links to gay and lesbian tour operators and other gay-themed travel links.

FOR SENIORS

Aruba's a great place for wise and seasoned travelers. In fact, a hefty portion of the island's guests, especially during the high season, are people over 50. If you're looking for a quiet environment with a more mature clientele, think about renting a unit in a timeshare. Most large hotels have plenty of older people, too. If you're revolted by the idea of being segregated from the youngsters, fear not: No resort, hotel, or timeshare caters to one type of person only. Most feature a nice mix of families and couples of all ages.

Mention your age when you begin planning your trip; many hotels and most airlines and cruise lines offer senior discounts. And don't hesitate to ask for discounts once you're on the island. Just be sure to have some kind of ID, such as a driver's license, especially if no one believes you're a day over 45.

Members of the **AARP,** 601 E St. NW, Washington, DC 20049 (© 800/424-3410; www.aarp.org), get discounts on hotels, airfares, and car rentals. Although **Mature Outlook** (© 800/336-6330) began as a travel organization for people over age 50, it now caters to people of all ages. Members receive hotel discounts. **Grand Circle Travel** (© 800/959-0405; www.gct.com) is one of hundreds of travel agencies that specialize in vacations for seniors.

7 Package Deals

Packages can save you a ton of money, and most people vacationing in Aruba came on a package deal. Don't be confused, though: Package tours are *not* escorted tours. You'll be on your own, but in most cases airfare, hotel, and transportation to and from the airport are included—and the whole kit and caboodle will cost you less than the hotel alone would if you booked it yourself. All of Aruba's hotels work closely with tour operators, so there's a money-saving package for you no matter where you want to stay.

Some packages cover meals. This can be cheaper, but it restricts your dining options. If you'd rather bounce around and sample the island's considerable gastronomic diversity, decline the meal plan or opt for a breakfast-only plan.

Start your search for a deal in the travel section of your local Sunday newspaper. Check the ads in national travel magazines like *Arthur Frommer's Budget Travel, National Geographic Traveler,* and *Travel Holiday,* too.

Powerhouse travel agencies offer some of the best deals. **American Express Vacations** (© 800/346-3607; www.americanexpress.com/travel) has offices nationwide. **Liberty Travel** (© 888/271-1584; www.libertytravel.com) is one of the biggest packagers in the Northeast, and usually takes out a full-page ad in Sunday papers.

The airlines themselves are another good resource. They often combine their flights with hotels at attractive prices. Try **American Airlines Vacations** (© 800/321-2121; www.aavacations.com), **Continental Airlines Vacations** (© 800/301-3800; www.coolvacations.com), **Delta Vacations** (© 800/654-6559; www.deltavacations.com), **United Vacations** (© 888/854-3899; www.unitedvacations.com), and **US Airways Vacations** (© 800/422-3861; www.usairways vacations.com).

To save time comparing the prices and value of hotel packages, contact **TourScan, Inc.** (© 800/962-2080 or 203/655-8091; www.tourscan.com). Every season, the company computerizes the contents of travel brochures that contain about 10,000 different vacations at 1,600 hotels in the Caribbean, including Aruba. TourScan selects the best-value vacation at each hotel. Don't use this as your only source, though. Published brochures don't always have the best prices available.

Large tour operators serving Aruba include **Apple Vacations** (**www.applevacations.com**; must be booked through your travel agent); **Funjet Vacations** (**www.funjet.com**; book online or through a travel agent listed on the Web page); **GOGO Worldwide Vacations** (**www.gogowwv.com**; must be booked through your travel agent); **GWV International** (**www.gwvtravel.com**; reservations must be made through your travel agent); **Inter Island Tours** (© 800/245-3434; www.interislandtours.com); **MCM Tours** (© 888/ARUBA-4-U; www.aruba4u.com); and **TNT Vacations** (© 800/262-0123 or 617/262-9200; www.tntvacations.com).

8 Getting There

Scheduled air service to Aruba from the United States expanded dramatically at the end of 2000. American Airlines once dominated the route, but Continental, Delta, United, and US Airways have joined the fray. There are no nonstop flights from Canada, but American, Continental, and Delta have connecting service. Although the number of flights generally increases during the high season, airlines may alter service depending on demand (and their own financial condition). Don't assume the flights mentioned below will be offered when you're ready to book.

Charter flights offer an alternative for both Canadians and Americans. If you've booked a package through a large tour operator, your flight might be a charter anyway. Charters serve Atlanta, Baltimore, Boston, Charlotte, Chicago, Cincinnati, Cleveland, Dallas, Detroit, Hartford, Louisville, Memphis, Milwaukee, Minneapolis, Nashville, New York, Philadelphia, Pittsburgh, St. Louis, and Toronto.

Before you book your airline tickets, read the section on "Package Deals," above—you can save yourself a bundle. Whether or not you choose a package, consider these rules of thumb:

- **When you fly makes a difference.** If you fly in spring, summer, or fall, you're guaranteed substantially reduced airfares to Aruba. You can also ask if it's cheaper to fly Monday through Thursday or to stay an extra day. Many airlines won't volunteer this information, so ask questions and be persistent.
- **Keep an eye out for sales.** Check your newspaper for advertised discounts or call the airlines and ask if promotional rates or special fares are available. You'll almost never see a sale during the peak winter vacation months of February and March, or during the Thanksgiving or Christmas seasons; but in periods of low-volume travel, discounted fares are common. If you already hold a ticket when a sale breaks, it may pay to exchange your ticket, even though it incurs a $50 to $75 charge. Remember, though, that the lowest-priced fares are often nonrefundable, require

advance purchase of 1 to 3 weeks and a certain length of stay, and carry penalties for changing dates of travel.

• **Check with consolidators.** Consolidators, or bucket shops, buy seats in bulk from the airlines and then sell them to the public at prices below the airlines' discounted rates. Make sure you know the airlines' current fares before buying from a consolidator. Before you pay, ask for a record locator number and confirm your seat with the airline itself. Also be aware that bucket-shop tickets are usually nonrefundable or rigged with stiff cancellation penalties, often as high as 50% to 75% of the ticket price.

  Reliable consolidators offer great deals. Try **Cheap Tickets** (② **888/922-8849;** www.cheaptickets.com); **Lowestfare.com** (② **888/278-8830;** www.lowestfare.com); **Cheap Seats** (② **800/675-7482;** www.cheapseatstravel.com); **Priceline. com** (www.priceline.com); and **1-800-FLY-CHEAP** (www.fly cheap.com). **STA Travel** (② **800/781-4040;** www.statravel. com) specializes in young travelers, but its bargain-basement prices are available to folks of all ages. (***Note:*** In 2002, STA bought competitors **Council Travel** and **USIT Campus** after they went bankrupt. It still operates some offices under the Council name.)

• **Search the Internet.** Check for deals online and compare your findings to the research of a dedicated travel agent, if you have one, especially if you're booking more than just a flight. **Travelocity** (**www.travelocity.com**) and **Microsoft Expedia** (**www.expedia.com**) are a couple of the better virtual travel agents. **Smarter Living** (**www.smarterliving.com**) is a great source for last-minute deals.

  American Airlines (② **800/433-7300;** www.aa.com) once dominated scheduled service from the United States to Aruba. It now offers a daily nonstop flight from New York's JFK airport (flight time is about 4½ hr.), two daily nonstops from Miami (2½ hr.), and one daily nonstop from San Juan, Puerto Rico (1½ hr.). Flights from Boston leave four times a week during the high season and twice a week the rest of the year. These nonstops take just under 5 hours.

  Continental Airlines (② **800/231-0856;** www.continental.com) leaves daily from Newark (5 hr.) and on Tuesday and Saturday from Houston (4½ hr.). Service from both cities is nonstop.

  Delta Air Lines (② **800/241-4141;** www.delta.com) offers daily nonstop service from Atlanta (4 hr.) and Saturday flights from New York's JFK (4½ hr.).

United (✆ 800/241-6522; www.united.com) offers daily service from Miami via Curaçao that takes 3½ hours. Saturday nonstop service departs from Chicago's O'Hare Airport and arrives at Aruba's Queen Beatrix International Airport 5 hours and 10 minutes later.

US Airways's (✆ 800/428-4322; www.usairways.com) nonstop service departs daily from Philadelphia (4½ hr.) and from Charlotte (3½ hr.).

Air ALM (✆ 800/327-7230; www.alm-airlines.com), an Antillean carrier, flies from Miami twice a day (except Tues, when there's one flight). Due to a stop in Curaçao, flight time is about 4½ hours.

Airlines with service from Canada include American, Continental, Delta, and US Airways. Each requires that you make connections in Miami, New York, or some other city in the U.S. **Air Canada** (✆ 888/247-2262 in the U.S and Canada; www.air canada.ca) can get you as far as Miami, Bermuda, or the Bahamas, where you'll have to switch carriers.

If you're departing from Europe, **KLM** (http://en.nederland.klm.com) is your best bet. Flights from Amsterdam leave daily and take 9½ hours.

9 Outdoor Pursuits

BIRDING Next to The Mill Resort and the Wyndham in the High-Rise area, the Bubali Bird Sanctuary attracts more than 80 ornithological species to its nutrient-rich ponds and wetlands. How many brown pelicans, black olivaceous cormorants, herons, and egrets can you spot? Farther afield, Arikok National Park features several diverse ecosystems in a compact area. Birds here include hummingbirds (common emerald and ruby-topaz), rufous-collared sparrows, tropical mockingbirds, ospreys, yellow orioles, American kestrels, black-faced grassquits, yellow warblers, Caribbean parakeets, long-tongued bats, common ground doves, troupials, crested caracaras, and Aruban burrowing owls. Captive birds can be depressing, but the Wyndham, Radisson, Hyatt, and Renaissance offer close encounters with a variety of showy tropical species like toucans, cockatoos, and macaws.

FISHING Local fishermen use simple hand lines (fishing line, hooks, and lead weights) to bring up red snapper and dolphin fish. Most activity takes place along the southwest coast, although some anglers occasionally venture to the north coast, where the rough seas trap fish in small pools carved out of the limestone bluffs. To try your hand at deep-sea fishing, charter one of the many skippered boats. Typical catches include barracuda, amberjack, sailfish, wahoo, blue and white marlin, kingfish, bonito, and black- and yellow-fin tuna.

GOLF   On the island's northern tip, Tierra del Sol is one of the Caribbean's best golf courses. The championship 18-hole, par-71 course was designed by Robert Trent Jones II and features stupendous views of the ocean and the California Lighthouse. Bunkers, cacti, and coral rock come into play throughout the course, while water hazards are confined to holes 13, 14, and 15. Gusting to speeds of 40 mph, the wind is the real challenge, though. Club selection is often crucial. Near San Nicolas, the Aruba Golf Club is Tierra del Sol's poor cousin. Originally built for oil executives at the nearby refinery, the 9-hole public course features 20 sand traps, 5 water traps, and desert terrain. The wind's a factor here, too, and the bands of roaming goats are an equally challenging hazard.

HIKING   The sun is hot, and the scant foliage offers little respite, but if you bring water and a wide-brimmed hat, traversing Aruba's hills and coastline is worth the effort. Arikok National Park has the best trails. Climb the island's highest hills, explore abandoned gold mines, poke around plantation ruins, trek through caves, and comb limestone cliffs for coral and small-animal bones (leave everything where you found it, please). The network of trails is clearly marked. Hiking boots are nice, but sneakers will do.

HORSEBACK RIDING   Aruba's coastline and outback are just as dramatic when viewed from the saddle. Several ranches offer early morning and midday excursions, or you can ride off into the sunset. As you wend your way through cacti and random boulders in the outback, watch for iguanas and skittish cottontails. Stop at Alto Vista Chapel and California Lighthouse, then ride along the shore. Or start at the crashing waves and sand dunes of the northern coast before heading for the Natural Pool. Keep your eyes open for bickering parakeets and hovering hummingbirds. That ominous bird circling over your head? Not to worry: It only looks like a vulture.

JET SKIING   Harleys of the sea—just as fast, just as noisy. Put on your black leather swimming trunks and head for Palm Beach, where several vendors have one- and two-seaters.

KAYAKING   The leeward (south) coast's calm waters are ideal for kayaking. Starting near the old fishing village of Savaneta, guided tours hug the coastal mangrove forests before crossing a lagoon to a small island, where you can have a bite to eat and snorkel.

PAINTBALL War is hell; simulated battle is fun. Armed with an air gun and biodegradable capsules filled with water-soluble paint, you and your team must save the free world by capturing the enemy's flag. Dodge your wily foes' fire: If splattered by a paint ball, you're dead. (Referee and protective clothing supplied.)

PARASAILING Aruba looks even better from 180m (600 ft.) in the air. Flight time is only 12 or 15 minutes, but secure in your boat-towed parachute, you're on top of the world. Several watersports centers along Palm Beach will be happy to put wind in your sails. Take a disposable waterproof camera along to show your friends back home that you've been there, done that.

SAILING Sailing adventures are available day and night. Some include watersports, others feature dinner. For night owls, dance-and-booze cruises include a midnight dip in the sea. If you have something special to celebrate, charter a private yacht. Catamarans, trimarans, and ketches are available. The calm waters along the southern coast are also ideal for extra-buoyant individual sailboats like Sunfish and Minifish.

SCUBA DIVING Aruba offers enough coral reefs, marine life, and wreck diving to keep most wetsuit-wearing folks happy. The water temperature averages 80°F (27°C), but during winter it can dip into the mid-70s. Due to currents and plankton, visibility varies, but at the leeward dive sites it usually ranges from 18m to 36m (60 ft.–120 ft.). The bountiful plankton nourishes a dense coral population, especially brain, sheet, finger, and mountainous star coral. Freshwater runoff is minimal. Sunken airplane fuselages and shipwrecks (including the largest in the Caribbean) are among the most popular destinations. In addition to snappers, grunts, angelfish, damselfish, and parrotfish, divers regularly spot less common species like frogfish, seahorses, nudibranchs, black crinoids, basket stars, scorpionfish, and eels. Barracudas, tarpons, and jacks also call Aruba's waters home.

SNORKELING Good visibility, several shallow reefs, and a couple of wrecks give snorkelers an array of options. All sites are on the southern, or leeward, coast. Slightly north of Palm Beach, Catalina Bay and Arashi Reef feature brain and star coral, sea fans, parrotfish, angelfish, and an occasional octopus; the 400-foot *Antilla* shipwreck is impossible to miss. East of Oranjestad and off the shore of Renaissance Island, a Beechcraft airplane rests in 4.5m to 6m (15 ft.–20 ft.) of water among a host of soft coral. De Palm Slope, off De Palm

Island, features magnificent coral as well. At Aruba's eastern tip, Baby Beach Reef boasts large elkhorn and sheet coral formations inhabited by crabs, octopuses, and lobsters.

UNDERWATER TOURING   Who says you have to be a certified scuba diver to experience life at the bottom of the sea? Board a submarine and descend 45m (150 ft.) to observe coral, shipwrecks, and some very curious fish. If you'd rather not have your vessel submerge completely, hop on a glass-bottom boat. The viewing deck is only 1.5m (5 ft.) below the surface, but a scuttled German freighter, encrusted with coral and teeming with other marine life, is just feet away. The sub leaves from a pier in front of the Crystal Casino in Oranjestad; the glass-bottom boat departs from Pelican Pier on Palm Beach.

WINDSURFING   Aruba's high-wind season is the longest in the Caribbean. Wind speeds are best in May, June, and July, when they average 20 to 25 knots. From December through April, they slow to 15 to 20 knots, and from September through November they range from 10 to 20 knots. Most launches are on the leeward side of the island, near the hotels and major beaches. The most popular site is off the northwest tip of the island on Malmok Beach, an area known as Fishermen's Huts. Near San Nicolas, Rodgers Beach, and Boca Grandi are alternatives to the hotel area.

10 Tips on Accommodations

HOTELS & RESORTS   Some travelers assume they can't afford the big hotels and resorts. With all the packages (see "Package Deals," earlier in this chapter) and sales, though, this isn't always true.

The rates included in this book are "rack rates"—the officially posted rates you'd be given if you walked in off the street. Hardly anyone actually pays these prices. Save yourself a bundle by asking your travel agent or the hotel's reservations agent about packages or discounts.

Some hotels are flexible about rates, and many offer discounts and upgrades whenever they have a big block of rooms to fill and few reservations. Smaller hotels are less likely to be generous with discounts, much less upgrades.

The best deals can be had during off-peak periods, which doesn't always mean from mid-April to mid-December only. Discounts are also available during certain slow periods, called "windows," most often after the New Year's holiday. If you want a winter vacation, choose January rather than February or the Christmas holidays, when prices are at their all-year high.

ALL-INCLUSIVES   Presumably, everything's paid for upfront at an "all-inclusive" resort, even drinks and watersports. Unfortunately, some packages cover a room and three meals a day only—drinks, sports, and whatever else are extra. Before you book, ask exactly what's included.

Generally speaking, the all-inclusive market is geared to the active traveler who likes lots of organized entertainment and activities, and unlimited food and drink. Aruba's all-inclusives also appeal to families (there's so much going on, the kids will never get bored) and young adults (plenty of fun times and other young adults). On the other hand, if you want to get out, see the island, and eat at different restaurants, or if you're not particularly interested in nonstop organized events, all-inclusives probably aren't for you.

TIMESHARES   Renting an apartment can be one of the least expensive ways to vacation in Aruba. It also offers privacy, independence, and, in most cases, peace and quiet. The island doesn't have many private-home rentals, but it's teeming with timeshare resorts.

All of Aruba's timeshare accommodations come with a kitchen, and most have a living room, a dining room, and a guest room or two. Some are freestanding villas; others are indistinguishable from regular resort complexes and feature all the facilities and amenities of a hotel, like a reception desk, restaurant and bar, and swimming pool. Most also include fresh linen and maid service, although housekeeping may be scaled back on Sunday or not include kitchen cleanup.

Because many tour operators work directly with timeshares that have rentals available, your travel agent may present a suite in a timeshare property as just another accommodation option. In addition, most individual timeshare resorts assist owners in renting their units, so call a property that interests you or visit its website. Some websites have owner bulletin boards with a listing of rentals available. And more general bulletin boards like **Aruba Bulletin Board** (**www.aruba-bb.com**) abound with timeshare rental opportunities, some at great prices.

2

Getting to Know Aruba

After several hours in flight, your plane approaches Aruba, and you get your first view of the small, unassuming island. Caressed by spectacularly colorful waters, the sun-drenched beaches look ready to warm and enfold your body. The cold and snow back home are a million miles away. In about an hour, you'll be sipping a tropical cocktail at your hotel's poolside bar. Because there's nothing jarringly unfamiliar about Aruba, a drink is about all the adjustment to the island you'll need. This is going to be stress-free: People speak English, most tourists are from the U.S. and Canada, prices are in dollars, driving's on the right side of the road, and you can drink the water. It's time to start your vacation. Full speed ahead.

1 Arriving

BY PLANE

Before Queen Beatrix International Airport was expanded and renovated in 2000, a blast of dry, warm air welcomed vacationers to Aruba as they descended the stairs of their plane to the tarmac. Nowadays, you walk from air-conditioned plane to air-conditioned terminal with no hint of the arid heat until you leave the building. Lots of folks miss that hot blast—shorthand for vacation—but it's hard to find fault with the airport otherwise. It's clean, modern, and organized. Unless your flight arrives with several others (it may on weekends), the lines through Immigration and Customs move rapidly. Luggage doesn't make it to the conveyer belts as fast as you'd like, but does it anywhere? Blame baggage delays on drug-sniffing canines (don't be alarmed; it's standard procedure). Plenty of free luggage carts are available.

The terminal has a bank and an ATM. Most stores are in the departing passenger lounges, but in the courtyard to your left as you leave the U.S. arrivals building, a handful of small shops sell books, souvenirs, and snacks. Plans to open more stores and a restaurant or two may be finalized by the time you arrive. Earlier talk of adding a small casino has waned.

Aruba

California Point

California Lighthouse

Malmok Beach

Hadicurari (Fishermen's Huts)

Palm Beach

2A
2B

Alto Vista Chapel

Eagle Beach

1A

Noord

1B

3B

Manchebo Beach

3A

Druif Beach

2A
2B

4A
4B

Bushiribana

6B
6A

Oranjestad

7B
7A

Natural Bridge

Queen Beatrix Airport

Hooiberg

Santa Cruz

7A
7B

Caribbean Sea

ARIKOK

Caves of Canashito

Spanish Lagoon

1A
1B

NATIONAL

Jamanota

Boca Prins
Sand Dunes

Fontein Cave

PARK

Quadirikiri Cave

Savaneta

1B
1A

7A
7B

San Nicolas

Boca Grandi

Caribbean Sea

Seroe Colorado

Rodger's Beach

Baby Beach

Colorado Point

Airport
Beach
Cruise Ship Dock
Lighthouse

0   3 mi

0   3 km

N

> **Tips Hassle-Free Return to the States**
>
> You just arrived, but remember this for later. Because U.S. Customs and Immigration agents are stationed at Aruba's airport, formalities for re-entry to the United States are taken care of before you board your plane for home. That means no long lines to wait in when you get back to the U.S.

In the interest of protecting cab drivers' livelihood, Aruban law precludes hotels from picking up guests at the airport. If you've come on a package tour, your ground transportation voucher gives you a seat on one of the privately operated, air-conditioned buses that take arriving passengers to the hotels. Otherwise, you can take a cab. Fixed, regulated fares are $9 to $10 to Oranjestad, $14 to $16 to the Low-Rise hotels, $17 to $19 to the High-Rises, and $21 to Tierra del Sol. Taxis line up outside the terminal. If you want to get behind the wheel of your own car, 20 or so car-rental kiosks await you on the other side of the taxis (see below for car-rental information). The drive from the airport to the hotels is 10 to 25 minutes, depending on traffic and the time of day.

BY CRUISE SHIP

Almost 340 cruise ships brought 580,000 visitors to Aruba in 2002. Celebrity, Holland America, Radisson, Royal Caribbean, and Windjammer ships begin itineraries in Aruba, and Carnival, Celebrity, Crystal, Holland America, Lindblad, Norwegian, Princess, Royal Caribbean, Silversea, and Windstar all have ships that make port calls here.

Cruisers arrive at the Aruba Port Authority, a modern terminal with a tourist information booth, ATMs, and plenty of shops. From the pier, it's a 5-minute walk to the immediately evident shopping districts of downtown Oranjestad. If you're not taking a shore excursion, you can make your way around on your own, allowing some time for the beach (just a 5- to 10-min. taxi ride away), lunch, and shopping. Taxis line up to take cruisers to the beach; if you want to save money, the bus terminal is practically as close as the cabs: Once you've walked to the main harborfront road, look for the large pastel complex to your left. Most buses serve the resort areas, but before boarding, ask the drivers if he's headed your way. The trip to the Low-Rise Area takes about 15 minutes; to the High-Rise Area, add another 5 to 10 minutes. Same-day round-trip fare between the beach hotels and the

Oranjestad station is $2; a one-way ride is $1.15. Make sure you have exact change. Still a large cargo port, Oranjestad is separating its cruise and cargo facilities and beefing up passenger terminal services. For more information, contact the **Cruise Tourism Authority,** Royal Plaza Mall, Suite 227, L. G. Smith Blvd. 94, Oranjestad (© **297/583-3648;** www.arubabycruise.com).

2 Getting Around

BY RENTAL CAR It's easy to rent a car in Aruba. Decent roads connect major tourist attractions, and all the major rental companies honor valid U.S. and Canadian driver's licenses. Most major U.S. car-rental companies and a variety of reputable local operators maintain offices at the airport and at major hotels; others have free delivery and pick-up service. There's no tax on car rentals, but even if you purchase a collision-damage waiver, you're responsible for the first $300 to $500 worth of damage. Rental rates for cars, usually Suzukis, Toyotas, Chryslers, Fords, or Volkswagens, vary from season to season and from dealer to dealer. Gas is expensive compared to North America. All service stations charge the same price, and there's no discount for self-service.

Is it necessary to rent a car? It depends. If you want to explore the island, go ahead and get one for a day or 2 or 3; many of the local agencies have 3-day specials. If you have no intention of leaving your resort except to dine, gamble, and shop, it's cheaper to take cabs or the reliable buses.

To rent a car, try **Avis,** Kolibristraat 14 (© **800/331-1212** in the U.S., or 297/582-8617 in Aruba; www.avis.com); **Budget Rent-a-Car,** Kolibristraat 1 (© **800/472-3325** in the U.S., or 297/582-5423

Tips Rules of the Road

As in the U.S. and Canada, driving is on the right side of the road. Traffic signs use international symbols: most are self-explanatory, but some aren't. Ask your car-rental agency for a sheet of the symbols, and take a few minutes to familiarize yourself with them. There are no right turns on red. Car speedometers and road signs are in kilometers. The speed limit in urban areas is 40kmph (about 25 mph); out of town it's 60kmph (about 37 mph), unless otherwise posted. Much of Oranjestad's traffic is one-way; at intersections where there are no road signs, traffic from your right has the right of way.

in Aruba; www.budgetrentacar.com); **Dollar Rent-a-Car,** at the airport (© **800/800-3665** in the U.S. or 297/582-5651 in Aruba; www.dollarcar.com); **Hertz,** Sabano Blanco 35 (© **800/654-3001** in the U.S., or 297/582-1845 in Aruba; www.hertz.com); **National,** at the airport (© **800/CAR-RENT** in the U.S., or 297/582-5451 in Aruba; www.nationalcar.com); or **Thrifty Car Rental,** at the airport (© **800/THRIFTY,** or 297/583-5335 in Aruba; www.thrifty.com). During the high season, expect to pay $40 to $65 per day for a compact car, $75 to $80 per day for a four-wheel-drive vehicle. During the low season, rates drop to $30 to $45 for a compact, $60 to $85 for a Jeep.

For a better deal, try one of the reputable local agencies, such as **Explore Car Rental,** Schotlandstraat 85 (© **877-803-9313** or 297/582-7202; www.explorecarrental.com); **Economy Car Rental,** Bushiri 27 (© **297/583-0200;** www.economyaruba.com); or **Carnaval Rent a Car,** Belgiestraat 2 (© **297/582-5295;** www.carnaval rent.com). You can make reservations online; look for online specials.

BY BUS   Aruba has an excellent public bus system, with regular, reliable service. Buses run roughly every half-hour from 6am to 6pm and every hour from 6pm to midnight, Monday through Saturday. On Sunday and holidays, service is less frequent: every hour between 6am and 6pm, every 2 hours between 6pm and midnight. Same-day round-trip fare between the beach hotels and Oranjestad is $2; a one-way ride is $1.15. Have exact change. Schedules are available at the **Arubus** office (© **297/582-7089**) at the central terminal on Zoutmanstraat in Oranjestad, but your hotel's reception desk will know when buses pass by. You'll seldom wait more than 20 to 30 minutes for the next coach. The trip into town takes 10 to 20 minutes. There's a stop in front of most hotels.

BY TAXI   Taxis are unmetered but rates are fixed, and every cab has a copy of the official rate schedule. Tell the driver where you're going and ask the fare before you get in. Hailing a taxi on the street is difficult, but you'll find plenty of cabs at hotels. To return to your resort from dinner, have the restaurant call for a car. The dispatch office is inland from the Low-Rises at Pos Abou z/n, behind the Eagle Bowling Palace on the Sasaki road (© **297/582-2116**). Tip 15% to 20%. Because it's next to impossible to find a taxi in remoter parts of the island, ask the driver who dropped you off to return for you at a certain time. Most drivers speak good English and are willing, even eager, to give you a tour of the island. Expect to pay $35 per hour for a maximum of four passengers. Following

---

Tips Driving Hazards

Most of Aruba's roads are pretty good, but the traffic signs leave much to be desired. Few streets outside of Oranjestad are marked, and signs to major tourist attractions look as if they were made by neighborhood kids decades ago. Try to keep your eye on the road, though, because iguanas and goats pose unusual traffic hazards. Arubans are considerate, cautious drivers for the most part, although they seem to drive either too fast or too slowly. For a small town, Oranjestad has big-city traffic much of the day.

---

are rates for the most common routes:

- From High-Rise hotels: $4 to $8 to Low-Rise hotels; $6 to $8 to Noord restaurants and Oranjestad; $17 to $18 to the airport
- From Low-Rise hotels: $4 to $8 to High-Rise hotels; $6 to $8 to Noord restaurants and Oranjestad; $14 to $16 to the airport
- From Oranjestad hotels: $6 to $8 to Low-Rise hotels; $8 to $9 to Noord restaurants and High-Rise hotels; $10 to the airport

Surcharges are added on Sunday ($1), holidays ($3), and after midnight ($2). The minimum fare is $4. Waiting time is $8 per 15 minutes. Shirtless, wet, or damp passengers are not allowed, and you're charged $50 for seat damage from wet clothing or sharp objects. U.S. bills in denominations larger than $20 are not accepted.

BY MOTORCYCLE & MOPED   Because Aruba's roads are good and the terrain is flat, mopeds and motorcycles are another transit option. They're available at **George's Cycle Center,** L. G. Smith Blvd. 136 (© **297/582-5975**), and **Nelson Motorcycle Rental,** Gasparito 10A, Noord (© **297/586-6801**). Scooters rent for $30 per day, motorcycles for $45 to $100. For $150 a day or $95 for 4 hours during the high season ($100 or $85 in the off season), you can go hog wild and rent a Harley (HOG members get a $10 discount during the high season). Call **Big Twin Aruba,** L. G. Smith Blvd. 124A (© **297/582-8660;** www.harleydavidson-aruba.com).

Melcor Cycle Rental, Bubali 106B (© **297/587-1787**), in front of the Adventure Golf Club, rents scooters for $32 per day. Prices for dirt bikes and street bikes begin at $45 per day. These are cash prices; add a 4% handling charge if you use a credit or charge card. You can also find rentals at **Semver Cycle Rental,** Noord 22 (© **297/ 586-6851**), where bikes begin at $25 per day.

FAST FACTS: **Aruba**

Banks Banks are open Monday to Friday from 8am to noon and 1:30 to 3:45pm. Oranjestad and Noord, the town inland from Palm Beach, have many branches. You can find ATMs at the airport, in Oranjestad, and at several hotels in the Low-Rise and High-Rise areas.

Business Hours Stores are open from 8am to 6pm, Monday through Saturday; some close for lunch between noon and 2pm. Shops in the malls and shopping centers have slightly different hours, from 9:30am to 6pm. When cruise ships are in port, some stores in Oranjestad open on Sunday and holidays. Office hours are generally Monday through Friday from 9am to 5pm.

Currency The coin of the realm is the **Aruba florin (AFl),** but U.S. dollars are universally accepted. See "Money," in chapter 1.

Documents Bring your passport or original birth certificate. See "Entry Requirements," in chapter 1.

Drinking The legal age for both drinking and gambling is 18.

Electricity Like the United States and Canada, Aruba uses 110 volts AC (60 cycles). No transformer or adapter is needed, so feel free to bring your electrical gadgets from home.

Emergencies As in the United States, dial ☎ **911** for police, medical, and fire emergencies.

Holidays See "When to Go," in chapter 1.

Language The official language is Dutch, but practically everybody speaks English. The language of the street is Papiamento, the local tongue that combines various European, African, and indigenous American languages. Spanish is also widely spoken.

Medical Emergencies Dial ☎ **911,** contact your hotel's reception desk, or go to the **Horacio Oduber Hospital,** L. G. Smith Boulevard, near Eagle Beach (☎ **297/587-4300**). See "Health & Insurance," in chapter 1.

Safety Aruba is one of the Caribbean's safest destinations. Don't leave your valuables unattended on the beach or in an unlocked car, though. You wouldn't at home.

Taxes & Service Charges The government of Aruba charges a 6% room tax and a $36 airport departure tax (included in the price of your ticket). Hotels and restaurants often add service charges of 10% to 12%. See "Money," in chapter 1.

Telephone To call Aruba from the United States, dial **011** (the international access code), then **297** (Aruba's country code), then **58** (the area code) and the five-digit local number. Once you're in Aruba, dial only the five-digit local number for locations on the island. AT&T customers can dial ℭ **800-8000** from special phones at the cruise docks and at the airport to get service; from other phones, dial ℭ **121** to place a collect or AT&T calling card call. International phone calls from hotels are exorbitantly expensive, about $1.50 a minute. There are no toll-free numbers; you'll pay $1.50 per minute even if you're dialing an 800 number. MCI's access number in Aruba is ℭ **800-8888**. Sprint's access number throughout the Caribbean is ℭ **001-800/877-8000**.

Time Aruba is on Atlantic Standard time year-round. For most of the year, the island is 1 hour ahead of Eastern Standard time (when it's noon in Aruba, it's 11am in New York, 10am in Chicago, and 8am in Los Angeles). When the United States is on daylight saving time, the time in New York and Aruba is the same.

Tipping See "Money," in chapter 1.

Water The water, which comes from the world's second-largest desalination plant, is pure and absolutely safe to drink.

3

Where to Stay

You'll be hard pressed to find a lemon among Aruba's hotels and resorts. At the very least, accommodations on the island are above average; in many cases, they're downright amazing. Hotels appreciate your business, and it shows, from the bend-over-backward service to the endless array of amenities.

Lodging is a competitive business on the island. When one hotel introduces a new feature, the others scramble to match or beat it. As a result, all of the upscale resorts have a casino, a fitness center, some kind of spa, an assortment of dining and drinking venues, lush gardens, and magnificent pools. Even modest lodges have amenities you wouldn't expect for the price.

So how do you decide where to stay?

If you'd rather be in the middle of the action than on an expansive beach, stay in Oranjestad. It's not a big town, but it has big-town casinos, restaurants, shopping, and nightlife. And it's no more than a 10-minute drive from the best beaches.

A 15-minute walk northwest from Oranjestad, the Low-Rise area has the feel of an unpretentious beach town. It's a mix of boutique hotels, peaceful timeshares, and large, low-lying resorts. Rooms here are generally a good value. As the lengthy, uncrowded beach moves up the coast, its name changes from Bushiri to Druif to Manchebo to Eagle. Not all the Low-Rise hotels are beachside—a small road separates several from the water—but that keeps the beach tranquil. Drink and snack bars are few and far between, motorized watersports are discouraged, piers are nowhere to be seen, and the beach is wide and generally uncrowded, but restaurants and other amenities are just across the road.

A brief limestone outcrop separates Eagle Beach from Palm Beach and the High-Rise area. A mix of Miami Beach and San Juan's Isla Verde, the glamorous High-Rise hotels usually have several stars next to their names in travel agent brochures. Most front the beach, all boast amenities that go on and on, and some rise as high as 18 stories. Despite the glitz associated with the area, moderately priced options are readily available. The mile-long strand here is as dazzling

---

(*Value* **Off-Season Savings**

Although occupancy rates during the low season (about mid-Apr to mid-Dec) remain high, prices plummet by up to 50%.

---

as Eagle Beach, but it's narrower and there's less room to isolate yourself. Smart bars and beachside restaurants line the strip. Piers projecting into the sea serve dive and fishing boats as well as other motorized equipment.

Hotels and timeshares inland from the Low-Rise and High-Rise areas lack the allure of instant beach access, but most are still within a 10- to 20-minute stroll of the sea. Naturally, their rates are lower.

In general, you'll find more Americans and a more mature crowd during the first 4 months of the year. After April, families, budget-conscious travelers, and Europeans make up an increasing part of the mix. South Americans have a greater presence during their winter (June, July, and Aug). Just a hop, skip, and a jump away from Aruba, Venezuelans and Colombians pop over for holiday weekends year-round. Recent economic and political crises, especially in Venezuela and Argentina, have hurt Aruba's South American business, though.

A word about rates: Some hotels have extremely complex rate schedules, with prices varying within certain months and several times a year. I've condensed some of these schedules in the listings below; of course, you'll always want to confirm rates before you book. Also know that the prices quoted are rack rates for two adults. Rack rates are the published prices that hotels charge customers who walk in off the street. In most cases, you can get an infinitely more affordable rate by opting for a package, offered by tour operators or the hotels themselves.

In the same vein, although hotels are grouped by price category, think of the groupings as ballpark figures. Hotels change rates at different times during the year and spontaneously to reflect supply and demand, so an "Expensive" hotel could be more affordable than a "Moderate" resort during a seasonal window of opportunity. Also, lumping traditional hotels and all-inclusives together is like comparing apples to mangos. To determine the relative value of an all-inclusive, you'll have to add the estimated cost of food, drink, and other amenities offered by the all-inclusive to the price of accommodations only at a traditional hotel.

One last point: Every hotel listed below provides room phones and ample free parking unless otherwise stated.

1 Oranjestad

EXPENSIVE

Renaissance Aruba Beach Resort & Casino ★★★ If this upscale resort's 40-acre private island, with its endless amenities, doesn't make you feel special enough, then book the private cove and enjoy your own secluded space, unlimited mimosas, and a personal butler. Oranjestad's main road, a marina, and an open-air shopping mall (replete with boutiques, restaurants, and a multiplex cinema) separate the hotel's two towers. The anchor of a second mall, the six-story Marina Tower is in the thick of the capital's bustle. It's popular with business travelers and vacationers alike. The compact rooms, beautifully refurbished in 2003, feature thick carpeting, modern color schemes, stylish rattan furniture, and step-out balconies. The bathrooms are a bit on the small side but have separate sink and bath areas and lighted, magnifying make-up mirrors. Overlooking the mall, atrium rooms are the quietest, but you'll forgo an ocean view. Get a corner room on the sixth floor if you like high ceilings. On the waterfront and favored by families, the five-floor Beach Tower feels more like a resort. It features a small man-made beach and 256 roomy, recently renovated one-bedroom suites with living rooms, dining areas, large bathrooms, full-size balconies or patios, and fully equipped wet bars. White tile, floral pastels, and glass brick brighten the rooms. Before hopping the free skiff to Renaissance Island (a 15-min. ride), catch the water, sound, and light show at the lobby lagoon. Also on the premises are two casinos (including the island's only 24-hr. facility) and a large theater that presents excellent Vegas-style shows.

L. G. Smith Blvd. 82, Oranjestad, Aruba. ② 800/468-3571 in the U.S. and Canada, or 297/583-6000. Fax 297/583-4389. www.marriott.com. 560 units. Christmas–Apr $230–$270 Marina Tower double, $350–$450 Marina Tower suite, $260–$290 Beach Tower suite; May–Dec $160–$200 Marina Tower double, $280–$380 Marina Tower suite, $190–$220 Beach Tower suite. Packages available. Children under 17 stay free in parent's room. AE, DISC, MC, V. Valet parking at Marina Tower ($5); free waterfront parking for guests of both towers. **Amenities:** 4 restaurants (international [L'Escale, one of Aruba's best; p. 64], breakfast buffet, casual, beachside); 4 bars; coffee bar; 2 casinos; 3 outdoor pools; 18-hole championship golf course nearby; tennis court; excellent health club and spa; separate fitness center on Renaissance Island; extensive watersports equipment/rentals; children's/teen programs; game room; concierge; tour/activities desk; car-rental desk; business center; shopping arcade; salon; 24-hr. room service; babysitting; coin-op laundry (Beach Tower); laundry/valet service; same-day dry cleaning; nonsmoking rooms; wheelchair-accessible rooms; theme nights. *In room:* A/C, TV, dataport, minibar, coffeemaker, hair dryer, iron, safe, robes.

INEXPENSIVE

Talk of the Town Beach Club *Value*   Between the airport and downtown Oranjestad, this unassuming hotel is Aruba's oldest operating resort. It books mostly Europeans, especially 20-somethings, and Dutch families. An outdoor restaurant and bar border one side of the good-size pool and deck area; palms and rooms line the other three sides. Parallel to a busy road, the standard rooms are the least desirable except during Carnival, when they offer prime parade views. The nicer and quieter superior rooms face the pool, are tropically decorated, and feature a refrigerator, microwave, and coffeemaker. All rooms have two doubles or one king-size bed; superior rooms also have a sofa bed. Apartments in the back have been converted to classrooms for the island's hotel school. The "beach club," across the street, features a small strand, towels, chairs, *palapas* (shade huts), a small pool, and a snack bar. Renovations at the complex since 1993 have been largely cosmetic, but the rooms are well maintained.

L. G. Smith Blvd. 2, Oranjestad, Aruba. ℭ 297/582-3380. Fax 297/582-0327. www. talkofthetownaruba.com. 51 units. Dec–Apr $120 standard, $135 superior; May–Nov $72 standard, $82 superior. Dive package available. AE, MC, V. **Amenities:** Bar and grill; outdoor pool; 18-hole championship golf course nearby; complimentary access to offsite health club (a 5-min. walk away); watersports equipment/rentals; tour/ activities desk; car-rental desk; babysitting; coin-op laundry. *In room:* A/C, TV.

2 High-Rise Hotels/Palm Beach/Noord

VERY EXPENSIVE

Aruba Marriott Resort & Stellaris Casino ★★★   The Marriott's airy, tastefully subdued rooms are the largest in any of Aruba's luxury high-rise hotels. Its 100-square-foot balconies are also the most commodious in the area. In fact, everything about the hotel is oversized: The bathrooms feature two sinks, counter space to spread your toiletries, and room for two to do jumping jacks. And as the last resort along Palm Beach, the Marriott boasts a spacious beach that's ideal for sunbathers craving space. Built in 1995 and under constant renovation, the hotel has a quiet and discerning tone. Guests run the gamut from honeymooners to retirees to corporate-incentive rewardees. There are plenty of families, too, but children here are well behaved. The eight-story complex forms a U that overlooks a large free-form pool, a waterfall, and lush palm, banana, and jacaranda trees. The Mandara Spa offers Aruba's most spiritually transformative indoor experience. Shopping arcades and a casino cater to your material needs.

L. G. Smith Blvd. 101, Palm Beach, Aruba. ℭ **800/223-6388** in the U.S. and Canada, or 297/586-9000. Fax 297/586-0649. www.marriott.com. 413 units. Christmas/New

Year's $450–$845 double, from $845 suite; Jan–Apr $390–$475 double, from $475 suite; May to mid-Dec $239–$324 double, from $324 suite. Packages available. Children under 12 stay free in parent's room. AE, DISC, MC, V. **Amenities:** 6 restaurants (coffee shop, Italian [Tuscany; p. 75], seafood, beachside grill, sushi, sports-themed); 3 bars; casino; large outdoor pool with waterfall; 18-hole championship golf course nearby; 2 tennis courts lit for night play; well-equipped health club and spa; extensive watersports equipment/rentals; children's center/program; game room; concierge; tour/activities desk; car-rental desk; fax/photocopy service; shopping arcades; salon; limited room service; babysitting; laundry service; same-day dry cleaning; nonsmoking rooms; ADA-compliant disabled-access rooms. *In room:* A/C, TV, dataport, minibar, coffeemaker, hair dryer, iron, safe.

Hyatt Regency Aruba Resort & Casino ☆☆☆   This elegant nine-story beachfront resort has stunning public spaces and a stellar reputation. Monumental cactus plants stud the refined lobby, and massive wrought-iron chandeliers give the grand, breezy entrance the air of an alcazar in Seville. Past the lobby, carpets of bougainvillea, moss-covered boulders, and towering palms spill down to a multilevel pool where exotic macaws and toucans doze. This full-service hotel offers first-rate amenities and some of the most elaborate guest programs on the island. Although attractively furnished with Deco-inspired furniture and modern carnival colors, the rooms are significantly smaller than the Marriott's. And the "Parisian" balconies offer just enough room for one person to stand. The good-size bathrooms were recently renovated. Overlooking the pool area, standard rooms have no balcony. Other rooms provide vistas of the pool and ocean, while garden units boast views of the lush tropical foliage. The 18 suites vary in size, but all are spacious, with good balconies, and some feature extras like stereo systems and in-room fitness equipment. Built in 1990, the hotel conducts ongoing renovations, and the room decor changes every 18 months.

J. E. Irausquin Blvd. 85, Palm Beach, Aruba. © **800/55-HYATT** in the U.S. and Canada, or 297/586-1234. Fax 297/586-1682. www.aruba.hyatt.com. 360 units. Christmas–New Year's $480–$630 double; Jan–Apr $400–$590 double; May–Nov $240–$365 double. Packages available. Children under 18 stay free in parent's room. AE, DISC, MC, V. **Amenities:** 4 restaurants (Spanish/tapas, international/seafood [Ruinas del Mar; p. 74], Italian, beachside grill); 4 bars; casino; 3-level outdoor pool/lagoon complex; 18-hole championship golf course nearby; 2 tennis courts lit for night play; state-of-the-art health club and spa; extensive watersports equipment/rentals; elaborate children's center/program; game room/video arcade; concierge; tour/activities desk; car-rental desk; full-service business center; shopping arcade; salon; 24-hr. room service; babysitting; laundry/valet service; same-day dry cleaning; nonsmoking rooms; concierge-level rooms; ADA-compliant disabled-access rooms. *In room:* A/C, TV, dataport, minibar, coffeemaker, hair dryer, iron, safe, makeup mirror.

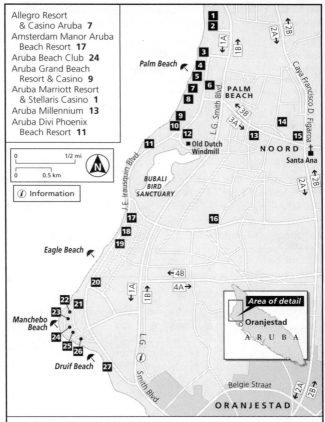

Allegro Resort
  & Casino Aruba **7**
Amsterdam Manor Aruba
  Beach Resort **17**
Aruba Beach Club **24**
Aruba Grand Beach
  Resort & Casino **9**
Aruba Marriott Resort
  & Stellaris Casino **1**
Aruba Millennium **13**
Aruba Divi Phoenix
  Beach Resort **11**

Palm Beach

PALM
BEACH

Old Dutch
Windmill

NOORD

Santa Ana

BUBALI
BIRD
SANCTUARY

(i) Information

Eagle Beach

Manchebo
Beach

Druif Beach

Area of detail

Oranjestad

A R U B A

Belgie Straat

(i)

ORANJESTAD

Arubiana Inn **16**
Best Western Manchebo
  Beach Resort Aruba **23**
Brickell Bay Beach Club Aruba **6**
Bucuti Beach Resort Aruba **22**
Caribbean Palm Village Resort **15**
Casa del Mar Beach Resort **25**
Coconut Inn **14**
Costa Linda Beach Resort **21**
Divi Aruba Beach Resort
  Mega All Inclusive **26**
Holiday Inn SunSpree Aruba
  Resort & Casino **3**

Hyatt Regency Aruba
  Resort & Casino **5**
La Cabana All-Suite
  Beach Resort & Casino **18**
La Quinta Beach Resort **20**
Marriott's Aruba Ocean Club **2**
The Mill Resort & Suites **12**
Paradise Beach Villas **19**
Playa Linda Beach Resort **4**
Radisson Aruba Resort & Casino **8**
Tamarijn Aruba Beach Resort **27**
Wyndham Aruba
  Beach Resort & Casino **10**

Marriott's Aruba Ocean Club 🏵🏵🏵   This is Aruba's newest and poshest timeshare resort featuring modern, comfortable one- and two-bedroom suites. (By 2004, it will be the island's second-newest timeshare; Marriott is building the even grander Surf Club next door.) Shaped like a giant U, the six-story building echoes the design of the Aruba Marriott hotel, its sister resort next door on Palm Beach's quietest stretch. The villas at the Ocean Club have a sumptuous, up-to-date look (they opened in 1999). Hardwoods, dark rattan, and tasteful fabrics create an elegant yet homey feel. All suites hold a full gourmet kitchen. Bar seating separates the kitchen from the semi-formal dining room and spacious living room, and an open whirlpool in the king-size bedroom beckons irresistibly. Vistas from the large balcony take in the ocean and the central rock-and-palm lagoon pool; two-room villas boast two balconies. The pricier ocean-front villas have even larger balconies with spectacular views. Ocean Club guests have full access to the Marriott hotel's impressive array of amenities, and the Mandara Spa, tucked away off the beaten path, is without peer on the island (see "Spa Retreats," below).

⎛Moments Spa Retreats

Diamonds may be a girl's best friend, but corporeal indulgence is a close second. The **Mandara Spa** at Marriott's Aruba Ocean Club, L. G. Smith Blvd. 99, Palm Beach (② **297/586-9000**), re-creates the tranquillity of a Javanese rainforest with Thai silk wall hangings, softly throbbing Balinese gamelan music, and the sweet scents of clove and cinnamon. Personal attention is the hallmark of this meditative retreat, which offers state-of-the-art massages, body wraps, and facials. Although most treatments reflect the spa's Indonesian roots, several highlight the restorative powers of Aruban aloe and the exfoliating properties of Bonairean salt. Specially designed programs cater to couples and men, who make up a hefty portion of the clientele. Aromatic masks, bath salts, and creams are for sale. Other upscale spas can be found at **Tierra del Sol** (② **297/586-4861**), the **Hyatt** (② **297/586-1234**), and the **Renaissance** (② **297/583-6000**). For a more rustic pampering experience, try **Cosmos Day Spa,** Savaneta 344 (② **297/584-5895**), a sanctuary by the sea featuring massages and other treatments in beachside cabanas in the village of Savaneta. The training of masseurs and masseuses on the island varies greatly. Be sure to ask for the most experienced person available.

L. G. Smith Blvd. 99, Palm Beach, Aruba. ℂ **297/586-9000.** Fax 297/586-0649. www.vacationclub.com. 218 units. Christmas–Jan $735–$770 1-bedroom, $975–$1,050 2-bedroom; Feb $525–$590 1-bedroom, $745–$825 2-bedroom; Mar–Apr $425–$485 1-bedroom, $625–$675 2-bedroom; May–Christmas $265–$315 1-bedroom, $385–$425 2-bedroom. AE, DISC, MC, V. **Amenities:** 5 restaurants (coffee shop, Italian, seafood, beachside grill, sports-themed); 3 bars; large outdoor pool; kiddie pool and play area with shipwreck theme; 18-hole championship golf course nearby; 2 tennis courts lit for night play; well-equipped health club and Aruba's best spa; outdoor Jacuzzis; extensive watersports equipment/rentals; children's center/program; game room/video arcade; concierge; tour/activities desk; car-rental desk; fax/photocopy services; shopping arcades; salon; limited room service; babysitting; coin-op laundry; laundry service; same-day dry cleaning; nonsmoking rooms; ADA-compliant disabled-access rooms. *In room:* A/C, TV/VCR, dataport.

Radisson Aruba Resort & Casino ⭐⭐⭐ This stunning eight-story resort has the most stylish and beautiful rooms in Aruba. Integrating Caribbean plantation and South Beach Art Deco elements throughout, the complex is both sophisticated and personal. Because the lush gardens, lagoons, and waterfalls ramble over more than 14 acres, the tone is tranquil and the feel is spacious even when the hotel's completely booked. The guest rooms aren't large, but they're remarkable. West Indian colonial louvered doors, rather than drapes, cover the terrace doors, and intricately carved finials crown the mahogany four-poster beds. The reading chair's retractable ottoman and floor lamp mix Bauhaus and plantation influences. The bathrooms reconfirm that space is not the strong point here, but the Italian marble floor, soapstone sink, and glass-enclosed tub argue that good things come in small packages. Elegance stretches out to the balconies, too, where mahogany slatted chairs and flagstone floors enhance the view over the gardens or turquoise sea. To create the warmth of a private home, the Radisson adds touches like frosted drinking glasses, silver ice buckets, and earthtone pottery. Originally built in 1959 as Aruba's first high-rise hotel, the complex closed in 1998 for a $55 million overhaul and reopened in 2000. It's now Radisson's flagship hotel, and it attracts a discerning clientele.

J. E. Irausquin Blvd. 81, Palm Beach, Aruba. ℂ **800/333-3333** in the U.S. and Canada, or 297/586-6555. Fax 297/586-3260. www.radisson.com/palmbeachaw. 358 units. Christmas–New Year's $425–$600 double, from $600 suite; Jan and Apr $340–$475 double, from $525 suite; Feb and Mar $360–$495 double, from $525 suite; May–Sep $210–$345 double, from $375 suite; Oct–Christmas $225–$345 double, from $375 suite. Children under 18 stay free in parent's room. Discounts for guests over age 50; packages available. AE, DISC, MC, V. **Amenities:** 3 restaurants (first-rate steak and seafood [Sunset Grille; p. 74], buffet/international, beach grill); 2 bars; casino; 2 large outdoor pools; 18-hole championship golf course nearby; 2 tennis courts lit for night play; modern health club/spa; 2 outdoor Jacuzzis; extensive watersports equipment/rentals; children's center/program; game room/video arcade; concierge; tour/activities desk; car-rental desk; business center; shopping arcade; salon; 24-hr. room service; babysitting; laundry service; same-day dry cleaning; nonsmoking rooms; concierge-level rooms; ADA-compliant disabled-access rooms. *In room:* A/C, TV, dataport, minibar, coffeemaker, hair dryer, iron, safe.

Wyndham Aruba Beach Resort & Casino 🟊🟊🟊 Talk about service. This hotel offers a personal vacation planner who'll arrange your dinner, tour, and tee-time reservations before you leave home. When you arrive, you'll have a friend waiting for you at the airport and a customized plan for your stay. Built in 1977, the hotel was most recently renovated in 2000, when $10 million went toward room refurbishment. It was money well spent. Olive, beige, and mustard fabrics accent the cherrywood and dark rattan furniture. Subtle carpeting and modern wrought-iron lamps add more style. The rooms are spacious, and all have Internet service (there's a $16 per day fee for unlimited minutes). The large bathrooms have phones, although the counter space could be more generous. The balconies are great: With 18 floors, this is Aruba's tallest building; a terrace anywhere near the top means superb ocean views and total privacy. The Wyndham's pool concierge service is in a class by itself. While you bask in the sun, you'll be misted with Evian water, offered a CD player, and given cool towels and stock quotes. The kids' program includes scuba-diving lessons in the pool. Guests include the usual suspects—couples, honeymooners, and families—and a fair number of business groups. The downside? The elevators can be slow, and you have to wait in line in the morning to reserve a beach hut.

J. E. Irausquin Blvd. 77, Palm Beach, Aruba. 📞 **800/WYNDHAM** in the U.S. or Canada, or 297/586-4466. Fax 297/586-8217. www.arubawyndham.com. 481 units. Dec–Apr $305–$420 double, from $455 suite; May–Sept and Nov $215–$299 double, from $309 suite; Oct $225–$325 double, from $345 suite. Meal plans and various packages (golf, romance, family) available. Children under 12 stay free in parent's room. AE, MC, V. **Amenities:** 5 restaurants (buffet, beachfront, Polynesian [Pago Pago, p. 70], Northern Italian, dinner/show); 3 bars; casino; large outdoor pool; 18-hole championship golf course nearby; 2 tennis courts lit for night play; health club/spa; extensive watersports equipment/rentals; elaborate children's center/program; game room/video arcade; concierge; tour/activities desk; car-rental desk; shopping arcade; salon; limited room service; babysitting; laundry service; same-day dry cleaning; nonsmoking rooms; wheelchair-accessible rooms. *In room:* A/C, TV, dataport, fridge, coffeemaker, hair dryer, iron, safe.

EXPENSIVE
Aruba Divi Phoenix Beach Resort 🟊 A quiet timeshare affiliated with Divi Resorts, the Phoenix has some distinctive features. Its triangular, totally private balconies offer unobstructed ocean views as good as any on the island. And its well-equipped health club is so

---

Tips Freebies for Kids

The One Cool Family Vacation program entices families to visit Aruba during the summer (June–Sept). Here's the deal: Kids under 13 get an assortment of freebies like bed and break- fast, daily activities, sightseeing tours, cruises, snorkeling, and scuba lessons. In addition, discounts are offered for a subma- rine ride, horseback riding, car rental, and even film develop- ing. The program covers two children for every paying adult. Contact the Aruba Tourism Authority (✆ **800/TO-ARUBA**; www.aruba.com) for a list of participating resorts.

---

inviting you'll be tempted to work up a sweat even if your exercise regimen usually consists of breathing—the light flooding through the high cathedral windows is inspiring. Not converted? Well, the rooms aren't too shabby, either. The 66 tower units feature rose-tile floors, sisal mats, rattan furniture, and kitchenettes or full kitchens; some one-bedroom units have an extra half-bath and a second bal- cony. Next to the tower, one- and two-bedroom villas boast enor- mous rooms, balconies that open off the master bedroom and living room, full kitchens, and living/dining areas. Some one-bedrooms have two bathrooms. Ask for a villa away from the noisy air-condi- tioning unit. Guests are independent and 30-plus, with a smatter- ing of kids. If you're coming from the Low-Rises, the 14-floor Phoenix tower marks the beginning of Palm Beach. Breakwaters protect the resort's large, peaceful oceanfront. Some say it's windier than farther up the High-Rise strip. That's a good thing on a really hot day, but when the gusts are extreme it's like getting sandblasted.

J. E. Irausquin Blvd. 75, Palm Beach, Aruba. ✆ **800/376-1072** in the U.S. and Canada, or 297/586-1170. Fax 297/586-1165. www.diviphoenix.com. 101 units. Jan–Mar $240 studio, $275 1-bedroom, $385 2-bedroom; Apr–Dec $115 studio, $165 1-bedroom, $250 2-bedroom. Children under 16 stay free in parent's room. Packages available. AE, DISC, MC, V. **Amenities:** Restaurant (international); bar; 2 outdoor pools; 18-hole championship golf course nearby; tennis courts nearby; excellent health club and spa; watersports equipment/rentals; children's activities; concierge; tour/activities desk; shops; salon; laundry service; dry cleaning; non- smoking rooms; ADA-compliant disabled-access rooms. *In room:* A/C, TV/VCR, kitchen or kitchenette, hair dryer, iron, safe.

Aruba Grand Beach Resort & Casino ⭐ This tranquil resort attracts low-key, independent guests—a senior crowd during the high season and lots of self-sufficient families at other times of the year. A full 80% are back for at least the second time, so the Grand's doing something right. Part hotel, part timeshare, the eight-story tower went up in 1968, but it's well maintained. The most recent renovations in 1999 toned down the color scheme and expanded the bathrooms in some rooms; ask for one of these units. The rooms are spacious, but there are no full-fledged balconies, just crescent-shaped step-outs. The recently enlarged bathrooms, with separate dressing areas, large walk-in closets, and guest robes, are noteworthy. Corner rooms have better layouts and more space, and the units overlooking the pool are worth the extra money. In two-story structures on the other side of the pool, the lanais are frequently sold out. They boast instant access to the beach; in fact, there's sand right outside room 120's door. The 41 one-and two-bedroom timeshare condominiums, which contain kitchens, are sometimes available for rental, too. If you swim for exercise, you'll love the huge lap pool; it's the only Olympic-style cement pond in the High-Rise area. Worth special mention, the Grand's 1,200-square-foot beach is relatively uncrowded for the area.

J. E. Irausquin Blvd., Palm Beach, Aruba. ⓒ **800/345-2782** in the U.S. and Canada, or 297/586-3900. Fax 297/586-1941. www.arubagrand.com. 171 units. Christmas–New Year's $335–$405 double, $445 junior suite, condominiums from $690; Jan–Mar $235–$300 double, $310 junior suite, condominiums from $525; Apr–Dec $155–$215 double, junior suite $235, condominiums from $330. Packages available. Children under 11 stay free in parent's room. AE, DISC, MC, V. **Amenities:** 3 restaurants (international, seafood/steak, poolside grill); Internet cafe; 2 bars; casino; Olympic-size outdoor pool; kiddie pool; 18-hole championship golf course nearby; 2 tennis courts; fitness center; spa; extensive watersports equipment/rentals; children's activities; recreation area; concierge; tour/activities desk; car-rental desk; salon; breakfast-only room service; babysitting; laundry/valet service; dry cleaning; nonsmoking rooms; wheelchair-accessible rooms. *In room:* A/C, TV, dataport, fridge, hair dryer, iron, safe.

Holiday Inn SunSpree Aruba Resort & Casino ⓐ (Value)   Like

Avis, this hotel tries harder. Holiday Inn reserves SunSpree status for its best resorts; this one completed a major transformation in 2000. Rooms were seriously renovated—furniture, drapes, bedspreads, and lighting were replaced—and new amenities, including a spa and humble 24-hour exercise room, were added. In the most evident change, the once uninviting lobby was opened to showcase Aruba's signature trade winds, which now blow freely through the louvered teak wood walls toward the palm trees, bright sand, and turquoise waters outside. The Holiday Inn can't compete with the ritziest hotels on the High-Rise strip, but it offers value—something many of its guests return to year after year. You'll find lots of families, couples, and honeymooners here, and many South Americans (although North Americans still account for more than 60% of guests). Distributed among three seven-story towers, the rooms feature wall-to-wall carpeting, handsome hardwood furniture, and cheerful colors. Some have sofa beds; all have full, if only average, bathrooms and balconies or patios. Refrigerators are available for $10 per day. Essentially identical in layout and furnishings, units are classified by view—garden or ocean. Because it's bounded by development on one side only, the Holiday Inn's beach is the largest in the High-Rise area.

J. E. Irausquin Blvd. 230, Palm Beach, Aruba. *✆* **800/HOLIDAY** in the U.S. and Canada, or 297/586-3600. Fax 297/586-5165. http://holidayinn-aruba.com. 600 units. Christmas–New Year's $295–$350 double; Jan–Apr $225–$275 double; May–Christmas $125–$175 double. Children under 18 stay free in parent's room. Children under 12 eat free with dining adult. Packages available. AE, MC, V. **Amenities:** 3 restaurants (breakfast/lunch buffet, beachside grill, international); 2 bars; casino; large outdoor pool; kiddie pool; 18-hole championship golf course nearby; 4 tennis courts lit for night play; small exercise room; spa; extensive watersports equipment/rentals; children's center/program; game/video room; playground; concierge; tour/activities desk; car-rental desk; small shopping arcade; salon; limited room service; babysitting; coin-op laundry; same-day dry cleaning; nonsmoking rooms; ADA-compliant disabled-access rooms. *In room:* A/C, dataport, coffeemaker, hair dryer, iron, safe.

Playa Linda Beach Resort *✿✿*   Centrally located on Palm Beach, this luxurious timeshare looks like a modern Maya pyramid. The terraced stories of the nine-floor, M-shaped building recede as the tower ascends, ensuring that all of the spacious accommodations have balconies or decks with impressive views. The tasteful furnishings vary by unit type; modern bamboo and rattan furniture, colorful fabrics, beige-tile floors, and sisal area rugs are prominent. Studios come with kitchenettes, and one-bedrooms have enhanced kitchens and living/dining areas. The one-bedroom lanais feature patios that open onto the pool area. Slightly larger than other one-bedroom units, they have spacious wooden decks and minigardens rather than balconies. The two-bedroom oceanfront units boast large master suites with king-size beds and two-sink bathrooms, guest rooms with two twin beds, kitchens, living and dining rooms, another full bathroom, and wraparound terraces with unbeatable vistas. Some have walk-in closets and bars; others feature separate master-suite balconies. Rooms facing away from the pool are generally quieter. Built in two phases (1983 and 1989), the resort is renovated continuously. In 2001, hallways were closed off and air-conditioned, gardens were embellished, and lanais were constructed. During the peak season, most guests are luxury-conscious and older. As the year progresses, families and honeymooners begin to predominate.

J. E. Irausquin Blvd. 87, Palm Beach, Aruba. *✆* **800/992-2015** in the U.S. and Canada, or 297/586-1000. Fax 297/586-3479. www.playalinda.com. 198 units. Jan–Apr $278 studio, $395 1-bedroom, $578 2-bedroom; May–Jun $145 studio,

$200 1-bedroom, $285 2-bedroom; Jul–Dec $185 studio, $255 1-bedroom, $365 2-bedroom. AE, DISC, MC, V. **Amenities:** 2 restaurants (international, seafood); 2 bars; outdoor lagoon pool; children's pool; 18-hole championship golf course nearby; 3 tennis courts lit for night play; sun-drenched fitness center; spa; extensive watersports equipment/rentals; children's program; game room; concierge; tour/activities desk; car-rental desk; business center; shopping arcade; salon; babysitting; coin-op laundry; same-day dry cleaning. *In room:* A/C, TV, kitchen or kitchenette, iron, safe.

MODERATE

Allegro Resort & Casino Aruba *(Kids* Here are a couple of things you should know about this conveniently located beachfront high-rise. First, it's a self-styled "cruise ship on land." If you're looking for a casual house-party atmosphere with lots of action and organized activities, this good-times place is for you. Second, and maybe most telling, the resort's many repeat guests are as happy as clams. Most people choose the all-inclusive package, which covers meals and snacks, unlimited beverages (including alcohol), all nonmotorized watersports, daily activities, tennis, scuba lessons in the pool, supervised kids' activities, nightly entertainment, and applicable taxes and gratuities. For the record, the food's okay if not remarkable. Lined with kids, young couples, middle-aged folks, and some grandparents, the hotel's pool is the busiest and loudest on Palm Beach. People staying here work hard for their vacation and make the most of it. About 80% come from the United States and Canada, and most use their rooms for nothing but crashing. They don't care that the accommodations are pretty standard affairs. Actually, many of the rooms could use a bit of a touch-up, so ask for one that's been recently renovated. You have a choice of garden, pool, or ocean view. The ground-floor lanai rooms (next to the pool) have terraces instead of small balconies and are great for families.

J. E. Irausquin Blvd. 83, Palm Beach, Aruba. ℂ **800/858-2258** in the U.S. and Canada, or 297/586-4500. Fax 297/586-3191. www.allegroresorts.com. 402 units. All-inclusive: Jan $228–$278 per person double, extra person $206–$257, children 2–12 $114–$139, suites from $417 per person; Feb $252–$303 per person double, extra person $231–$282, children 2–12 $126–$152, suites from $442 per person; Mar–Apr $228–$278 per person double, extra person $206–$257, children 2–12 $114–$139, suites from $417 per person; Easter week $252–$303 per person double, extra person $231–$282, children 2–12 $126–$152, suites from $442 per person; May–Aug $185–$262 per person double, extra person $163–$240, children 2–12 $92–$131, suites from $400 per person; Sept–Christmas $200–$262 per person double, extra person $178–$240, children 2–12 $100–$131, suites from $400 per person. Children under 2 stay free in parent's room. Packages available. AE, DISC, MC, V. **Amenities:** 4 restaurants (dinner/show, snack, Italian, Caribbean); 3 bars; casino; outdoor pool; 18-hole championship golf course nearby; 2 tennis courts lit for night play; exercise room; spa; extensive watersports equipment/rentals; children's center/program (enclosed playground); tour/activities desk; car-rental desk; fax services; shopping arcade; salon; room service (breakfast only); babysitting; laundry/dry cleaning service; nonsmoking rooms; wheelchair-accessible rooms. *In room:* A/C, TV, fridge on request, hair dryer, iron, safe.

Caribbean Palm Village Resort   Close to Santa Anna Church, the three-story Caribbean Palm Village Resort rests in the town of Noord, a 15- to 20-minute walk inland from Palm Beach. Because units in this timeshare are completely sold out, vacation rentals are limited. The attractive Spanish mission–style buildings, first opened in 1987, feature white stucco walls, terra cotta–tile roofs, and plenty of columns and arches. The spacious rooms feature cane and glass furniture, fabrics in soothing shades, and white-tile floors. All units have roomy full bathrooms and queen- or king-size beds. Each studio has a kitchenette, and the airy, bright one- and two-bedroom suites come with full kitchens and sofa beds. Attractive gardens surround the two pool areas. Because the front pool is the center of activity, rooms adjacent to the back pool are quieter. The resort's a hike from the sea, but the beach shuttle is free.

Palm Beach 43E, Noord, Aruba. © 297/586-2700. Fax 297/586-2380. 228 units. Dec–Mar $185–$210 double, $250–$275 1-bedroom suite, $310–$335 2-bedroom suite; Apr–Nov $110–$120 double, $125–$140 1-bedroom suite, $165–$185 2-bedroom suite. AE, DISC, MC, V. **Amenities:** Restaurant (Italian [Valentino's; p. 75]); bar; 2 outdoor pools; 18-hole championship golf course nearby; tennis court; car-rental desk; coin-op laundry; barbecue grills. *In room:* A/C, TV, kitchenette or kitchen, safe.

The Mill Resort & Suites ★ *(Finds)*   The only low-rise in the High-Rise area, this resort combines Dutch efficiency and Aruban warmth. Opened in 1990, the two-story complex lies opposite Palm Beach and the Wyndham, next to the kitschy Dutch windmill. Its strengths include personal service, easy access to amenities, and comparatively reasonable prices. Most guests tend to be honeymooning or celebrating a longer romance, but others are looking to meet people and have a good time. Families, who appreciate the value, are welcome as well. The sunny, spotless units feature near-retro bamboo furniture, watercolor fabrics, and tile floors. Junior rooms have a king-size bed, full bathroom, sitting area with sofa bed, good-size porch or balcony, and gleaming kitchenette. Budget-friendly studios have two double beds, a shower-only bathroom, dining/sitting area, and fully equipped kitchen, but no balcony. An open Jacuzzi is steps away from a king-size bed in the Royal rooms, which also boast a vanity area with two sinks, a separate bathroom with shower, a sitting area, and a porch or balcony, but no kitchenette. Garden- and pool-view rooms cost the same; the pool's party atmosphere wanes later in the day, but garden rooms are quieter around the clock. Although the Mill has no beachfront, it offers a towel hut and chairs on the beach, a 3-minute walk away.

J. E. Irausquin Blvd. 330, Palm Beach, Aruba. ⓒ 800/992-2015 in the U.S. and Canada, or 297/586-7700. Fax 297/586-7271. www.millresort.com. 200 units. Dec–Mar $180–$200 studio, from $320 suite; Apr–Nov $85–$120 studio, from $170 suite. Children under 15 stay free in parent's room. Packages available. AE, DISC, MC, V. **Amenities:** Restaurant; bar; 2 pools (1 for children); 18-hole championship golf course nearby; 2 tennis courts lit for night play; exercise room and spa; children's program; concierge; tour/activities desk; car-rental desk; babysitting; coin-op laundry; same-day dry cleaning; wheelchair-accessible room. *In room:* A/C, TV, hair dryer, iron, safe.

INEXPENSIVE

Aruba Millennium This appealing two-story motel is a 10-minute walk inland from Palm Beach. The studios and one-bedroom units, each with kitchenette, face either the small pool or one of two cozy courtyards. Each verdant garden features two Jacuzzis with small wooden decks. All rooms boast either a balcony or a raised rustic-wood terrace with patio furniture and blue-and-white-striped awning. Inside, colorful geometric prints accent the white wicker and bamboo furniture. White-tile floors run throughout the small dining areas and functional bathrooms. The poolside bar serves drinks, continental breakfast, and snacks; the minimart can further satisfy your thirst or hunger. Restaurants and other shops are within easy walking distance. The motel's quiet ambience makes it popular with budget-conscious families and couples looking to zone out by the pool.

Palm Beach 33, Palm Beach, Aruba. ⓒ 297/586-1120. Fax 297/586-2506. www. arubamillenniumresort.com. 22 units. Dec–Apr $130 studio, $172 1-bedroom; May–Nov $60 studio, $95 1-bedroom; Dec–Apr $770 studio weekly, $1,000 1-bedroom weekly; May–Nov $350 studio weekly, $500 1-bedroom weekly. Children under 12 stay free in parent's room. AE, MC, V. **Amenities:** Snack bar; bar; small outdoor pool; 18-hole championship golf course nearby. *In room:* A/C, TV, kitchenette, coffeemaker.

Brickell Bay Beach Club Aruba *(Value* Aruba's newest hotel, this four-story complex is much like an American-style chain motel, but its cleanliness and proximity to the action make it the island's best budget option. Across the street from the Allegro, it has no beach-front, but the sea is no more than a 5-minute walk away, and the pool is inviting. Although the rooms have cookie-cutter uniformity, the walls, carpet, and furnishings are cheerfully colored. All rooms have either two double beds or one king. The bathrooms are bright and functional if not luxuriously spacious. Many guests are here for the nearby casinos, but the hotel also has dive and honeymoon packages.

J. E. Irausquin Blvd. 370, Palm Beach, Aruba. © **800/324-6965** in the U.S. and Canada, or 297/586-0900. Fax 297/586-4957. www.brickellbayaruba.com. 101 units. Jan–Feb $150 double; Mar–Dec $80 double. Packages available. AE, MC, V. **Amenities:** Restaurant; bar; pool; 18-hole championship golf course nearby; tour/activities desk; car-rental desk; Internet desk; babysitting; coin-op laundry. *In room:* A/C, TV, fridge on request, coffeemaker, hair dryer, iron, safe.

Coconut Inn   This budget bed-and-breakfast is about a 20-minute walk inland from Palm Beach, in a hamlet near Santa Anna Church. Brick pathways lined by coconut palms border the five bright yellow-and-white stucco buildings built between 1975 and 1996. The corrugated metal rooftops are painted to look like terra-cotta tile. Wood decks front the ground-floor rooms; second-floor units have balconies. The basic accommodations feature white-tile floors and cheerful fabrics. All rooms have a kitchenette or full kitchen, and the motel's small restaurant serves complimentary breakfast. Shops and restaurants are nearby.

Noord 31, Noord, Aruba. © **297/586-6288.** Fax 297/586-5433. www.coconutinn. com. 40 units. Christmas–Apr $80 superior studio double, $95 deluxe studio or 1-bedroom apt double; May–Christmas $65 superior studio double, $75 deluxe studio or 1-bedroom apt double; Christmas–Apr $525 superior studio double weekly, $630 deluxe studio or 1-bedroom apt double weekly; May–Christmas $430 superior studio double weekly, $455 deluxe studio or 1-bedroom apt double weekly. Rates include breakfast. Children under 12 stay free in parent's room. MC, V. **Amenities:** Restaurant/bar; small outdoor pool; 18-hole championship golf course nearby; coin-op laundry. *In room:* A/C, TV, kitchen or kitchenette.

3 Low-Rise Hotels/Eagle & Manchebo Beaches

VERY EXPENSIVE

Costa Linda Beach Resort ⟨⟨⟨   On a glorious 600-foot stretch of Eagle Beach, this timeshare offers some of Aruba's most impressive accommodations. Its five-story Dutch-Caribbean buildings feature sunny ochre walls with white trim and terra cotta–tile roofs. Inside, tropical colors, split-cane furniture, and light tile floors brighten the enormous two- and three-bedroom suites. All units have expansive living/dining rooms, fully equipped kitchens, at least two TVs, a master suite with raised Roman tub and separate shower, guest bedroom with twin beds and full bathroom, and large private balcony with ocean view. The two-bedroom suites have 348 sq. m (1,160 sq. ft.) of space and can accommodate six people. The three-bedroom suites will make your jaw drop. In addition to every two-bedroom suite appointment, they boast a second guest room with its own kitchenette, TV, and bathroom; original oil paintings; slatted-wood ceilings; glass-brick room dividers; and an enormous balcony. Big enough to entertain 20 to 30 cocktail guests, these ocean-facing terraces feature two distinct sections reached from the living room or master suite. There's patio furniture for eight, a raised Jacuzzi for four, and a party-size BBQ grill. With 900 sq. m (3,000 sq. ft.) of space, the three bedrooms accommodate eight people with ease. Built in 1991, the resort undergoes constant refurbishment and promotes environmental consciousness: Recycling bins and posted exhortations to conserve are everywhere. Obviously, guests are luxury conscious. If you're looking for a chink in the Costa Linda's armor, maid service on Sundays is skeletal.

J. E. Irausquin Blvd. 59, Eagle Beach, Aruba. ✆ **800/992-2015** in the U.S. and Canada, or 297/583-8000. Fax 297/583-6040. www.costalinda-aruba.com. 155 units. Christmas–New Year's $715 2-bedroom suite, $1,397 3-bedroom suite; Jan–Apr $561 2-bedroom suite, $1,243 3-bedroom suite; May–Christmas $360 2-bedroom suite, $715 3-bedroom suite. AE, DISC, MC, V. **Amenities:** 2 restaurants (breakfast buffet, seafood/international); 2 bars; large outdoor pool; kiddie pool; 18-hole championship golf course nearby; 2 tennis courts lit for night play; good-size exercise room; water-sports equipment/rentals nearby; children's program; teen program; game room; concierge; tour/activities desk; car-rental desk; shopping arcade; babysitting; coin-op laundry; same-day dry cleaning; beach wheelchair available; barbecue facilities. *In room:* A/C, TV, dataport, kitchen, hair dryer, safe.

EXPENSIVE

Bucuti Beach Resort Aruba ✦✦✦ *(Finds*

This elegant oasis provides Aruba's most adult ambience. Set on one of the Caribbean's best beaches, a serene 14-acre expanse of sugary white sand, it's a favored retreat for sophisticated couples of all ages, especially honeymooners. About half are from Europe, and most are independent and well traveled. And while most guests are straight, the Bucuti is both appealing and welcoming to gay couples. Carnival and West Indian–plantation motifs enliven the spacious rooms. The stylish drapes and bedspreads blaze with colors like mango, lemon yellow, and cobalt blue, but the taupe-tile floors, pastel area rugs, and warm cherrywood louvered furniture have a calming effect. The bathrooms feature plenty of counter space, and the large balconies overlook gardens or the beach. Suites have kitchenettes. Because the Bucuti's owner-manager is the driving force behind many environmental initiatives, the hotel is one of Aruba's greenest. Recycling bins, water-conservation measures, and beachwide clean-ups are part of the effort. Beach lovers appreciate the Bucuti's *palapa*-to-guest ratio—it's the highest on the island (you'll always have shade if you want it). Once the sun sets, you can dine intimately at a torch-lit table on the beach. At the breezy, open-air fitness center, nature and exercise go hand in hand. Built in 1987, the three-story Spanish mission–style resort was comprehensively refurbished in 1998. The new wing of 39 oceanfront suites scheduled to open in March 2004 promises to raise the comfort level to stratospheric levels, with in-room Internet connections and a separate concierge lounge.

L. G. Smith Blvd. 55B, Eagle Beach, Aruba. ✆ **800/223-1108** in the U.S. and Canada, or 297/583-1100. Fax 297/582-5272. www.bucuti.com. 63 units. Christmas–Apr $240–$270 double, $330 suite; May–Christmas $140–$160 double, $215 suite. Packages available. AE, DISC, MC, V. **Amenities:** Restaurant; bar; outdoor landscaped pool; 18-hole championship golf course nearby; open-air health club; bike rental; concierge; tour/activities desk; car-rental desk; 24-hr. business center; coin-op laundry; laundry/valet service; same-day dry cleaning; nonsmoking rooms. *In room:* A/C, ceiling fan, remote-control cable TV, minibar/fridge, microwave, coffeemaker, hair dryer, iron, safe, magnifying vanity mirror.

Casa del Mar Beach Resort ★   On Manchebo Beach, across from the Alhambra Casino, this timeshare resort is closely affiliated with the Aruba Beach Club next door; amenities at either complex are available to guests at both. Casa del Mar consists of two four-story buildings (each with a pool) separated by a quiet street. The vast majority of the timeshare owners and rental guests are North American families. Constructed in 1986 on the beach, the two-bedroom presidential suites feature two TVs and fully equipped kitchens. Both the living rooms and master bedrooms open to the large square balconies. The master suites have queen-size beds, huge vanity areas with make-up mirrors worthy of Hollywood, large open bathtubs with faux-marble bench seating, and separate showers. The guest rooms have two twin beds and full bathrooms. Pleasant dark-rattan furniture, muted solid colors, and off-white tile floors decorate the spacious living/dining area. Ocean- and island-view suites cost the same; ocean views are prettier, but the island-view units are quieter. Built across the street in 1991, the newer ambassador wing has no beachfront. The tranquil one-bedroom suites here also have

Sustainable Tourism

A kind of environmental Good Housekeeping seal of approval, the Green Globe 21 certificate recognizes hotels around the world that develop and implement sound, eco-friendly policies. The Amsterdam Manor Aruba Beach Resort was Aruba's first resort to be certified, followed quickly by the Bucuti Beach Resort Aruba and the Costa Linda Beach Resort. La Cabana All-Suite Beach Resort & Casino is the latest hotel to make the list.

two TVs, but the kitchen/dining/living area is more compact, and the decor is less subdued. The full bathrooms are large but no match for the elaborate ones in the presidential wing. The good-size balconies face the pool.

J. E. Irausquin Boulevard 51, Punta Brabo Beach, Aruba. ℭ **297/582-7000.** Fax 297/582-9044. www.casadelmar-aruba.com. 147 units. Dec–Mar $425 presidential double, $190 ambassador double; Apr–Nov $300 presidential double, $140 ambassador double. AE, DISC, MC, V. **Amenities:** Beachside restaurant; Internet cafe; pool bar; 2 outdoor pools; kiddie pool; 18-hole championship golf course nearby; 4 tennis courts lit for night play; exercise room; poolside Jacuzzis; extensive watersports equipment/rentals; children's program; tour/activities desk; car-rental desk; shopping arcade; salon; babysitting; coin-op laundry; wheelchair-accessible rooms. *In room:* A/C, TV, dataport, kitchen or kitchenette, iron, safe.

MODERATE

Amsterdam Manor Aruba Beach Resort ⟨★★⟩ *Finds*   Next to La Cabana, this cheerful gem is a refreshing alternative to cookie-cutter uniformity. With a strong European accent and couples-friendly slant, the Amsterdam Manor features a quiet atmosphere and boutique size that's perfect for independent, curious travelers. The last low-rise resort on the road to the high-rises, the hotel's across a small road from a prime strip of Eagle Beach. The colors of the well-maintained three-floor complex are tropical, but the architecture is Dutch—gingerbread ornamentation, quaint gabled roofs, and whimsical turrets. Scattered around a series of intimate courtyards, the studios and one- and two-bedroom suites feature oak furniture from Holland and European cabinetry and fixtures, dark solid fabrics, and beige-tile floors. All units feature a balcony or terrace and a kitchen or kitchenette. The standard studios have shower-only bathrooms, but they're flooded with light and slightly larger than superior studios. On the other hand, the superior units have a Jacuzzi and an ocean view. The one- and two-bedroom suites have comfortable living rooms and complete kitchens. Suites on the top floor boast high barn ceilings. An environmental leader, the resort is Green Globe–certified. Cyberphiles love the free Internet access at a couple of outdoor terminals. Note that package deals booked through a tour operator are even cheaper than rooms booked online.

J. E. Irausquin Blvd. 252, Oranjestad, Aruba. ℭ **800/932-6509** in the U.S. and Canada, or 297/587-1492. Fax 297/587-1463. www.amsterdammanor.com. 72 units. Dec–Mar $199–$209 studio double, $269 1-bedroom suite, $334 2-bedroom suite; Apr–Nov $130–$140 studio double, $170 1-bedroom suite, $240 2-bedroom suite. Packages available. 15% Internet discount. Up to 2 children under age 12 stay free in same room with 2 paying adults. AE, DISC, MC, V. **Amenities:** Restaurant; 2 bars; outdoor pool; kiddie pool; 18-hole championship golf course nearby; extensive watersports equipment/rentals; playground; concierge; tour/activities desk; car-rental desk; minimart;

babysitting; coin-op laundry; same-day dry cleaning; nonsmoking rooms; wheelchair-accessible rooms. *In room:* A/C, TV, kitchen or kitchenette, iron, safe.

Aruba Beach Club Rather than dazzle guests with an array of activities, this intimate, family-friendly resort and timeshare charms with friendliness and service. Each spacious room has two queen-size beds and large balconies or terraces. The good-size bathrooms have a vanity chair and lots of counter space. Studios have a large, shower-only bathroom and a kitchenette. The units on the second floor have much higher ceilings. Deluxe and royal superb one-bedroom suites boast a dining area, comfortable living room, and a full kitchen; royal superb rooms have two bathrooms. Guests are free to avail themselves of all amenities offered by the adjacent Casa del Mar Beach Resort.

J. E. Irausquin Boulevard 53, Punta Brabo Beach, Aruba. © **297/582-3000.** Fax 297/583-8191. www.arubabeachclub.com. 131 units. Dec–Apr $200 studio double, $265 deluxe suite, $300 royal superb suite; May–Nov $140 studio double, $175 deluxe suite, $195 royal superb suite. AE, DISC, MC, V. **Amenities:** Restaurant; Internet cafe; bar; large outdoor pool; kiddie pool; 18-hole championship golf course nearby; 4 tennis courts lit for night play; exercise room; extensive water-sports equipment/rentals; children's program; tour/activities desk; car-rental desk; shopping arcade; salon; babysitting; laundry service; wheelchair-accessible rooms. *In room:* A/C, TV, VCR rental, dataport, kitchen or kitchenette, safe.

Best Western Manchebo Beach Resort Aruba ⚲ *(Value)* Next to the Bucuti Beach Resort on a fabled stretch of Eagle Beach, this little hotel offers good value and friendly, personal service. It's a Best Western, but there's nothing franchise about it. The glorious 10-acre beach speaks for itself, but the Manchebo's cheerful 1960s Florida decor with Route 66 influences is a charming retro touch not seen elsewhere on the island. Too restrained to be kitschy, both of the two-story wings feature white stucco walls, pink and turquoise accents, and whimsical painted embellishments over the doorways. The rooms aren't spectacular, but they're pristine, with gleaming bathrooms, and each one has a private patio or balcony with wide-strip railings and a garden or ocean view. Members of the staff have been at the hotel for an average of more than a decade: Obviously liking what they do, they welcome guests—lots of honeymooners and repeat visitors—as family members. The open-air beachside wedding chapel is as grand as a tropical cathedral and continues the Florida-inspired color scheme, this time with turquoise and white. Built in 1967, the Manchebo is constantly renovated, but it retains its aura of a simpler time.

J. E. Irausquin Blvd. 55, Oranjestad, Aruba. © **800/528-1234** in the U.S. and Canada, or 297/582-3444. Fax 297/583-2446. www.manchebo.com. 71 units. Dec–Mar $199–$225 double; Apr–Nov $129–$144 double. Packages available. Children under 12 stay free in parent's room. AE, DISC, MC, V. **Amenities:** 3 restaurants (steak/seafood [The French Steakhouse; p. 81], tropical garden, beachside grill); 2 bars; outdoor pool; 18-hole championship golf course nearby; watersports equipment/rentals; concierge; tour/activities desk; car-rental desk; coin-op laundry; non-smoking rooms available. *In room:* A/C, TV, fridge, coffeemaker, hair dryer, safe.

Divi Aruba Beach Resort Mega All Inclusive

This all-inclusive resort on Druif Beach is popular with families who don't want hidden costs. It's also Aruba's top hotel for honeymoon bookings. The Divi's all-inclusive package includes unlimited food and beverages at five restaurants, two snack stations, and six bars, unlimited nonmotorized watersports, bicycles, tennis, nightly entertainment, activities, taxes, service charges, and access to all the amenities of the nearby Tamarijn Resort. All of the recently refurbished, identically configured rooms boast balconies, decks, or porches; price variations are based on location. Ask for a room away from the noisy air-conditioning units and laundry room. Garden rooms are cheaper and farther from the beach than oceanview and oceanfront units, but they're quieter and have Jacuzzis. Rooms in the single-story lanai building open directly onto a narrow beach, while *casitas* face small courtyards just steps from the beach. Built in the early 1970s, the resort is constantly being renovated. Free trolley service connects it with the Tamarijn, its sister resort just a stretch of beach away. How to choose between the Divi and the Tamarijn? The food at both is decent. The Divi's closer to other low-rise amenities and has a better beach, but the Tam has more activities, and all its rooms are oceanfront.

J. E. Irausquin Blvd. 45, Druif Beach, Aruba. (C) **800/554-2008** in the U.S. and Canada, or 297/582-3300. Fax 297/583-4002. www.diviaruba.com. 203 units. All-inclusive rates per person based on double occupancy: Christmas–New Year's and Feb $235–$275; Jan and Mar $215–$240; Apr–Christmas $170–$220. Christmas–Apr children under age 12 free all inclusive in parent's room; May–Nov children under age 18 free all inclusive in parent's room/additional children's room $135 per night (maximum 4 children per room). Packages available. AE, DISC, MC, V. **Amenities:** 5 restaurants (buffet, international, pizza/sandwiches, Italian, grill, pool deck); 6 bars; 3 outdoor pools; 9-hole golf course on-site; 18-hole championship golf course nearby; 3 tennis courts (2 lit for night play); exercise room; extensive watersports equipment; bikes; children's center/program; game room/video arcade; concierge; tour/activities desk; car-rental desk; shopping arcade; salon; babysitting; coin-op laundry; laundry service; same-day dry cleaning; wheelchair-accessible rooms. *In room:* A/C, TV, fridge available, safe ($2 per day).

La Cabana All-Suite Beach Resort & Casino *Kids*

You could spend a week here and still not know all the amenities and activities available. It's a great place for families—there are tons of kids here—but there's ample room for privacy, so couples and honeymooners are abundant, too. Spreading over acres of landscaped grounds, the self-contained village's two main complexes feature spacious accommodations, all with balconies and whirlpool tubs. The rooms are in tip-top shape (every room is taken out of service 1 week per year for a major overhaul). The studios and one-bedroom suites in the front four-story building (built in 1990) form a U around an expansive courtyard and busy pool. These units, most popular with families and couples drawn to the action, come with fully equipped kitchenettes. Those refurbished in 2001 feature muted floral prints and darker-wood furniture. The five-floor complex in back was built in 1994. The one-, two-, and three-bedroom suites here are larger and quieter than those in front, but they're farther from the beach. Enclosing a large patio with two pools, they have good-size kitchens. The sunny bedrooms and dining/living areas sparkle with tropical floral prints, white bamboo furniture, and white tile. Across a relatively sleepy road from a prime section of Eagle Beach, La Cabana boasts distinctive extras like a home shopping service (order groceries online before you arrive), "blue phones" that offer international calls at U.S. rates, and all-inclusive packages.

J. E. Irausquin Blvd. 250, Oranjestad, Aruba. © **800/835-7193** in the U.S. and Canada, or 297/587-9000. Fax 297/587-5474. www.lacabana.com/resort. 811 units. Winter $219–$302 studio double, $260–$379 1-bedroom suite, $520–$741 2-bedroom suite, $765–$980 3-bedroom suite; Summer $132–$174 studio double, $174–$231 1-bedroom suite, $331–$468 2-bedroom suite, $499–$578 3-bedroom suite. Packages available. Children under 12 stay free in parent's room. AE, DISC, MC, V. **Amenities:** 6 restaurants (Caribbean seafood, poolside grill, buffet/international, Spanish tapas, sushi bar, poolside pizza); 4 bars; disco; casino; 3 large outdoor pools; 18-hole championship golf course nearby; 5 tennis courts lit for night play; large health club and spa; extensive watersports equipment/rentals; children's center/program; teen program; game room/video arcade; concierge; tour/activities desk; car-rental desk; business center; shopping arcade; salon; babysitting; coin-op laundry; laundry/valet service; same-day dry cleaning; nonsmoking rooms; barbecue grills. *In room:* A/C, TV, kitchenette, hair dryer, iron, safe.

Paradise Beach Villas ✪ Next to La Cabana and across the street from one of Eagle Beach's nicest sections, this quiet, welcoming timeshare boasts large studios and suites in Spanish mission–style two- and three-story buildings. Because many owners come back year after year, the place has the air of a family reunion. You'll see lots of American couples in their 30s, 40s, and 50s, often joined by children and grandkids during the high season. Independent rental guests enjoy the laid-back atmosphere and absence of nonstop activities. White-tile floors, tropical pastel colors, and wicker-bamboo furniture brighten every unit. Balconies are large, and the full bathrooms hold a Jacuzzi. Studios have a small kitchenette, while suites have a deluxe, fully equipped kitchen. In the two- and three-bedroom suites, guest rooms feature two single beds; the large adjacent bathrooms have a roomy shower. The master bedrooms have a queen- or king-size bed and a bathroom with two sinks. In townhouses, a spiral staircase ascends to the master suite. Bar seating separates the kitchen from the dining and living room, which opens to a spacious balcony. The more expensive Phase II units are closer to the beach and have a roomier kitchen and living room. The Phase II pool is also larger than the original.

J. E. Irausquin Blvd. z/n, Eagle Beach, Aruba. © **297/587-4000.** Fax 297/587-0071. www.paradisebeachvillas.com. 80 units. Dec–Mar $170 studio double, $235–$325 1-bedroom suite, $340–$475 2-bedroom suite, $665 3-bedroom suite; Apr–May and Oct–Nov $125 studio double, $175–$265 1-bedroom suite, $265–$375 2-bedroom suite, $520 3-bedroom suite; Jun–Sept $112 studio double, $155–$225 1-bedroom suite, $240–$340 2-bedroom suite, $470 3-bedroom suite. Children under age 12 stay free in parent's room. AE, DISC, MC, V. **Amenities:** 2 restaurants (seafood/steak, breakfast/lunch casual); bar; 2 large free-form outdoor pools/lagoons; 18-hole championship golf course nearby; exercise room; poolside Jacuzzis; bike rental; tour/activities desk; car-rental desk; shops; babysitting; coin-op laundry; wheelchair-accessible rooms. *In room:* A/C, TV, VCR on request, kitchenette or kitchen, iron available, safe.

Tamarijn Aruba Beach Resort

What's bigger than all-inclusive? Why, mega all-inclusive, of course. Guests at this casual, low-key Druif Beach resort can enhance their dining, drinking, and activity options by upgrading to "mega" status (about $25 per person per day), which entitles them not only to the Tamarijn's amenities but also to those next door at the Divi Aruba Beach Resort. If you opt for the simple all-inclusive package, you get an oceanfront room, unlimited food and beverages at three restaurants and three bars, all the non-motorized watersports you can handle, bicycles, tennis, activities, and nightly entertainment. If you book as a "mega" guest, you can eat, drink, and be merry at the Divi as well. All rooms at the Tamarijn are oceanfront, but the beach directly in front of the resort is narrow and rocky; the beaches on either side of the complex are wider and sandier. The spacious rooms in the two-story buildings feature warm colors, rattan furniture, and tile floors. Every unit has a nice-size balcony or terrace. Built in 1977, the resort is kept up with ongoing renovations; ask for a recently refurbished room. The Tamarijn has more activities than the Divi—a plus for kids and other active vacationers—but it's still low-key enough to attract older guests.

J. E. Irausquin Blvd. 41, Druif Beach, Aruba. © **800/554-2008** in the U.S. and Canada, or 297/582-3300. Fax 297/583-4002. www.tamarijnaruba.com. 236 units. All-inclusive rates per person based on double occupancy: Christmas–New Year's and Feb $215; Jan and Mar $195; Apr–Christmas $160. Mega all-inclusive rates per person based on double occupancy: Christmas–New Year's and Feb $235; Jan and Mar $215; Apr–Christmas $190. Christmas–Apr children under 12 free all-inclusive in parent's room. May–Nov children under 18 free all-inclusive in parent's room; additional children's room $130 per night (maximum 4 children per room). Packages available. AE, DISC, MC, V. **Amenities:** 3 restaurants (buffet, terrace grill, Italian); 3 bars; outdoor pool; 9-hole golf course on site; 18-hole championship golf course nearby; 2 tennis courts lit for night play; exercise room; watersports equipment; bikes; children's center/program; game room/video arcade; concierge; tour/activities desk; car-rental desk; shopping arcade; salon; babysitting; coin-op laundry; laundry service; same-day dry cleaning; wheelchair-accessible rooms. *In room:* A/C, TV, fridge available, safe ($2 per day).

INEXPENSIVE

Arubiana Inn *Value*   A 15-minute walk inland from Eagle Beach, this quiet, tidy motel lies in wild, cactus-covered terrain a few hundred feet from a main road. The single-story structure of coral stucco and terra-cotta tile encloses a central pool area that boasts plenty of chairs and tables. Each of the squeaky-clean studio units opens to the palm-lined pool and courtyard. The cozy rooms feature white tile floors, white wicker furniture, and pastel floral prints. The small bathrooms are blindingly white with salmon accents. Next to the pool, the quiet, open-air bar is open throughout the day, and a minimart supplies food and other items. Restaurants, a supermarket, and miniature golf are a few minutes away by foot.

Bubali 74, Noord, Aruba. © **297/587-7700.** Fax 297/587-1770. www.arubianainn. com. 16 units. Dec–Apr $85 double; May–Nov $55 double; Mar–Apr $500 weekly; May–Feb $345 weekly. Children under 12 stay free in parent's room. AE, MC, V. **Amenities:** Bar; small outdoor pool; 18-hole championship golf course nearby. *In room:* A/C, TV, cable TV, fridge, microwave.

La Quinta Beach Resort   Built in 1991, this small timeshare next to Le Dôme Restaurant is across the road from Eagle Beach. Most owners are older couples, but there are a fair number of families as well. The atmosphere at the two five-floor buildings is sedate. All units boast large balconies, but the closets are small. The furnishings are tropical and modular—lots of bamboo, pink tile, and nondescript floral prints. The wooden louvered windows and paned windows and doors are a nice touch, though. All units have a kitchenette, and two-bedroom deluxe units have a loft bedroom. The deluxe building's suites are smaller and have pinched corners, but they're closer to the beach. A small parking lot separates the deluxe units from the more expensive executive building, where suites have nicer kitchens. The pool in the executive complex is also much larger than the one in front. For those looking for a touch of luxury, some of the one-bedroom executive suites have a balcony Jacuzzi.

J. E. Irausquin Blvd. 228, Eagle Beach, Aruba. © **297/587-5010.** Fax 297/587-6263. 54 units. Winter $115–$150 double, $175–$250 1-bedroom suite,

$250–$400 2-bedroom suite, $475 3-bedroom suite; Summer $75–$85 double, $100–$135 1-bedroom suite, $145–$205 2-bedroom suite, $255 3-bedroom suite. AE, DISC, MC, V. **Amenities:** Restaurant; bar; 2 outdoor pools; 18-hole championship golf course nearby; Jacuzzis; car-rental desk; babysitting; coin-op laundry. *In room:* A/C, TV/VCR, kitchen or kitchenette, hair dryer, video rentals.

4 Tierra Del Sol

VERY EXPENSIVE

Tierra del Sol Aruba Resort & Country Club ⟨⟨   If you think more about sand traps than sand castles, Tierra del Sol tops the leaderboard. This resort combines the sun and golf of Scottsdale with the waves and dunes of Aruba's north coast. The finishing touch is a picturesque lighthouse. The 18-hole championship golf course features lush greens and cacti. The accommodations are spectacular, too. In addition to two- and three-bedroom condominiums, the complex boasts two- and three-bedroom freestanding villas spread over acres of desert landscaping. Individually owned, each unit has a distinct decor, but all have a golf-course or ocean view, a spacious living room, dining room, custom kitchen, a large master suite with a full bathroom, one or two guest rooms with another bathroom, a covered terrace with patio furniture, and a washer and dryer. Most two- and three-bedroom villas also feature walk-in closets, an additional half bath, a sauna, a second-story balcony, an outdoor Jacuzzi, a private pool, and a garage. You can open the door to a fully stocked kitchen by ordering items online before you leave for Aruba. Because you'll want a car here—everything's a schlep away—the resort offers rentals at significantly discounted rates. If you decide against a car, the hotel operates a shuttle to nearby Arashi Beach.

Malmokweg z/n, Oranjestad, Aruba. ℂ **800/992-2015** in the U.S. and Canada, 297/586-7800. Fax 297/586-4970. www.tierradelsol.com. 77 villas, 37 condos (not all units are rented at all times). Accommodations only: Jan–Mar $300 2-bedroom condo, $425 2-bedroom villa; Apr–Dec $199 2-bedroom condo, $325 2-bedroom villa. Unlimited golf and accommodations: Jan–Mar $375 2-bedroom condo, $525 3-bedroom condo, $575 2-bedroom villa, $680 3-bedroom villa; Apr–Dec $275 2-bedroom condo, $400 3-bedroom condo or 2-bedroom villa, $480 3-bedroom villa. $50 extra per night for 2- and 3-bedroom villas with pool. 3 night minimum stay. 10% online discount (packages are still cheaper). AE, DISC, MC, V. **Amenities:** 2 restaurants (international/seafood [Ventanas del Mar; p. 83], grill); 3 bars; outdoor pool; 2 tennis courts lit for night play; excellent fitness center and spa; 18-hole championship golf course; concierge; tour/activities desk; informal business center in resort office. *In room:* A/C, TV, kitchen, iron.

4

Where to Dine

If you're like lots of folks vacationing in Aruba, you'll spend all day on the beach thinking about where to dine that night. The options are prodigious. Few places as small as Aruba can boast such a variety of quality restaurants. In fact, with the exception of the French islands and Puerto Rico, Aruba leaves most of the Caribbean in the dust.

This is due in large part to fierce competition. Most restaurateurs never stop thinking of new ways to bring you through their doors. Many add a personal touch, taking the time to chat and thank you for your visit. And most are loath to leave anyone behind, so there's usually something for vegetarians, kids, and couples celebrating special occasions (how about a romantic private room or a table on the beach?). Because some form of entertainment has become almost *de rigueur*, expect to be serenaded by live bands, jazz saxophonists, or singing waiters. Frequent culinary competitions spur chefs to experiment and hone their skills, constantly raising the quality bar. And over the past few years, ethnic spots have burgeoned: When you're not feasting on steak, seafood, or Aruban specialties, you can try something Argentinean, French, Caribbean, Indonesian, Cuban, Belgian, Mexican, Japanese, Chinese, or Indian.

Restaurant prices are a bit steep in Aruba, but with good reason. Almost nothing grows on the arid island, so most edibles, with the exception of seafood, are imported. That gets to be expensive. Fruits and vegetables come primarily from Venezuela, but some make the trip from as far away as Europe. Beef is flown in from Argentina and the U.S. Portions are large, though, if that's any consolation.

Most restaurants are a $6 to $10 taxi ride from your hotel, but many are within easy walking distance of the major resorts. If you have a car, call for explicit directions: Inadequate street signs and substandard navigation skills inevitably lead to wrong turns and missed reservations. Another caveat: If you're going into Oranjestad from the hotel areas, allow yourself some time to get there. Traffic into the capital is absurd at times, and parking can be hard to find.

It's tough to find a restaurant that's open for lunch on Sunday. Some are, of course, especially hotel restaurants, but double-check before you set out.

1 Oranjestad

EXPENSIVE

Chez Mathilde ⭐⭐⭐ FRENCH FUSION Opulence and first-rate French cuisine make Chez Mathilde a superb choice for special occasions. The restaurant's ambience is classically elegant, and although the service is formal, it's never intimidating. The glorious front dining room features black-and-white tile floors and bentwood chairs with brocade upholstery; a stunning Art Nouveau stained-glass window serves as the front room's focal point. The much larger back room has a sultry, luxurious feel and exuberant foliage. Enclosed by a Belle Epoque glass ceiling, it smells of old money. The food is equally evocative. Appetizers include Beluga caviar, *pâté de foie gras,* and paper-thin prosciutto with roasted potatoes. Delicious pan-fried trout rests on a bed of peppers, curly endive, and buttons of *haricots verts* in a heady lobster vinaigrette. Bathed in curry-infused mushroom sauce, the succulent grilled chicken breasts come with sautéed spinach and puréed potatoes. Or you can feast on chateaubriand, veal, wild boar, or ostrich. For dessert, the custardy crème brûlée or strawberries marinated in strawberry and lemon juice are unbeatable. Finish with an espresso (send it back if it's too weak), dark chocolates, and cognac. What a shame that the service, though usually stellar, can sometimes be distracted, imprecise, or slow.

Havenstraat 23, downtown Oranjestad. ℂ **297/583-4968.** Reservations recommended. Proper attire required (no shorts). Main courses $25–$40 at dinner, $15–$22 at lunch. AE, DISC, MC, V. Mon–Sat 11:30am–2:30pm; daily 6–11pm.

L'Escale ⭐⭐⭐ INTERNATIONAL/STEAK/SEAFOOD There are many contenders, but L'Escale may be Aruba's most romantic restaurant. Beyond a wall of windows, the sun descends and the lights of Oranjestad harbor emerge as a saxophonist plays cool jazz. The gold-damask tablecloths, chandeliers, and voluptuous botanical drawings are traditionally elegant, but for all the refinement, there's nothing stuffy about L'Escale. And the cuisine can be inventive and adventurous. Consider the avocado and shrimp salad to start. Arranged as a whimsical pinwheel, it is served with a fine cilantro and orange dressing. The Aruban *vol au vent* (puff pastry with curried chicken and sautéed mushrooms) is succulent and complex. Meditating on a frosted-glass lily, mango sorbet ushers in the main courses.

Dining Details

What to Wear?   Dress is almost always casual. At many places, dinner dress is elegant casual (sundresses for women, long pants for men). A couple of restaurants enforce a "no-shorts" policy, but they usually have a supply of clean long pants on hand in case you arrive unaware.

How Much to Tip?   Many, but not all, restaurants add a service charge, ranging from 10% to 15%, to your bill. This money's distributed among all restaurant employees. If you feel your waiter or waitress has earned a little extra, don't hesitate to show your largesse. If no service charge is automatically added, tip 15% to 20%.

What About Reservations?   Reservations are universally appreciated. During the high season, they're necessary at the most popular places. Your hotel concierge will be happy to make reservations for you.

The dramatic mahimahi filet, grilled with thyme and served with puréed red pepper, is garnished with flavorful julienned vegetables and a dome of rice. An architectural wonder, the rack of lamb balanced on roasted potatoes is peerless. Save room for the Grand Marnier soufflé. The restaurant offers a special deal for diners who also want to take in the show at the Crystal Palace. This package offers value, but L'Escale's best dishes aren't on the theater menu. To fully appreciate the cuisine, come early and order off the main menu.

At the Renaissance Aruba Beach Resort, L. G. Smith Blvd. 82, downtown Oranjestad. (©) **297/583-6000.** Reservations recommended. Main courses $20–$55. AE, DISC, MC, V. Mon–Sun 6–11pm; Sun brunch 10am–2pm.

MODERATE

Driftwood 🐟 ARUBAN SEAFOOD   Authentic Aruban seafood doesn't get any fresher or better than the fare at this rustic restaurant tucked away on a side street. Keeping with its name, this cozy venue is full of gnarled driftwood posts and slats laced with ship lanterns and Captain Nemo underwater helmets. The owner wakes up early every morning, hops on his boat, and stalks the coast for your dinner. Depending on what he snags, you might enjoy lobster, shrimp, octopus, squid, grouper, or mahimahi. Tender octopus marinated in vinegar and aromatic spices is a good way to kick the meal off, although Aruban seafood soup with fish, shrimp, scallops, and vegetables is a more authentic taste of the island. Lightly floured wahoo sautéed in garlic and served with cilantro-butter sauce is unfussy and delicious. Pan-fried snapper in creole sauce (tomatoes, onions, bell peppers, and the local version of basil) is equally pleasant. Just about everything comes with the local corn bread, *pan bati.*

Klipstraat 12, downtown Oranjestad. ℂ **297/583-2515.** Reservations recommended. Main courses $16–$35. AE, MC, V. Wed–Mon 5:30–11pm.

El Gaucho Argentine Grill ℛ STEAK/SEAFOOD   Although it's not exactly home on the range—or The French Steakhouse or Sunset Grille (see reviews later in this chapter)—El Gaucho serves buffalo-size portions of Argentine beef. Open for more than 25 years, the restaurant looks like a hacienda on the pampas—ranchero leather chairs, cowhide artwork, rough-hewn log crossbeams, and warm stucco walls. You're likely to have beef as the main course, so start with conch harbor style (pounded till tender and flavored with onion) or squid Buenos Aires, in a delicate broth. They're even better with garlic parsley sauce or marinated onions. Pace yourself, though, because the signature dishes—charcoal-grilled sirloin steak, shish kebab, and the Argentinean grill (ribs, beef tenderloin, pork tenderloin, and pork sausage)—are massive. They're also served with several tasty sides. Not big on red meat? The Caribbean seafood mix lets you gorge on conch, squid, shrimp, and fish. If you can stomach dessert, order the Argentine ice cream. It's served with caramel and a dense sweet-potato paste. While you're digesting, nurse a cognac or brandy.

Wilhelminastraat 80, downtown Oranjestad. ℂ **297/582-3677.** Reservations recommended. Main courses $18–$28. AE, DISC, MC, V. Mon–Sat 11:30am–11pm. Closed the first 2 weeks of Aug.

Kowloon CHINESE/INDONESIAN   Aruba's Chinese restaurants are generally disappointing, but Kowloon is one of the best. This elegant spot boasts two red-and-black dining rooms, accented with lacquered hardwoods and Chinese lamps that overlook one of the capital's thoroughfares. Skilled at preparing Hunan, Szechuan, and Shanghai cuisine, chefs here also offer Indonesian staples such as *nasi goreng* and *bami goreng,* made with rice or noodles and shreds of pork, vegetables, and shrimp. Other favorites include *saté* (grilled strips of beef or chicken in spicy peanut sauce) and a variety of curries. The elaborate *rijsttafel* combines dozens of appetizer-size dishes that range from vegetables to seafood, pork, beef, and goat. The house special seafood dish combines fish, scallops, lobster, shrimp, and Szechuan-style black-bean sauce.

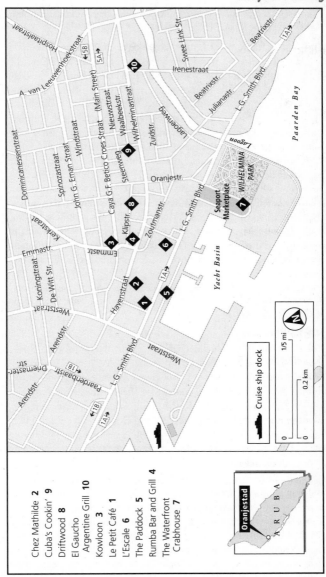

Chez Mathilde **2**
Cuba's Cookin' **9**
Driftwood **8**
El Gaucho
Argentine Grill **10**
Kowloon **3**
Le Petit Café **1**
L'Escale **6**
The Paddock **5**
Rumba Bar and Grill **4**
The Waterfront
Crabhouse **7**

Emmastraat 11, Oranjestad. © **297/582-4950**. Reservations recommended. Main courses $17–$24; *Rijsttafel* for 2 $36–56. AE, MC, V. Daily 11am–10pm.

The Waterfront Crabhouse *(Kids* SEAFOOD   Here's a kid-friendly place that won't cause you to regress. Colorful murals of happy dolphins adorn the walls inside, and just in front of the outdoor terrace, two white tigers—real, not painted—loll behind Plexiglas (take your picture with the felines later). The kids' menu looks like a coloring-book page and comes with crayons. Time-honored treats for finicky eaters include grilled-cheese sandwiches cut into fours (with or without the crust) and "psketti." I can't vouch for the deliciousness of these meals, but the more sophisticated adult fare features local and not-so-local seafood. The red snapper and grouper are caught off the Aruban coast; York Harbor fishermen supply the Maine lobster. You can pass a death sentence on any crustacean in the lobster tank, but crabs are king here. The tasty snow crabs are prepared with herbs, garlic, and butter. In season, soft-shell crabs come lightly fried with fresh tartar sauce. The sandwiches at lunch are pretty standard. The service is accommodating, and the '80s retro decor is fun.

L. G. Smith Blvd., Seaport Marketplace, downtown Oranjestad. © **297/583-5858**. Reservations recommended. Main courses $18–$40; kids' menu $3.95–$8.95; lunch $7–$22. AE, DISC, MC, V. Daily 8am–11pm.

INEXPENSIVE

Cuba's Cookin' *(Finds* CUBAN   This fun, informal spot, though set in an old *cunucu* (farm) house, is plenty hip. Original art captures whimsical scenes of Latin street life, while up-tempo music from the *Buena Vista Social Club* keeps the warm staff smiling. Sip a mint, rum, and sugar-laced *mojito* and start with the yucca chips. Earthier than tortilla chips, they're great with the *muy picante* salsa,

---

Tips Food Fairs

The Bon Bini Festival, a folkloric event that features arts, crafts, and local food, takes place year-round every Tuesday, from 6:30 to 8:30pm at Fort Zoutman in Oranjestad.

The Watapana Food & Art Festival enlivens Wednesdays between early April and late September. In addition to food from some of the island's best eateries, there's live entertainment, music, and local art. The party takes place between the Allegro Resort & Casino and Hyatt Regency, in the midst of the High-Rise hotels. Get there between 6 and 8pm.

a mix of jalapeño, habanero, cilantro, garlic, and olive oil. Your conga cocktail appetizer should arrive just in time to extinguish the fire in your mouth. Served in a half shell, the cool appetizer features chopped lobster, crab, red onions, and carrots in a light vinaigrette. The seafood boat is a winning main course: Lightly grilled shrimp, calamari, conch, and mussels rise from a flavorful ragout of green and red peppers, onions, garlic, tomatoes, and cucumbers. Other Cuban specialties include *ropa vieja* (shredded skirt steak sautéed in tomatoes, onions, and green peppers) and *picadillo de res* (ground beef with raisins and olives). For dessert, try *tres leches* pound cake drenched with sweet, milky syrup and topped with whipped cream. Then light up a Cuban cigar with your *café con leche.*

Wilhelminastraat 27 (across from the police station), downtown Oranjestad. ℭ **297/ 588-0627.** Reservations recommended. Main courses $8–$21 at lunch, $15–$29 at dinner. AE, MC, V. Mon–Sat noon–2:30pm and 5:30–11pm.

Le Petit Café SEAFOOD/STEAK   When they say the plate's hot, they mean it. Le Petit Café offers seafood and beef served on stone platters as hot as molten lava. With the "stove" at your table, you determine how much your meal's cooked, and the "on the stone" method makes for healthy dishes. A boon on breezy evenings, the hot plates are a mistake during the heat of the day unless you'd just as soon be lunching in a sweat lodge. Thankfully, the kitchen prepares several menu items. The restaurant's second-floor outdoor terrace features faux-archaic inlaid-tile tables and blue-and-white striped awning. The pink and turquoise stucco walls fit right in with the confectionery architecture of the surrounding buildings. Start with a Crazy Monkey. Boasting vodka, Bailey's Irish cream, Kahlúa, crème de banana, and amaretto, it covers three of the food major groups. The crispy conch fritters and popcorn shrimp are good appetizers. For the main course, jumbo shrimp "on the stone," marinated in olive oil and enough garlic to keep vampires at bay, tastes like it just came off the barbie. The lobster, shrimp, and beef tenderloin combo is just as flavorful.

3 locations: Royal Plaza Mall (downtown Oranjestad); Playa Linda Beach Resort (Palm Beach); Paradise Beach Villas (Eagle Beach). ℭ **297/586-1234** for reservations. Reservations recommended. Main courses $9–$30. AE, DISC, MC, V. Mon–Sat 11am–midnight; Sun 6–11pm.

The Paddock INTERNATIONAL   In the heart of Oranjestad, this cafe and bistro overlooks the harbor, a short walk from virtually every shop in town. Much of the staff is blond, hip, and European, and the atmosphere is decidedly Dutch. No one minds whether you opt for a drink, a cup of tea or coffee, a snack of sliced sausage and

Gouda cheese, or a full-fledged meal. The menu offers crab, salmon, shrimp, and tuna sandwiches; salads; pita-bread sandwiches stuffed with sliced beef and an herb sauce with plenty of tang; fresh poached or sautéed fish; and glazed tenderloin of pork. Happy hours change frequently; when they're offered, a festive crowd packs the place.

L. G. Smith Blvd. 13, Oranjestad. © 297/583-2334. Sandwiches, snacks, and salads $4–$7; main courses $10–$15. AE, MC, V. Mon–Thurs 10:30am–2am; Fri–Sun 10:30am–3am.

Rumba Bar and Grill EUROPEAN GRILL   This languid spot offers seafood and steak with a slight European accent. Split-cane blinds screen the tile-inlaid tables on the outdoor terrace from the midday sun, but the inside dining room is still your best bet: It's 10 degrees cooler. Moroccan rugs, rustic vases, bullfight posters, and a starburst mosaic tile floor set a Mediterranean tone, while the blue glass-brick bar adds a touch of urbanity. Rumba is a great place to regain your strength during an extended daytime shopping venture in Oranjestad. The inexpensive ($4–$8) salads and sandwiches feature ingredients like curry, brie, pesto, and crab; full-blown seafood, steak, and chicken meals are also available. Live music in the evening argues for an extended dining experience over dishes like grilled tuna steak, chicken cordon bleu, grilled beef tenderloin, or grilled rack of lamb with béarnaise, Provençale, tomato-basil, or "devil" sauce.

Havenstraat 4 (behind the Renaissance), downtown Oranjestad. © 297/588-7900. Dinner reservations recommended. Main courses $12–$28. AE, MC, V. Mon–Fri 11:30am–11pm; Sat 5–11pm.

2 High-Rise Hotels/Palm Beach/Noord

Just inland from Palm Beach and the High-Rise hotels but virtually indistinguishable from the immediate resort area, the town of Noord is home to many popular restaurants.

EXPENSIVE

Pago Pago 𝕽𝕽𝕽 SEAFOOD   The elegant South Sea fantasy of Pago Pago begins with hibiscus-print tablecloths and Polynesia-inspired oil paintings that blaze through subdued but dramatic lighting. The piano and bass combo adds sophistication, while the restaurant's multi-tiered spaciousness whispers luxury. Expectancy and promise hang in the air, fueled by the dramatic first course: fried plantain chips, 6 inches long, served with a subtle sauce of orange, ginger, honey, and chile. The firecracker lobster spring roll (served fresh in a nest of fried rice noodles) and tropical shrimp cocktail (seasoned with a refreshingly tart mango relish) score. But they can

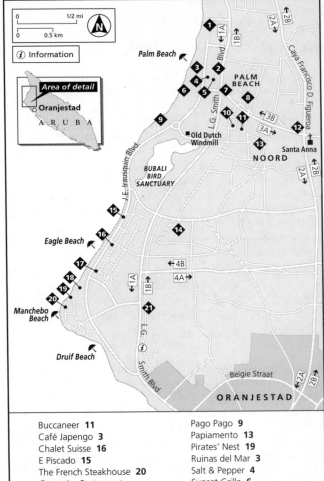

Buccaneer **11**	Pago Pago **9**
Café Japengo **3**	Papiamento **13**
Chalet Suisse **16**	Pirates' Nest **19**
E Piscado **15**	Ruinas del Mar **3**
The French Steakhouse **20**	Salt & Pepper **4**
Gasparito Restaurant	Sunset Grille **6**
and Art Gallery **10**	Tango Argentine Grill **5**
Hostaria da' Vittorio **2**	The Turtle's Nest **18**
La Dolce Vita **21**	Tuscany **1**
Le Dôme **17**	Twinkletone's **7**
Madame Janette **14**	Valentino's **12**
The Old Cunucu House **8**	

What's Cookin' in Aruba?

Don't go home without sampling the worthwhile local cuisine. Here's some help with the menu:

Sopito Fish soup made with coconut milk, salt pork or corned beef, whole fish, shellfish, greens, potatoes, onions, tomatoes, garlic, peppers, fresh cream, and spices

Pan Bati A thick, sweet, corn bread–like pancake

Bitterballen Deep-fried croquettes made with beef, pork, chicken, or shrimp

Krokechi Deep-fried fish croquettes; longer than bitterballen

Pastechi Crescent-shaped, deep-fried turnovers filled with spicy meat, shrimp, fish, or cheese; popular for breakfast and as a snack

Empanadas Similar to pastechis but smaller and made with cornmeal rather than flour

Funchi Cornmeal polenta

Tutu Funchi jazzed up with bacon and black-eyed peas

Giambo A thick gumbo made with fish filets, salted beef, okra, fresh basil *(yerba di hole),* and shrimp

barely hint at the perfection of the main courses: Twice-cooked pork roast with lime-honey glaze is tender and succulent; macadamia-crusted grouper with papaya-lime-cilantro salsa is flawless down to the jasmine rice and julienned vegetable side dishes. The climax? Will it be delectable coconut mousse that's as dense as cheesecake, or lighter chocolate mousse cake? Or both?

At the Wyndham Aruba Beach Resort and Casino, J. E. Irausquin Blvd. 77, Palm Beach. ℭ **297/586-4466.** Reservations recommended. Main courses $22–$40. AE, DISC, MC, V. Daily 6–10:30pm.

Papiamento ☆☆ INTERNATIONAL/CARIBBEAN/SEAFOOD
Originally from Holland, the Ellis family has served award-winning Caribbean food in their 175-year-old *cunucu* (farm) home for almost 2 decades. Over the years, tables have spilled out from the thick-walled, antiques-filled interiors to the large fairy-lit palm garden. At twilight, birds serenade outdoor diners around the luminescent

Keshi Yena Edam or Gouda cheese rinds stuffed with beef, chicken, fish, or shrimp, embellished with raisins, grated cheese, bread crumbs, olives, capers, and spices; created by frugal Dutch colonists who had to stretch their provisions to last until the next ship arrived, this recipe ensured that nothing would be wasted

Passaat Lamb roasted over a charcoal fire fanned by the trade winds

Stoba Hearty stew made with chicken, beef, goat, conch, or fish

Madame Janette chile pepper Considerably hotter than the jalapeño and Aruba's favorite way to spice up almost anything; better known as the Scotch bonnet pepper, it's an integral ingredient in the Creole relish that accompanies any dish prepared "Arubiana"

Kesio Eggy caramel custard

Pudin di Coco Coconut pudding made with rum and served with lime sauce

Ponche Crema Creamy eggnoglike drink laced with rum and flavored with nutmeg

pool. Diaphanous cotton swathes the rattan chairs, and white eyelet tablecloths add to the tropical elegance. When Beatrix, queen of the Netherlands, is in Aruba, she sups inside on the former verandah, now dubbed the Queen's Room. Capers, caviar, basil, passion fruit, and radicchio garnish the smoked salmon appetizer. The crudités platter features prosciutto, aged Gouda, and marinated peppers and onions. If you're lucky enough to be around during the season, order Brazil fish, a luscious, snapperlike delicacy that's caught only in March and April. Lightly seasoned with pepper and garlic, it's cooked and served on a stone that's heated in a 600°F (315°C) oven. Mango, onion, and chile pepper chutney accompanies *pisca arubiana* (fish Aruban style). Best bets for dessert are cocobana, an ephemeral coconut mousse, and flaky-crusted Dutch apple pie. Coffee snobs, take note: Papiamento's espresso may be the island's best.

Washington 61, Noord. © 297/586-4544. Reservations recommended. Main courses $22–$35. AE, MC, V. Tues–Sun 6–10:30pm.

Ruinas del Mar ★★ INTERNATIONAL/SEAFOOD   A table for two in the Garden of Eden? Dining on the crescent-shaped patio of this romantic restaurant is like spending an hour or two before the fall. Unperturbed by the muffled waterfalls nearby, serene black swans and Japanese koi fish glide through the terrace-side lagoon, while tropical birds in the luxuriant foliage serenade the setting sun. It's an artificial environment—if only the white-stone walls were covered with moss—but in lieu of paradise, it will do. There's nothing fake about the food, though. Start with the shrimp and crab gazpacho cocktail, or barbecued duck tostadas with avocado and mango salsa. The grilled veal chop with fig confit and Marsala sauce is a good main course, as is grilled grouper with cardamom baked sweet potatoes Other possibilities include stuffed chicken breast with goat cheese, spinach, cremini mushrooms, and sun-dried tomatoes; and sugar cane–skewered jumbo shrimp with crushed coriander seeds, pumpkin risotto, and citrus cream. Key lime pie is perfect to top it off. Unfortunately, the crowded Sunday brunch is more like boarding Noah's Ark than relaxing in paradise.

At the Hyatt Regency Aruba Resort & Casino, J. E. Irausquin Blvd. 85, Palm Beach. ℰ 297/586-1234. Reservations recommended. Main courses $25–$48. AE, DISC, MC, V. Daily 5:30–10:30pm; Sun brunch 9am–2pm.

Sunset Grille ★★★ AMERICAN STEAK/SEAFOOD   This chic restaurant's bold Art Deco design and 21st century color palette honor the architectural splendor of Miami's South Beach. Many diners rave about the outside terrace with its view overlooking a garden and lagoon, but the gorgeous interior dining room deserves attention, too. The hammered-copper surfaces, illuminated blue-glass partitions, and reflective mosaic pillars are richly modern. The pale mustard, salmon, and olive accents are cool and muted, and the daringly asymmetrical banquettes are dramatic. The stunning decor could overwhelm the food, but the Sunset's Angus beef and succulent seafood are outstanding. The refrigerated case in front displays main course options: choose your cut or filet. The generously portioned sushi is a good start, as is the mountain of iced shrimp, scallops, mussels, lobster tail, and crab legs with mango sauce. If it's beef you came for—there's no better steak on the island—savor filet mignon or New York sirloin strip. A delicious seafood choice, pan-seared ruby-red sushi-grade tuna, is encrusted with peppercorns and flavored with wasabi-soy sauce. To end the evening on a perfect note, moan over the tropical citrus cannoli.

At the Radisson Aruba Resort & Casino, J. E. Irausquin Blvd. 81, Palm Beach. ✆ 297/586-6555. Reservations recommended. Main courses $20–$50. AE, DISC, MC, V. Daily 6–11pm; Sun brunch 11am–2:30pm.

Tuscany 🏵🏵 REGIONAL ITALIAN   As the name implies, this top-notch restaurant features Tuscan cuisine, especially dishes from Florence. The sonorous live piano and etched glass walls at the entrance set an elegant tone, but the Liberace-inspired statuary adds a not-too-serious touch, and the ceiling pipes are anything but musical. Start with antipasti Toscana, an assortment of time-tested appetizers like tomato, mozzarella, and basil *caprese;* prosciutto and melon drizzled with pesto oil; and Tuscan vegetables marinated in olive oil and rosemary. Flash-grilled shrimp tossed in a frascati, lemon, and caper sauce is lighter but equally satisfying. For the main course, try chicken breast roulade stuffed with shallots, prosciutto, wild mushrooms, spinach, and mozzarella, spiced with sun-dried tomato sauce, or Parmesan-crusted sea bass in basil-butter sauce. For dessert, who can resist flaky profiteroles filled with amaretto gelato and topped with chocolate and toasted almonds? The cordial servers are attentive but never overbearing.

At the Aruba Marriott Beach Resort & Stellaris Casino, L. G. Smith Blvd. 101, Palm Beach. ✆ 297/586-9000. Reservations recommended. Main courses $22–$40. AE, MC, V. Daily 6–11pm.

Valentino's 🏵 REGIONAL ITALIAN   One of Aruba's more elegant Italian restaurants, Valentino's features regional specialties from Campania, Rome, Piedmont, Lombardy, Liguria, and the Adriatic coast. You can start with a cocktail at the bar on the first level before ascending the central staircase to the cozy, peak-ceilinged dining room. Large windows make for great views of the palms, courtyards, and pools outside. The bustling, glass-enclosed kitchen is a spectacle in itself. Start your feast with hearts of palm salad or *mozzarella in carozza* (Italian bread and mozzarella cheese dipped in egg and milk, rolled in bread crumbs, then fried in olive oil and crowned with marinara sauce). *Trittico,* the house main-course pasta specialty, combines three kinds of homemade pasta: cheese ravioli in pomodoro sauce, penne with broccoli and shrimp, and tortellini in a heavy cream and Parmesan sauce. The chef is especially proud of the tenderloin stuffed with roasted garlic in Polvechio red wine sauce, and linguine *pescatore,* an array of seafood in marinara sauce. Numerous veal, chicken, and beef dishes round out the menu. For dessert, ask for profiterole or tiramisu.

Noord 43–E, at Caribbean Palm Village, near Santa Anna Church, Noord. ✆ 297/586-4777. Reservations recommended. Main courses $22–$50. AE, MC, V. Mon–Sat 6–11pm.

MODERATE

Buccaneer SEAFOOD/INTERNATIONAL   In a rustic stone building in the hamlet of Noord, Buccaneer is one of Aruba's most popular seafood restaurants. The nautical decor, which features hanging fishnets, portholes, and 12 bubbling aquariums chock-full of colorful fish, creates the watery atmosphere of a sunken ship. Another dining area has the feel of an underwater cave and boasts a 5,000-gallon seawater tank. Menu items include crabmeat cocktail, escargots in herb-garlic-butter sauce, shrimp in Pernod sauce, seafood Thermidor, and a land-and-sea platter with fish, shrimp, and beef tenderloin. If you're looking for something that sticks to the ribs, try smoked pork cutlets, sausage, sauerkraut, and potatoes. The food is hearty and delicious. The spacious bar area is a great place to linger over a drink or two.

Gasparito 11-C, Noord. ℭ **297/586-6172.** Reservations not accepted. Main courses $14–$32. AE, DISC, MC, V. Mon–Sat 5:30–10pm.

Café Japengo ℛ ASIAN FUSION   Located in the Hyatt, this minimalist cafe serves innovative pan-Asian cuisine and specializes in fresh seafood and sushi. Red, white, and black Japanese kites adorn the simple walls, providing only temporary distraction from the busy sushi chefs, who command attention in the cozy space. Start with fried shrimp and ginger dumplings or spicy seafood soup with bean sprouts and lemongrass-fish broth. For the main event, try seared, herbed tuna over soba noodles and shiitake mushrooms, or seared and oven-roasted sea bass with roasted sweet potatoes. The fish of the day might include mahimahi, grouper, swordfish, and red snapper bathed in ponzu, criollo, or citrus tamarind chutney. There's also oven-roasted duck, seared ginger beef, and cashew chicken, and more than enough green tea to slake any thirst.

At the Hyatt Regency Aruba Resort & Casino, J. E. Irausquin Blvd. 85, Palm Beach. ℭ **297/586-1234.** Reservations recommended. Main courses $16–$28. AE, DISC, MC, V. Tues–Sun 6–10:30pm.

Gasparito Restaurant and Art Gallery ℛℛ SEAFOOD/ARUBAN   Here's a favorite with people in love. Located in a restored *cunucu* (farm) home—the well out front is especially picturesque—Gasparito features intimate dining rooms inside (where the air-conditioning can be too efficient) and a breezy outdoor patio and bar. The tinkling of a fountain, modern rattan chairs, and lambent candlelight enhance the courtyard's warmth. Inside, vaulted ceilings embrace cozy rooms made more romantic by the sounds of classical piano. Local art, much of it for sale, graces the interior walls. Start with *pan bati,* a flat, pleasingly spongy corn bread. The *keri keri* ravioli, a favorite appetizer, features shredded barracuda (dry like *bacalāo*) in a creamy tomato and basil sauce. Main courses focus on seafood and Aruban dishes, but the menu makes a special nod to vegetarians, and the filet mignon has vocal fans. The precise staff is happy to give you detailed information about each dish. How about shrimp in coconut milk and brandy sprinkled with seasoned coconut flakes? Or seafood *keshi yena,* a casserole of scallops, shrimp, squid, and fish in Newburg sauce topped with melted Gouda cheese. For dessert you can't go wrong with *banana na forno,* a whole banana baked with cinnamon.

Gasparito 3, Noord. ✆ **297/586-7044.** Reservations recommended. Main courses $15–$33. AE, DISC, MC, V. Mon–Sat 5–11pm.

Hostaria da' Vittorio ✿✿ REGIONAL ITALIAN

It's hard to imagine a trattoria in Aruba, but this relative newcomer to the island's dining scene does a yeoman's job of recreating a Mediterranean atmosphere. The new building can't claim any old-world authenticity, but the sunny colors, arched doorways, and copper pots hanging over the open kitchen warm the columned dining area. Where to begin? How about raw salmon with olive oil, pink peppercorns, and Parmesan cheese, or baked artichokes with olive oil, white wine, and black olives? Vegetarians can choose from the island's most extensive risotto list or from a variety of pastas (cheese ravioli in walnut-cheese sauce or maybe gnocchi with fresh tomatoes, garlic, basil, and mozzarella). Featured main courses include sea bass baked in a crust of salt, dover sole sautéed in butter lemon sauce, and *osso buco.* In case you need a late-night snack, the shop at the restaurant's entrance sells a nice selection of Italian food and beverage specialties.

L. G. Smith Blvd. 380 (across from the Hyatt Regency), Palm Beach. ✆ **297/586-3838.** Dinner reservations recommended. Main courses $18–$35. AE, MC, V. Daily 11am–3pm and 6–11pm.

La Dolce Vita ✿ NORTHERN ITALIAN

La Dolce Vita has long been among the most acclaimed Italian restaurants in Aruba, and although it's not as traditionally elegant as Valentino's, its food is just as satisfying. The creative menu includes most of the usual favorites and a few unusual dishes. Start with aromatic *stracciatella,* an Italian version of egg-drop soup enhanced with diced vegetables and served over fettuccine. Pasta dishes include rigatoni in a piquant *arrabiata* sauce and linguine Calabrese seasoned with olive oil, anchovies, black olives, and walnuts. Main courses include chicken baked with spinach and ricotta and mozzarella cheeses, and the catch of the day simmered in marinara sauce with clams and mussels. A veal dish is topped with eggplant and mozzarella and smothered in marinara sauce.

Sasakiweg 46, Palm Beach. (C) 297/588-5592. Reservations recommended. Main courses $14–$47. AE, DISC, MC, V. Daily 11:30am–2:30pm and 5:30–11pm.

The Old Cunucu House ARUBAN/INTERNATIONAL   This warm, appealing restaurant showcases home-cooked Aruban specialties. Set in a traditional island homestead built almost a century ago, the Old Cunucu House boasts thick, whitewashed walls, Shaker-like furniture, and checkerboard tile floors. Cocktails are served out front, where tables overlook a desert garden. The intimate interior dining rooms are neat and informal. So is the food. Aruban fish soup with lemongrass, *mezze* (fish cakes), and cheese *pastechis* (deep-fried turnovers) are good appetizers. Recommended main courses include lobster, fish, shrimp, scallops, and squid in wine-and-Pernod cream sauce, and the popular *keshi yena* (chicken and Gouda cheese baked with onions, peppers, olives, raisins, and cashews). Most dishes come with *funchi* (corn polenta) and *pan bati* (corn bread). Have caramel flan or cheesecake for dessert. On Friday, guitarists make the rounds. On Saturday, you can partake of the all-you-can-eat fajita buffet while enjoying the mariachi band.

Palm Beach 150, Noord. (C) 297/586-1666. Reservations recommended. Main courses $17–$32. AE, DISC, MC, V. Mon–Sat 6–10:30pm.

Tango Argentine Grill ARGENTINE/STEAK/SEAFOOD   A short walk from most of the High-Rise hotels, Tango features sexy Argentine dance inside, live music and shopping kiosks outside, and decent food. The flavor here is South American, from the *churrasco* beef to the bilingual menu and Chilean wines. The large interior dining room features splayed cowhides and views of the 9-foot-long open grill. On the stage near the entrance, live tango dancers smolder before a backdrop painted to resemble a Buenos Aires street; a few lucky diners get brief lessons. The pleasant outside terrace overlooks a brick plaza, where live music fills the air from 8 to 11pm. For a light start, try tasty Caesar salad or octopus marinated in lime vinegar. The enormous barbecued beef dishes get mixed reviews, but all are better with *chimichurri* sauce, a savory blend of garlic, parsley, and olive oil. Don't get anything well done; it can be overdone. Shrimp in garlic and olive oil is a hit and comes with rice, fried plantains, and corn on the cob. Ice cream crowns the buttery Tango dessert crepe. It's filled with *dulce de leche*, a caramel confection.

J. E. Irausquin Blvd. 370 (across from the Allegro Resort), Palm Beach. ℂ 297/586-8600. Reservations recommended. Main courses $17–$32. AE, MC, V. Mon–Sat 5–11pm.

Twinkletone's *Kids* SEAFOOD/STEAK   If Mickey Rooney and Judy Garland had spent their teen years in Aruba, Twinkletone's is where they'd have put on their show. The warmth and can-do enthusiasm of the singing waiters and chefs at this family-friendly restaurant are impossible to resist. And the food's good, too. Special menus cater to kids, vegetarians, and early birds, but seafood and steak are the main attractions. Start with garlic toast or sweet bread pudding, then try coconut shrimp. Encrusted with unsweetened coconut and flash-fried, it's less sweet than you think. Next, sample red snapper with tomato, garlic, and onion *criollo* sauce. Room for dessert? Indulge in an Aruban banana. Big enough for two, it's rolled in coconut, deep fried, and served with ice cream and chocolate sauce. Now it's time for the show. The production values are no match for Las Vegas, but who needs fancy lighting and glittery costumes when you're having so much fun? Dad can flirt with the beauty singing "Big Spender." Mom can retaliate by dancing with the chef, while Sis merengues with the dreamy waiter. Enter a jaded cynic; leave with a smile and thawed heart.

Noord 186 (slightly inland from the Allegro Resort), Palm Beach. ℂ 297/586-9806. Reservations recommended. Main courses $18–$34; children's dinners $9.99. AE, DISC, MC, V. Mon–Sat 5:30–10:30pm.

Tips **Epicurean & Eclectic**

The Aruba Gastronomic Association (AGA), a group of more than 30 of the island's restaurants—including such recommended spots as Brisas del Mar, The French Steakhouse, Gasparito, and Pago Pago—offers a "Dine-Around" program with three options. For $109, you get coupons good for three dinners; $177 gets you five dinners; and for $245, you can have one dinner every day of the week. Children under 13 pay half price. The coupons are good at any of the AGA's member restaurants. Each dinner includes an appetizer, main course, dessert, coffee or tea, and service charges. For more information contact the AGA, L. G. Smith Blvd. 160, Sun Plaza Mall, Suite 401-I, Oranjestad (ℂ 800/793-6028 in the U.S., 297/588-5700 in Aruba, or fill out the online fax order form at www.arubadining.com or www.aruba.com).

INEXPENSIVE

Salt & Pepper SPANISH TAPAS   This fresh, appealing spot serves light meals such as salads, burgers, and sandwiches—but tapas are its specialty. Most of the 30 appetizer-size dishes have a Spanish accent, but others speak Cantonese, Italian, French, or Dutch. What sounds good to you? Pan-fried shrimp in mango sauce? Sautéed mushrooms with Parmesan cheese? Paella? Garlic potatoes? Dutch sausage spiced up for the islands? Fried brie? Black-olive spread? Nothing's too fancy or complicated, but better snacks are hard to find. With prices ranging from $2.50 to $5 per item, you can have a feast for less than the price of a simple entree at most restaurants in the neighborhood. Live entertainment begins at 8pm.

J. E. Irausquin Blvd. 368 A (across from the Allegro Resort), Palm Beach. ℃ 297/586-3301. Main courses $8–$18. AE, DISC, MC, V. Mon–Sun 8am–midnight; bar until 1am.

3 Low-Rise Hotels/Eagle & Manchebo Beaches

MODERATE TO EXPENSIVE

Chalet Suisse SWISS/INTERNATIONAL   Along the road that borders Eagle Beach, a short stroll from La Cabana resort, this alpine-chalet restaurant has the feel of an old-fashioned Swiss dining room. In deliberate contrast to the arid scrublands that surround it, the 15-year-old institution is an air-conditioned refuge of thick plaster walls, pinewood panels, and good old Teutonic *gemütlichkeit* (well-being). Appetizers include *bündnerfleisch* (thinly sliced dried beef with tangy horseradish sauce), escargots in herbal garlic butter with shallots, and Dutch pea soup. Main courses include beef stroganoff, pasta, Wiener schnitzel, roast duckling with orange sauce, and red snapper with Creole sauce. The array of high-calorie desserts include Swiss and German standards like apple strudel and Toblerone chocolate fondue. The hearty Swiss fare is a nice change for Arubans and expatriates; tourists may find it a bit heavy.

J. E. Irausquin Blvd. 246, Eagle Beach. ℃ 297/587-5054. Reservations recommended. Main courses $15–$42. AE, MC, V. Mon–Sat 6–10:30pm.

E Piscado CARIBBEAN SEAFOOD   La Cabana Beach Resort's entry in the fine dining category, E Piscado rests on a breeze-cooled garden terrace and boasts live piano and bass guitar music. The restaurant's name means "the fisherman" in Papiamento, and island seafood is the featured cuisine. Caribbean crab cake with papaya salsa is a favorite appetizer, as is chicken curry topped with garlic shrimp. There's also crisp-fried squid in spicy tomato sauce, and smoked salmon. For the main event, try Caribbean paella or the house specialty, seafood fiesta, a cornucopia of crab, mussels, scallops, and shrimp in a refreshing lime sauce. There are plenty of lamb, beef, and pork dishes as well. Most dishes come with *funchi* (corn polenta) and *pan bati* (corn bread).

At La Cabana All-Suite Beach Resort & Casino, J. E. Irausquin Blvd. 250, Eagle Beach. (© **297/587-9000.** Reservations recommended. Main courses $16–$33. AE, DISC, MC, V. Daily 5:30–10:30pm.

The French Steakhouse ☆☆ INTERNATIONAL/STEAK/SEAFOOD

Several Aruban restaurants feature *churrasco,* the distinctive Argentine beef, but none compares to The French Steakhouse for overall excellence. Despite the emphasis on the South American specialty, the dining room feels like a 1950s French country bistro—cafe curtains and brick accents decorate the windows, hand-painted tiles border the walls, and gold wrought iron gives the Louis XV–inspired chairs a rustic flavor. The live piano music is mellow, the lighting dim. Start with the old standard, shrimp cocktail (it couldn't be more refreshing), or mushroom caps stuffed with rich, herb-flavored crab and grated Gouda. For the main event, carnivores can't resist the extremely tender, 2-inch-thick *churrasco.* It's presented with the restaurant's signature fanfare: A bell rings and your waiter moans "ooh la la." The seafood platter, a feast of deep-fried jumbo shrimp, juicy scallops, tender calamari, and the catch of the day, is equally outstanding. Rich ice cream crowns the not-too-sweet apple strudel, a real treat with the strong and flavorful coffee. Value-conscious diners love the $30 Ambassador's Five-Course Dinner, which even includes a bottle of very decent wine (per couple).

At the Manchebo Beach Resort, J. E. Irausquin Blvd. 55, Manchebo Beach. (© **297/582-3444.** Reservations recommended. Main courses $13–$32. AE, DISC, MC, V. Daily 5:30–11pm.

Le Dôme ☆☆ BELGIAN/FRENCH

The award for the restaurant with the strongest European flavor goes to this auberge, hosted and owned by three Belgians. Opened in 1997, the restaurant flourished immediately, and in 2000 Queen Beatrix gave her royal seal of approval: She enjoyed her shrimp so much, she asked for the recipe. The newish building can't match the authentic antiquity of Chez Mathilde, but the establishment boasts four dining areas. One feels like a rustic, bourgeois home in Provence; another features antiques; Salvador Dalí lithographs grace the walls of a third; and diners on the outdoor terrace enjoy views of the sea. Start with scampi Le Dôme—*crème fraiche* makes the aromatic curry sauce special. As a main course, pan-fried turbot in a sauce of island spices and pineapple is a good example of the chef's rich but light cooking. Prime-cut beef, another specialty, comes with port sauce and goose-liver mousse; rosemary and garlic flavor the veal chop. The wine, liqueur, and cigar menus are voluminous, and you have a choice of 25 desserts. The mixed berry compote with ice cream is divine. No one would think of rushing you, so ask for your check. It comes with Leonidas truffles fresh from Brussels.

J. E. Irausquin Blvd. 224 (across from Eagle Beach). ℂ **297/587-1517.** Reservations recommended. Shorts permitted on outdoor terrace only. Main courses $16–$35. AE, DISC, MC, V. Tues–Sun noon–midnight.

Madame Janette ✦ INTERNATIONAL/CARIBBEAN Especially popular with Aruba's Dutch residents, Madame Janette weds an unlikely pair: the cuisines of northern Europe and the Caribbean. Although the fusion usually works, it's sometimes a shotgun wedding. The restaurant's outdoor dining areas spill down steps and around corners, some areas protected by reed-mat awnings, others open to the stars. The smoky house gravlax appetizer is pure Nordic: salmon marinated in dill and capers served on toast with hollandaise sauce. Rustic potato and leek soup with garlic croutons is also nice. Madame's hot shrimps show the chefs' ingenuity—juicy prawns baked in a flavorful marinara sauce topped with melted Gouda and Gorgonzola— but also the problem—the strong cheeses overwhelm the shrimp. Toasted almond grouper in light spinach cream sauce is an unqualified success, but pork tenderloin, seasoned with onions and Madagascar peppercorns, can be as dry as Bubby's brisket. The au gratin potatoes are perfect. For dessert, try Dutch apple pie a la mode. The food's hit or miss, but kudos to the chefs for experimenting. Once they settle into their successes, Madame Janette will be dynamite.

Cunucu Abao 37 (inland from La Cabana, next to the Blue Village Villas) Bubali. ℂ **297/587-0184.** Reservations recommended. Main courses $14–$31. AE, MC, V. Wed–Mon 6–10pm.

Pirates' Nest SEAFOOD/INTERNATIONAL Open-air, beachside dining is the allure of this breezy restaurant at the Bucuti Beach Resort. Built to resemble a 16th-century Dutch galleon, the structure glows with soft light at night, and from a distance looks afloat although it's more than 30m (100 ft.) from the sea. The extensive menu ranges from inexpensive soups, salads, and sandwiches to more substantial fare (mostly seafood). Start with oak-smoked Scottish salmon with onions and capers, or ice-cold shrimp cocktail. Sautéed jumbo shrimp in creamy chile, garlic, and cognac sauce is a zesty main course; other marine options include mahimahi, grouper, sea bass, and red snapper. Not everything served comes from the sea, however. There's beef stroganoff, filet mignon, pork, and chicken; several vegetarian dishes round out the menu. Call in advance for a private table on the beach.

At the Bucuti Beach Resort, L. G. Smith Blvd. 55B, Manchebo Beach. ✆ 297/583-1100. Dinner reservations recommended. Main courses $11–$49. AE, DISC, MC, V. Daily 7am–10:30pm.

The Turtle's Nest (Kids SEAFOOD/INTERNATIONAL Within earshot of the sea, this unpretentious but polished spot features al fresco dining and reliably good seafood. The sister establishment of the Waterfront Crabhouse (p. 68), it's just as kid-friendly, and main courses on the menu for the little ones start at an adult-friendly $3.95. Appetizers for grown-ups include standards like shrimp cocktail, fried squid, and Caesar salad. Main events include pastas, steaks, barbecued chicken, duck à l'orange, and hearty paella. Seafood is usually the ticket, though, and there are shrimp and fresh fish specials every day, depending on what inspires the chef. Nobody frowns if you order a mere sandwich or salad, and the pizza also makes a great snack. The best tables are at the extreme back, near the palm trees and the turquoise waves.

At the Costa Linda Beach Resort, J. E. Irausquin Blvd. 59, Eagle Beach. ✆ 297/583-8000. Reservations recommended. Main courses $12–$27. AE, MC, V. Daily noon–10pm.

4 California Lighthouse/Tierra Del Sol

EXPENSIVE

Ventanas del Mar ★★ INTERNATIONAL/SEAFOOD When you've got it, you don't have to flaunt it. Flavor combinations at this stylish restaurant are masterful and sophisticated. Each ingredient contributes subtly and in its own time, never overwhelming the star attraction. The interior dining rooms feature ochre walls and vaulted wooden ceilings, but the outside views dominate. Curved windows overlook the cacti and fairways of the adjacent golf course. The outdoor terrace, bordered by lush bougainvillea, palm trees, and a gentle colonnade, is steps above poolside tables that dream in a world of their own. Sweet lump crab cakes are a good start. Served with arugula and wispy carrots, they're accented with a Madame Janette pepper rémoulade. The grilled tuna main course, seasoned with refreshing mango-tomato chutney and soy sauce, is accompanied by garlic mashed potatoes that have a smoky, roasted flavor. The chef's signature dish, crispy fried whole snapper, comes with stir-fried vegetables and ginger soy sauce. Because the portion sizes have humans, not bears, in mind, you'll have room for dessert. Mango-scented coconut mousse dances to a medley of fresh melons. *Ponche crema* ice cream tastes like creamy, rum-infused eggnog.

At the Tierra del Sol Resort and Country Club, Malmok. ℂ **297/586-0879.** Reservations recommended. Main courses $18–$39. AE, DISC, MC, V. Daily 11am–3pm; Tues–Sun 6–10pm.

MODERATE

La Trattoria El Faro Blanco ITALIAN   Isolated at the top of a hill on the island's northernmost tip, this popular restaurant affords unbeatable vistas. A 360° scan takes in the expansive sea, windswept sand dunes, an emerald golf course, and the California Lighthouse. Just steps from the much-photographed beacon, the restaurant's original structure (which has since expanded) once housed the local lighthouse keeper, and the interior dining rooms retain a residential coziness. Seating on the terrace features unobstructed views of the sea. The fare covers a full range of Italian cuisine, with a good helping of Neapolitan specialties. Baby octopus, cooked with garlic, tomato, olive oil, and parsley, is a good way to kick things off. For a seafood main course, try grouper encrusted with pistachios, pink peppercorns, and Parmesan. Carnivores should try the excellent *osso buco* or filet mignon with porcini mushrooms. Desserts include tiramisu and pears poached in red wine. The outdoor bar is a favorite stop for golfers. Pizza is served between 3 and 6pm.

At the California Lighthouse, North Aruba. ℂ **297/586-0786.** Reservations recommended. Main courses $19–$36. Pizza from $12. AE, DISC, MC, V. Daily 11am–3pm and 6–11pm; bar daily 11am–11pm.

5 Savaneta

MODERATE

Brisas del Mar 🍴 *Kids* SEAFOOD/ARUBAN   Conventional wisdom has it that this decades-old, family-run restaurant is a prime place to watch the sun set. It's hard to argue with that: The open-air terrace overlooks the sea, and the sea breezes soothe sunburned skin. But at lunch on weekends, the restaurant offers a completely different experience: You can witness authentic Aruban family life. Sundays, when the local churches let out, are best. That's when multigenerational extended families, 15 or 20 people strong, feast on fresh, home-cooked Aruban seafood. Plus, there's no better place to sample the local sea's bounty or traditional Aruban side dishes like *keri keri* (shredded barracuda), *pan bati* (sweet, flat corn bread), and *funchi* (corn polenta). The crispy conch fritters come with marinated onions and Madame Janette peppers. Anything prepared Aruban style is smothered in onions and sweet red peppers.

Savaneta 222 A (between Oranjestad and San Nicolas). ✆ 297/584-7718. Reservations recommended. Main courses $10–$26. AE, MC, V. Tues–Sun noon–2:30pm and 6:30–9:30pm.

Flying Fishbone ✿ NOUVELLE INTERNATIONAL This intimate beachside restaurant is perfect for a moonlit dinner in the old fishing village of Savaneta. Many tables line the rustic wooden deck, but if you call a week in advance, you can get a spot so close to the sea that your feet may get wet. Swaying palm trees and starlight glittering in the sea are the stage for the restaurant's dramatically presented nouvelle cuisine. Duck liver terrine with walnuts, beets, and apples in beetroot dressing may not be for everyone, but grilled shrimp with mushrooms and mild pesto oil is a winner. Shrimp roti and smoked duck with cantaloupe are other good appetizers. Main courses include braised wahoo with papaya chutney and turmeric mayonnaise, and rock lobster poached in brandy stock with garden herbs and butter sauce. The portions are nouvelle, too, which means you'll have room for mango mousse or pineapple-coconut pie.

Savaneta 344 (between Oranjestad and San Nicolas). ✆ 297/584-2506. Reservations recommended. Main courses $16–$30. MC, V. Mon–Sat 6–10pm.

6 San Nicolas

MODERATE

Charlie's Bar and Restaurant SEAFOOD/ARUBAN Opened in 1941 by a crusty but lovable Dutchman and his saintly wife, Charlie's has survived several economic recessions as well as Nazi torpedoes (next to Aruba's oil refinery, it was vulnerable to Axis attacks during World War II). A sailor and oil-worker dive for 35 years, the place metamorphosed into a literary and tourist haunt that's now an Aruban treasure. The decor is Early American attic, and every inch of wall and ceiling is encrusted with some kind of memorabilia. Charlie's is a watering hole, but the clientele is on the discreet side of rowdy, and the staff can be downright gentle. The tasty food's just what you'd expect at a seaside bar—fresh shrimp, fish, and squid. Typical main courses come smothered in garlic, stewed peppers, and celery. Beef tips, spiced with tangy brown sauce, come with hearty steak fries. Don't pass on the Honeymoon

Sauce, a three-alarm blend of scotch bonnet peppers, onions, carrots, sweet peppers, coriander, and vinegar.

Zeppenveldstraat 56 (Main St.), San Nicolas (follow the signs). (**297/584-5086.**
Main courses $12–$30 (prices in Aruban florins; dollars accepted). No credit cards.
Kitchen Mon–Sat noon–9:30pm; bar until 10:30pm or later. Closed holidays.

The Promenade   SEAFOOD/INTERNATIONAL/ARUBAN
This oasis of provincial comfort is your best bet for civilized dining in San Nicolas. Although the Promenade has a reputation for being expensive, the prices are reasonable by Aruba standards. Don't expect the polish of the fanciest restaurants in Oranjestad; just savor the calm atmosphere, attentive service, and well-executed cuisine. Kick things off with seafood tempera. Featuring chilled chunks of calamari, crab, and octopus, it's seasoned with onions and a light chile-pepper vinaigrette. The excellent butterfly shrimp main course, sprinkled with toasted almonds, is bathed in a complex curry sauce that hits a series of flavor tones, from sweet to hot. Pepper steak flambéed with brandy and topped with green-pepper sauce is another favorite. The velvety crème caramel comes with lemony strawberry sauce.

Zeppenveldstraat 15 (Main St., near the refinery), San Nicolas. (**297/584-3131.**
Reservations recommended. Main courses $11–$21 (prices in Aruban florins). AE, MC, V. Tues–Sun noon–2:30pm and 6–10:30pm.

5

Fun in the Surf & Sun:
Beaches & Active Pursuits

Warm sunshine and beautiful beaches are Aruba's major attractions. The seemingly endless strips of white, sugary sand along the southwestern coast rank among the Caribbean's widest and most beautiful, and the shallow aqua surf is ideal for swimming. Toys like jet skis, waverunners, parasails, and banana boats are plentiful. Near the island's western tip, steady winds draw windsurfers, while the shallow waters and abundant marine life attract snorkelers. Shipwrecks, sunken planes, and coral reefs dot the entire leeward coast, keeping scuba divers happy, and along the south-central coast, mangrove forests, barrier islands, and calm seas combine for favorable kayaking conditions. For those who prefer to see the wonders of the sea without getting wet, submarines and glass-bottom boats make daily excursions. Anglers can struggle with barracuda, wahoo, marlin, and tuna in the deep waters not far from the coast.

Although dramatically beautiful, the northern coast of the island is pounded with waves. The stunning vistas and craggy limestone bluffs are great for hikes and picnics, but playing in the current is treacherous and strongly discouraged.

Land-based activities include bicycling, golf, hiking, horseback riding, paintball, and tennis. How many can you fit in?

1 Beaches

All of Aruba's beaches are public, but chairs and *palapas* (shade huts) provided by resorts are the property of the hotels and for guest use only. If you use them at a hotel other than your own, expect to be charged. Few of the smaller beaches have facilities other than a shade hut or two, so if you venture afar for privacy, bring your own food, water, and gear. Beer cans and charcoal ash litter a few remote areas, but Aruba's beaches are expansive, and trash is easily avoided. This beach tour starts at the island's northwest tip, near the California Lighthouse, and moves counterclockwise.

The calm surf and sandy bottom make **Arashi Beach,** near the California Lighthouse at the island's northwestern tip, one of Aruba's best swimming sites. Snorkelers like it for the elkhorn coral, while sunbathers spend lazy minutes watching pelicans fish. The white sand is soft, but look out for pebbles and stones. Although there are no facilities in the immediate area, a few beach huts provide shade.

Just a few minutes south, **Boca Catalina,** with its gentle, shallow water and plentiful fish, is another good spot for snorkeling. The sand is white, with some pebbles and shells, but the real hazard is horse manure left behind by some horseback-riding tours. This beach has no facilities, but it offers seclusion and tranquillity.

A bit farther south, **Malmok Beach** is another popular swimming and snorkeling spot with tiny coves, white sand, vast shallow waters, and abundant fish. This strand has no facilities, but you can fantasize about the accommodations in the nearby mansions. A scuttled German freighter on the seabed not far from the coast attracts divers. The steady winds make the beach extremely popular with windsurfers.

The island's mecca of windsurfing, though, is just minutes south at **Hadicurari,** or Fishermen's Huts. Every June, this site hosts the Hi-Winds World Challenge, an important pro-am windsurfing competition, but on any day, you can watch the brilliantly colored boards and sails dance along the waves. The shallow water is also excellent for swimming. Facilities include picnic tables and shade huts, but the white powder-sand beach is flecked with pebbles and shells at the water's edge.

Home of the High-Rise hotels, **Palm Beach** 🐾🐾 is Aruba's best spot for people-watching. This stretch of white sand, adjacent to Hadicurari, is also great for swimming, sunbathing, sailing, fishing, and snorkeling. The resorts sift the sand daily to get rid of pebbles and sharp shells, ensuring a beach as soft as talcum powder. Located smack dab in the heart of things, it can get crowded, though, and hotel guests stake out the scores of *palapas* sprouting from the sand early in the morning. With two piers and numerous watersports operators, Palm Beach is also busier and noisier than Aruba's other beaches. The least crowded areas are to the north, between the Holiday Inn and the Marriott, and to the south, between the Wyndham and the Divi Phoenix. (Potential drawbacks in those areas are the massive timeshare complex Marriott is building just north of the Holiday Inn, where you may want to avoid construction noise, and the wind around the Phoenix, which is sometimes powerful.) On the other hand, as you walk along the shore, you can wander through the splendid gardens of the beachfront resorts, watch the

California Lighthouse
California Point
Arashi Beach
Boca Catalina
Malmok Beach
Hadicurari (Fishermen's Huts)
Palm Beach
2A
2B
Alto Vista Chapel
Caribbean Sea
Noord
1A
1B
Eagle Beach
Manchebo Beach
Druif Beach
3B
3A
2A
2B
4A
4B
6B
6A
Bushiribana
Oranjestad
Surfside Beach
Sonesta Island
7A
7B
Natural Bridge
Queen Beatrix Airport
Hooiberg
Santa Cruz
1A
1B
ARIKOK
Caves of Canashito
7A
7B
De Palm Island
Spanish Lagoon
Jamanota
NATIONAL
Dos Playa
Boca Prins Sand Dunes
Boca Prins
Fontein Cave
Mangel Halto
Caribbean Sea
PARK
Quadirikiri Cave
Savaneta
1A
1B
7A
7B
San Nicolas

✈ Airport
🏖 Beach
🔦 Lighthouse

0   3 mi
0   3 km

N

Boca Grandi
Seroe Colorado
Rodger's Beach
Baby Beach
Colorado Point

thriving bird and iguana life, and stop for a cold tropical drink at one of the many open-air bars. The eponymous trees, coconut and date palms, were planted in 1917.

Separated from Palm Beach by a brief outcrop of limestone that's home to a splendid green flock of parakeets, **Eagle Beach** 🐟🐟🐟 is across a small road from the La Cabana resort and several timeshare resorts. The wide beach here stretches as far as the eye can see. The sugar-white sand and gentle surf are ideal for swimming, and although the nearby hotels offer watersports and beach activities, the ambience is relaxed and quiet. A couple of bars, as well as numerous *palapas* and chairs maintained by the hotels, punctuate the expansive strand. Shaded picnic areas are provided for the public, and the beach is popular with tourists and locals alike on weekends. Prime sand conditions are directly in front of La Cabana and the Amsterdam Manor.

For sheer tranquillity and open space, **Manchebo Beach** 🐟🐟🐟, also known as Punto Brabo, is top-notch. Because the sand here stretches 110m (120 yd.) from the shore to the hotels, congestion is never a problem. The handful of smaller resorts that occupy this coveted location, next to Eagle Beach, offer beverages and food, and the discreet atmosphere makes Manchebo one of Aruba's only tops-optional beaches. The white-powder sand is spectacular, but the surf is steady and brisk. With no watersports in the area, serenity is guaranteed. The premier spots are in front of the Bucuti Beach and Manchebo Beach resorts.

Druif Beach meets Manchebo Beach farther east along the coast. The sand remains white but the strand narrows considerably, and the surf becomes more restless. Rocks and pebbles come out in profusion here. The beach between the Divi Aruba Beach Resort and the Tamarijn resort is the widest stretch in the area; the strip south of the Tamarijn is also nice.

South of Oranjestad and across the street from the Talk of the Town Beach Resort, **Surfside Beach** is sleepy and intimate. Although the hotel operates a bar and provides towels and beach chairs for guests, the small strip is also popular with Arubans, especially residents of nearby Oranjestad. The calm waters are great for swimming, but there are prettier beaches; Surfside's proximity to the capital is its major selling point.

The beaches of **Renaissance Island** are restricted to guests of the Renaissance resort, who board a skiff in the hotel's lobby in downtown Oranjestad for the 15-minute trip to the private island. The 40-acre tropical retreat features cozy white-sand beaches, intimate coves, and protected swimming areas. One secluded area is tops-optional.

Hammocks span the palm trees, and beach chairs are also provided. The resident iguanas and flamingos are always ready to strike a pose.

In the hamlet of Pos Chiquito between Oranjestad and Savaneta, **Mangel Halto** is a favorite picnic spot. Its white-powder sand and shallow water are additional enticements for Aruban families, especially on weekends.

The charm of **Rodger's Beach,** south of San Nicolas, is initially overwhelmed by the gigantic oil refinery looming on the western horizon. Like something out of Orwell's *1984* or Dr. Frankenstein's lab, the smoke-belching towers contrast bizarrely with the idyllically beautiful Caribbean waters. The refinery is harmless (they say)—no obvious water pollution, no stench (if the wind's blowing in the right direction)—and the gentle, protected waters are ideal for swimming. The narrow strip of soft, white-powder sand is popular with locals, but tourists who want to get away from the more familiar sites show up as well. *Palapas* and giant sea-grape bushes provide shade. There's also a small bar and grill, an array of colorful fishing boats, and shower facilities. Bring your own equipment, including snorkeling gear: The water is shallow for almost 15m (50 ft.) out, and multicolored fish and coral formations are easy to spot.

Baby Beach ⟨⟨, near Aruba's easternmost tip, is a prime destination for families with young children. Like a great big bathtub, this shallow bowl of warm turquoise water is perfect for inexperienced swimmers, thanks to the protection of rock breakwaters. The water is never deeper than 1.5m (5 ft.), and the powdery sand is friendly to bare feet. Be on the lookout for gnarled driftwood and sharp shells, though. Giant sea grape bushes offer protection from the sun. Facilities are restricted to a refreshment stand and washrooms. On weekends, the beach is very popular with Arubans, who party with music and barbecues. Coral reefs farther out are popular with snorkelers, but the surf is rough outside the protected lagoon; keep an eye on the kids if they tend to stray. Bring your own towels and snorkeling gear.

If you find yourself sometimes snarling at children, avoid Baby Beach and drive north a few minutes to **Boca Grandi** ⟨⟨, a virtually deserted expanse of dramatic sand dunes and sea grasses. The salt air and terrain are reminiscent of Cape Cod, but the aqua, azure, and sapphire waters are unmistakably Caribbean. A penitentiary crowns limestone bluffs rising behind the dunes, and the inmates suffer the ultimate punishment: viewing the ocean and beach and knowing they can't enjoy it. The low-lying sea grapes provide next to no protection from the sun, and pockets of trash and jetsam mar some of the intimate coves. The sand has pebbles, too, but the steady breeze and rolling surf are excellent for advanced windsurfing. Because the surf is riled up most of the time, Boca Grandi is appropriate for strong swimmers only.

Boca Prins ⚑, in Arikok National Park on the north coast, also boasts dunes and hardy seaside vegetation, but the rough-and-tumble waters here make swimming out of the question. You'll need a car, preferably an all-terrain vehicle, to get here on the dirt roads. Plan a picnic lunch, walk along the limestone cliffs, and slide down the dunes instead of risking the water.

Dos Playa, a 15-minute walk west along the coast from Boca Prins, is an even more popular picnic spot. With huge crashing waves and a rugged limestone coast, it too is picturesque but unsuitable for swimming.

2 Hitting the Water

BOATING

Aruba offers sailing adventures on yachts and catamarans day and night. Some include snorkeling, swimming, and lunch; others feature sunset vistas. For night owls, dinner-dance-and-booze cruises include a midnight dip in the sea (see chapter 8). If you have something special to celebrate, you may want to charter a private yacht (about $175–$200 per hr.).

CatPeople (℡ 297/993-2750; www.arubacatpeople.com) offers high-speed adventures on a 21m-long (70-ft.) catamaran. Departing from the Seaport Marina in Oranjestad, the speedster makes trips to Venezuela and back (3½ hr., $75), to the California Lighthouse and Arashi Beach for snorkeling (3½ hr., $65), to Rodger's Beach for snorkeling (4 hr., $65), and completely around Aruba (7 hr., $175). All trips include snacks and drinks. Schedules vary, so call for specific information. Private charters are available (2½ hr., maximum of 6 persons $495; 3½ hr., maximum of 6 persons $695).

De Palm Tours (℡ 297/582-4400; www.depalm.com) offers more sailing options than anyone else—six different snorkel sails on catamarans and trimarans, and several sail-only cruises. Some cruises feature dinner catered by Le Dôme (see chapter 4); others offer "snuba," a cross between scuba and snorkeling. Ranging from 2 to 5 hours in length, the trips depart daily in the morning and afternoon and at sunset. Prices start at $35 and climb to $79.

Boarding at the Hadicurari Pier between the Holiday Inn and Marriott, **Jolly Pirates** (℡ 297/583-7355) features 3½-hour sail, snorkel, and rope-swing (think Tarzan plunging into the sea) cruises (daily; $50, including barbecue lunch); 2-hour sunset trips (Mon and Fri, $26); and 3-hour afternoon sail and snorkel tours (Tues–Thurs and Sat, $30). All three options include an open bar.

Mi Dushi Sailing Adventures (© 297/586-2010; www.aruba adventures.com) offers three cruises on a 23m (78-ft.) sailing vessel built in 1925. The 5-hour morning cruise combines sailing, snorkeling, swimming, and a rope swing, with continental breakfast, surf-and-turf lunch, and open bar. The boat departs from the De Palm Pier Monday through Friday at 9:30am. The price is $69, $35 for children 6 to 12, free for children under 6. Also featuring shallow reef snorkeling and swimming, the 3-hour sundown cruise sets sail at 3:30pm from the same pier on Tuesday and Thursday, and costs $39, $20 for children; the price includes snacks and an open bar for adults. On Wednesday and Friday, the boat leaves at 5pm for a 2-hour all-you-can-drink sunset sail. This adult-only party is $35.

Pelican Adventures (© 297/587-2302; www.pelican-aruba.com) offers morning, afternoon, and sunset cruises on two different catamarans. The 2½-hour snorkel cruise departs daily at 2pm and includes snacks and open bar ($30; $15 for children). The 3½-hour brunch cruise features continental breakfast, barbecue lunch, snorkeling, and open bar (Wed and Fri, 9:30am, $50; $35 for children). The sunset booze cruise lasts 2 hours and includes snacks and drinks (Tues, Thurs, and Sat, 5pm, $30; $15 for children). The 4-hour dinner cruise leaves at 5pm; the $50 charge ($35 for children) includes the meal and unlimited drinks. All trips leave from the Pelican Pier near the Holiday Inn, and private charters can be arranged.

Red Sail Sports (© 877-RED-SAIL in the U.S. and Canada, 297/586-1603 in Aruba; www.redsail.com) boasts two large catamarans and several sailing options. The 4-hour morning snorkel sail visits three snorkeling sites and includes deli lunch and an open bar (daily at 9:15am; $56, children 3–12 $28). The 2½-hour afternoon snorkel sail includes snacks and beverages (daily at 2:30pm; $40, children $20). The 1½-hour sunset cruise features snacks and rum punch (daily at 5:30pm; $35, children $18). On full-moon nights only, the 2-hour moonlight sail includes wine and cheese (7:30pm; $40, children $20). All trips leave from De Palm Pier, and group charters are available.

Operated by the same folks who own Mi Dushi, *Tattoo* (© 297/586-2010; www.arubaadventures.com) conducts nocturnal booze and dance cruises with dinner buffet and $1 and $2 drinks (Tues–Sat, 8pm–midnight; $49, adults only). On Wednesday and

Friday, it offers a 4-hour snorkeling and swimming cruise that departs from De Palm Pier at 11:30am. The $35 price ($20 for children) includes a barbecue lunch, but alcoholic drinks are extra ($2–$3 per drink). All Tattoo cruises feature a rope swing and three-level water slide.

How about a yacht cruise? Family-owned *Tranquilo* (© 297/585-7533; www.visitaruba.com/tranquilo) has several programs. On Tuesday, Thursday, and Friday, a 6-hour lunch cruise features snorkeling, fishing, lunch, and drinks during a trip down Aruba's southeast coast (10am; $50). Available upon request for a minimum of eight people, the 2-hour sunset sail is $25 per person. An exclusive 3-hour sail for two is offered on Wednesday and Saturday at 5pm. It includes a menu of lobster, shrimp, or Argentine steak and total privacy ($475 for you and your love). Charter cruises, available on request, start at $120 per hour.

Catamaran cruises from the Pelican Pier (behind the Holiday Inn) are conducted by **Wave Dancer Cruises** (© 297/582-5520; www.arubawavedancer.com). A 4-hour trip with three snorkeling stops, snacks, lunch, and drinks is $50; a 2-hour tour hits one snorkeling reef and includes snacks and drinks for $25; and a 2-hour sunset cruise is an extended happy hour at sea ($25).

DEEP-SEA FISHING

In the deep waters off the coast of Aruba you can test your skill and wits against barracuda, amberjack, sailfish, wahoo, blue and white marlin, kingfish, bonito, and black- and yellow-fin tuna. Chartered boats, with captain, crew, advice, tackle, bait, and soft drinks, usually accommodate four to six anglers. **De Palm Tours** (© 297/582-4400; www.depalm.com) books half-day tours beginning at $250 per boat. The price for full-day trips goes as high as $600. **Pelican Adventures**'s (© 297/587-2302; www.pelican-aruba.com) half-day rates are about $300; full-day excursions range from $440 to $600. **Red Sail Sports** (© 877-RED-SAIL, or 297/586-1603 in Aruba; www.redsail.com) offers half-day expeditions for $350 and full-day trips for $700 for a maximum of four. You can also try your luck with **Mahi Mahi Fishing Charters** (© 297/587-0538; www.aruba-mahimahi.com), **Rainbow Runner** (© 297/586-4259; www.rainbowseekers.com), **Teaser Charters** (© 297/582-5088; www.teasercharters.com), or any of the other individually owned boats docked at the **Seaport Marina,** Seaport Marketplace 204, Oranjestad (© 297/583-9190); their captains offer slightly cheaper prices.

PLAYING WITH WATER TOYS

How many different toys will you try out this vacation? Choose from jet skis ($45 single, $55 double per ½ hr.), banana boat or tube rides (both towed behind a speed boat, $15), Sunfish sailboats ($20 per hr.), waverunners (high-speed jet boats, $45 single, $55 double per ½ hr.), water skis ($35 per 15 min.), paddle boats ($15 per hr.), and floatbeds (sturdier than a raft; $5 per day). Check out any of the watersports operators along Palm Beach or contact **De Palm Tours** (© 297/582-4400; www.depalm.com), **Island Watersports** (© 297/593-5436), **Pelican Adventures** (© 297/587-2302; www.pelican-aruba.com), **Red Sail Sports** (© 877-RED-SAIL, or 297/586-1603 in Aruba; www.redsail.com), or **Unique Sports of Aruba** (© 297/586-0096; www.visitaruba.com/uniquesports).

KAYAKING

Aruba Kayak Adventures, Ponton 90 or the activities desk at the Costa Linda (© 297/582-5520; www.arubawavedancer.com/arubakayak), offers a leisurely 4-hour kayak tour along the southern coast. Boats launch not far from Savaneta Monday through Saturday at 9:30am, then hug the coastal mangroves, past Pos Chiquito, Mangel Halto, and Spanish Lagoon, formerly a pirate hideout. After crossing the calm lagoon to De Palm Island, paddlers can snorkel, sunbathe, and lunch at the island's restaurant before kayaking the final leg to Barcadera Beach. The $77 price includes hotel pick-up and drop-off, training, boat and snorkeling equipment, and lunch.

KITE SURFING

With the help of large inflatable kites, about 27m (90 ft.) of flying line, and small surfboards with foot straps, kite boarders at Malmok Beach skim across the water at 48kmph (30 mph) and launch 3m to 15m (10 ft.–50 ft.) in the air. Kite surfing has many of the same elements and thrills as snowboarding and windsurfing, but with a relatively easier learning curve. Aruba's calm, shallow waters make the island ideal for giving it a whirl. **Kite Surfing Aruba** (© 297/586-5025; www.kitesurfingaruba.2get2u.com) has 2-hour introductory lessons for $100. Only comfortable swimmers at least 10 years old need apply. **Vela Windsurf and Kite Surf Center,** next to the Marriott, is a joint operation of **Pelican Adventures** (© 297/587-2302; www.pelican-aruba.com) and **Vela Windsurf** (© 800/223-5443; www.velawindsurf.com). It offers a suite of introductory classes that break the art into specialized segments (which means more instruction time and a higher price tag).

PARASAILING

You can ascend 180m (600 ft.) above the sea in a boat-towed parachute after making arrangements with one of the watersports centers along Palm Beach or by calling **Caribbean Parasail** (© 297/586-0505), **Island Watersports** (© 297/593-5436), **Pelican Adventures** (© 297/587-2302; www.pelican-aruba.com), or **Red Sail Sports** (© 877-RED-SAIL, or 297/586-1603 in Aruba; www.redsail.com). Although flight time is only 12 or 15 minutes, the exhilaration lasts all day. Expect to pay about $40 for a single-seater, $70 for a parachute built for two. Some operators restrict flights to persons weighing between 100 and 200 pounds only. Bring a waterproof camera.

SCUBA DIVING & SNORKELING

Aruba offers enough coral reefs, marine life, and wreck diving to keep scuba divers and snorkelers busy. The coastal waters have an average temperature of 80°F (27°C), and visibility ranges from 18m to 30m (60 ft.–100 ft.). Snorkelers: Be forewarned that waves can be choppy at times in some locations. Divers should wear wet suits, especially for deeper dives (the water doesn't always feel like 80°F). Plankton feeds the dense coral population, and freshwater runoff is minimal. The best snorkeling sites are around Malmok Beach and Boca Catalina, where the water is calm and shallow, and visible and kinetic marine life is plentiful. Dive sites stretch along the entire southern, leeward coast.

THE OPERATORS

Pelican Adventures (© 297/587-2302; www.pelican-aruba.com), probably the island's premier dive and snorkeling operation, has desks at the Aruba Beach Club, Holiday Inn, La Cabana, Playa Linda, Radisson, and Wyndham. The full-service, 5-Star PADI-certified Gold Palm operator has two dive boats (one can handle up to 25 divers) and an array of diving options. Two-tank morning boat dives are $55, one-tank morning or afternoon boat dives are $35, and one-tank night dives are $39. Packages include 6 days of unlimited diving for $325 (try out an operator before committing to a package, though; Pelican is recommended, but judge for yourself). Non-diving boat passengers pay $20 to $25, space permitting. Snorkeling cruises include instructions, equipment, stops at three sites, snacks, and an open bar for $30. Pelican also conducts 1-day introductory scuba courses ($70) and full-fledged PADI open-water certification instructions ($350).

Red Sail Sports ✿ (℃ **877/RED-SAIL,** or 297/586-1603 in Aruba; www.redsail.com), another full-service, 5-Star PADI-certified Gold Palm operator, has locations at the Allegro, Hyatt, La Cabana, Marriott, and Renaissance. Its dive prices are slightly higher than Pelican's: Two-tank morning boat dives are $65, one-tank morning or afternoon boat dives are $40, and one-tank night dives are $45. Packages include unlimited diving within a 7-day period for $300, a better value than Pelican's 6-day package (there are blackout dates and a 10% service charge). Non-diving boat passengers pay $18, space permitting. Snorkelers are charged $22, including equipment, but Pelican, Red Sail, and other operators offer an array of snorkeling-only excursions that visit multiple sites. Red Sail also offers 1-day introductory scuba and refresher courses that include instructions, a morning pool session, a one-tank boat dive, and all equipment for $79. Pool-only introductory courses are available for children ($40). The PADI open-water certification course is $350.

Only two other operators boast PADI affiliation. **Unique Sports of Aruba** (℃ **297/586-0096;** www.visitaruba.com/uniquesports), on Palm Beach at the Aruba Grand, is another popular operation. Its two boats can accommodate a maximum of 16 divers, and its rates are slightly cheaper than those of Pelican and Red Sail. Although **S. E. Aruba Fly 'n Dive** (℃ **297/587-8759;** www.searuba.com) operates out of Oranjestad harbor, it specializes in dives along the

---

Tips Take the Plunge

If you weren't born with gills, you'll have to learn certain skills and gain an understanding of your equipment before you scuba dive. Contact PADI, NAUI, or SSI for instruction. Certifying 70% of U.S. divers and 55% of divers worldwide, **PADI (Professional Association of Diving Instructors),** 30151 Tomas St., Rancho Santa Margarita, CA 92688-2125 (℃ **800/729-7234;** www.padi.com), is the world's largest diving organization. Equally respected but less of a marketing powerhouse, **NAUI (National Association of Underwater Instructors),** 1232 Tech Blvd., Tampa, FL 33619-7832 (℃ **800/553-6284;** www.naui.org), is a not-for-profit association that's been around for 40 years. The last of the Big Three is **SSI (Scuba Schools International),** 2619 Canton Ct., Ft. Collins, CO 80525-4498 (℃ **970/482-0883;** www.ssiusa.com).

island's southeast coast. The "fly" part of the company's name refers to its package dive tours to Aruba's sister islands, Bonaire and Curaçao. The weekend special to Bonaire, a veritable diver's paradise, includes 2 nights' accommodations, a two-tank boat dive, unlimited shore dives, and round-trip air transportation on Fly 'n Dive's own plane. Open to certified divers only, the package is $335 during the high season, $320 at other times (air tax and equipment are included).

Two other dive shops operate in the resort area. **Aruba Pro Dive** (© 297/582-5520; www.arubaprodive.com), with a desk at the Costa Linda, specializes in small groups. **Mermaid Sport Divers** (© 297/583-5546; www.scubadivers-aruba.com) is located between the Bucuti Beach and Manchebo Beach resorts and offers a free dive to anyone who spots a sea horse.

See "Boating," earlier in this chapter, for a comprehensive list of snorkeling operators.

THE SITES

At the island's extreme northeast point, the *California* **wreck** has haunted the ocean floor for almost 100 years. While traveling from Liverpool to Central America, the wooden passenger ship ran aground, its merchandise, clothing, and furniture eventually washing ashore. Tour guides often circulate the romantic notion that the ship was the only vessel to have heard the *Titanic*'s distress signal. It's a nice story but a bunch of malarkey. The ship that ignored the *Titanic*'s flares was the *Californian,* which was torpedoed by a German submarine off the coast of Greece in 1915. About 14m (45 ft.) beneath the ocean's surface, Aruba's *California* is draped in orange and yellow sponges, plate coral, and anemones. Grouper, jewfish, lobster, and barracuda make frequent appearances, and a dense reef of staghorn and pillar corals forms a breakwater beyond the ship. Due to strong currents and choppy seas, this dive is strictly for advanced divers, and only when the water is unusually calm.

At **Arashi Reef** ⟨ℛ⟩, around the island's northern tip from the *California,* a Lockheed Lodestar has permanently landed on the silty bottom of tranquil Arashi Bay. The wings, cockpit, and front half of the fuselage sit upright in a frozen take-off position. Maybe the plane's waiting for the neighborhood angelfish, parrotfish, sergeant majors, yellowtail snappers, caesar grunts, gray chromis, and blue tangs to clear the runway. Just south of the plane, brain coral, star coral, and sea rods dot the strip before dropping off to a ledge painted with sea fans and multicolored encrusting sponges. The plane's depth of 11m to 12m (35 ft.–40 ft.) is ideal for novice divers and snorkelers.

Just south of Arashi Reef, the 120m-long (400-ft.) ***Antilla*** **wreck** ⊛⊛ is the Caribbean's largest shipwreck. Once a German freighter, the ship was scuttled in 1941 when threatened by Allied forces. The wide compartments make diver penetration easy. It's one of the island's most popular dives, though, so you may have to wait in line to have your photo taken in the captain's bathtub. Covered by giant tube sponges and coral formations, the 18m-deep (60-ft.) ghost ship is swarmed by angelfish, yellowtail snapper, silversides, moray eels, and the occasional lobster. Octopus, sergeant majors, and puffers can also be spotted.

Leaf and brain coral await you at **Malmok Reef,** just south of the *Antilla.* This 21m-deep (70-ft.) bottom reef's dozing lobsters and stingrays are popular with underwater paparazzi, and the giant purple, orange, and green barrel sponges pose for the camera as well. The *Debbie II,* a 36m (120-ft.) fuel barge sunk in 1992, attracts schools of fish and barracudas.

Southwest of Malmok Reef, the mangled midsection is all that remains of the ***Pedernales,*** an American flat-bottomed oil tanker torpedoed by a German submarine in 1942. Cabins, washbasins, lavatories, toilets, and pipelines are exposed for easy viewing. The bow and stern were hauled back to the United States, refitted with a new hull, and used to transport troops for the Normandy invasion. Chunks of the hull, supports, and cross beams litter the sandy bottom. The wreckage attracts caesar grunts, squirrelfish, trumpet fish, groupers, parrotfish, angelfish, silversides, and yellowtail snappers. Keep an eye open for snake eels and spotted eagle rays, too. White tunicates and orange cup corals coat the metal undersides. At a depth of only 6m to 9m (20 ft.–30 ft.), the *Pedernales* is popular with novice divers and snorkelers.

Off the coast of Oranjestad, **Harbor Reef** features an abundance of plant and soft coral formations, including giant brain coral and orange, black, and blue sponges. Nearby, the aging **pilot boat wreck** is encrusted with sponges and brain, star, and sheet coral. The queen angels, parrotfish, and Spanish hogfish bathe the 11m (35-ft.) vessel in fiesta colors, while a barracuda and a pair of green morays keep divers alert. You may also spot the occasional stingray or spotted eagle ray.

Two twin-engine aircraft wrecks—both unclaimed drug runners—form an artificial reef 46m (50 yd.) from **Renaissance Island**'s main beach. The Beechcraft 18 and Convair 400 are intact;

divers can sit in the cockpits, but octopuses, moray eels, lobsters, and crabs would prefer they didn't. The fuselages feature a veneer of clinging corals and hydroids, while elkhorn, staghorn, and fan corals preside nearby. Snorkelers can see the 4.5m-deep (15-ft.) Beechcraft from the surface, but the 12m-deep (40-ft.) Convair is better viewed by divers. In only 4m (12 ft.) of water and a bit farther off Renaissance Island's main beach, a sunken barge with crowds of swarming fish is also perfect for snorkeling.

Just east of the airplanes, **Sponge Reef** is the home of a remarkable array of sponges, including orange elephant ears, purple and yellow tubes, vases, and small baskets. Interesting leaf and plate coral formations are also found in the area.

Farther east but still only 4 miles southwest of Oranjestad, **Barcadera Reef** stretches from depths of 6m to 27m (20 ft.–90 ft.), accommodating both divers and snorkelers. Dense clusters of elkhorn, staghorn, and finger corals populate the reef, and along the sandy bottom, brain corals and huge sea fans hold sway. Wrasses, scorpionfish, blue and stoplight parrotfish, French angelfish, damselfish, and pink-tipped anemones also set up house in the area.

West of Barcadera Reef at a depth of 27m (90 ft.), the *Jane Sea* **wreck** rests in a thick grove of star, boulder, plate, and brain coral. This 75m (250-ft.) Venezuelan cement freighter was sunk to form an artificial reef after it was caught with a cargo of cocaine. Blanketed with hydroids, fire coral, and encrusting sponge, the anchor chain is completely rigid. The ship's sides are orange with cup corals and home to French and queen angels. Keep your eyes peeled for barracudas, green morays, lobsters, tropicals, and gorgonians, and watch your head when entering the radio room and mess hall.

Even before snorkelers leave the dock of **De Palm Island** (east of the *Jane Sea* wreck), savvy blue parrotfish looking for a snack greet them. Feel free to feed them, but watch your fingers. More adventurous snorkelers can swim out 27m (30 yd.) for a dense coral reef that supports blue tangs, triggerfish, sergeant majors, yellowtail, grunts, and blue and stoplight parrotfish. Sleeping nurse sharks are around as well. Water depths start at 1.2m (4 ft.) at the dock but drop off to 36m (120 ft.) by the time you're 364m (400 yd.) out. Divers, who usually reach the reef by boat, are likely to spot a barracuda or two.

Off the central coast of De Palm Island, **Mike's Reef** ⋆⋆ offers one of Aruba's best reef dives. Enormous clusters of gorgonians, brain coral, flower coral, and star coral dominate the environment, while brilliant purple and orange sponges direct the procession of rainbow runners and barracuda. This reef is especially popular with macro photographers (underwater photographers who specialize in close-up and extreme close-up shots).

Just east of Mike's Reef and 110m (120 yd.) out from Mangel Halto Beach, **Mangel Halto Reef** 𝕽𝕽 slopes from 4.5m (15 ft.) to ledges and ridges that plunge to depths of 33m (110 ft.). The area boasts an array of deep-water gorgonians, anemones, and sponges. Mobile marine life includes copper sweepers, grunts, sergeant majors, lobsters, blue tangs, butterfly fish, stingrays, yellow tails, and jacks. You may even spot a sea horse. At the greater depths, octopuses, green morays, nurse sharks, tarpons, and large barracuda inhabit small caves and overhangs. In early spring, magically graceful sea turtles appear on their way to lay eggs on the nearby beaches.

Continuing east along the coast, **Isla de Oro Reef** rests off the old fishing village of Savaneta. Close to the mangrove-lined shore, the reef is usually swept by a running current, and visibility is excellent. Beginning at 6m (20 ft.), yellow stingrays, lobster, Spanish hogfish, and French angelfish dart along the walls of staghorn, star, brain, and plate corals. Toward the ultimate depth of 36m (120 ft.), sheet and leaf corals form ledges and caves—home to large morays, coral crabs, and parrotfish.

A bit farther east, **Commandeurs Reef** slopes from 12m to 27m (40 ft.–90 ft.) below the surface. Sheet and leaf coral here attract extensive marine life such as snappers, groupers, grunts, and French and queen angels. On occasion, runners and barracuda patrol the area.

UNDERWATER TOURING

If you loved Captain Nemo and *20,000 Leagues Under the Sea,* don't miss your chance to cruise 45m (150 ft.) below the sea in a submarine. **Atlantis Adventures** (𝒞 **800/253-0493** in the U.S., or 297/588-6881; www.atlantisaruba.com) operates a spacious, modern ship with large portholes for maximum ogling. After a comprehensive orientation on shore, you board a catamaran for the 30-minute sail to deeper water, then transfer to the *Atlantis VI,* a 20m-long (65-ft.), fully pressurized vessel. During the gentle descent, you'll pass scuba divers, coral reefs, shipwrecks, and hundreds of curious sergeant majors, blue chromis, creole wrasse, damselfish, parrotfish, and angelfish. Brain and sheet coral, sea whips, and tube and barrel sponges are just as easy to spot during the hour you're submerged. The crew's commentary is expert, informative, and very wry. Depending on the season, trips depart 3 to 6 times each day. The cost is $74 for adults, $68 for persons over 60, and $35 for children younger than 16. All passengers must be at least .9m (3 ft.) tall. It's worth the splurge, but for a cheaper option consider Atlantis's other ship, the *Seaworld Explorer.* This glass-bottom boat remains above sea level, but its observatory is 1.5m (5 ft.) below the surface. The narrated tour covers Arashi Reef and features an up-close encounter with a scuttled German freighter, encrusted with coral and teeming with other marine life. The daily voyages are $37 for adults, $20 for children under 12, gratis for anyone under 2. The *Atlantis VI* trip leaves from a pier in front of the Crystal Casino in Oranjestad; the *Seaworld Explorer* excursion departs from Pelican Pier on Palm Beach.

If you don't mind getting a little wet but have no desire to learn to scuba dive, consider the Sea Trek "helmet dive" offered by **De Palm Tours** (② **297/582-4400;** www.depalm.com). Donning a wet suit and a TeleTubbies-inspired helmet that supplies a continuous flow of air, you'll descend 6m (20 ft.) beneath the sea to a 105m (350-ft.) walkway, where you can feed the fish, view a sunken Piper Cub, and generally experience life underwater. If you can walk and breathe, don't deprive yourself of the fun. The 20- to 25-minute stroll is $89. The CD-ROM featuring you in full aquanaut regalia seated at an underwater cafe is another $35, but worth it. (*A word to the wise:* Although Sea Trek is on De Palm Island, don't let anyone convince you to spend all day there. Its beaches are rocky and generally dismal compared to those of the main island.)

WINDSURFING

Aruba's world-class windsurfing conditions attract competitors from around the world every June for the Hi-Winds World Challenge, one of the region's most popular windsurfing competitions and the only Professional Windsurfing Association Grand Prix event in the Caribbean. Wind speeds on the island are best in May, June, and July, when they average 20 to 25 knots, and calmest from September through November, when they range from 10 to 20 knots.

The area around **Malmok Beach** and Hadicurari, or Fishermen's Huts, is the most popular windsurfing spot on the island. Sailed by novices and pros alike, it features slightly gusty offshore winds, minimal current, and moderate chop. The water is shallow more than 60m (200 ft.) out from the shore. **Boca Grandi,** on the extreme eastern coast, is for advanced and expert wave sailors only. The very strong current here moves out to sea, and on-shore waves rise from 1 foot to mast high on the outer reefs. Around the island's eastern tip, the calmer waters of **Rodger's Beach** are excellent for beginner and intermediate windsurfers. Offshore winds are moderate, the current is slight, and the waves have negligible chop.

Most windsurfing operations cluster around Malmok Beach, where equipment rental averages $35 to $40 for 2 hours, $45 for half a day, and $55 to $60 for a full day. Two-hour beginner lessons with equipment are about $50; 6-hour introductory courses are $135. Operators include **Aruba Boardsailing Productions,** L. G. Smith Blvd. 486 (© **297/586-3940;** www.arubawindsurfing.com); **Aruba Sailboard Vacations,** L. G. Smith Blvd. 462 (© **297/586-2527;** www.aruba sailboardvacations.com); **Unique Sports of Aruba,** J. E. Irausquin Blvd. 79 (© **297/586-0096;** www.visitaruba.com/uniquesports); and **Vela College of Windsurfing,** next to the Marriott, a joint operation of **Pelican Adventures** (© **297/587-2302;** www.pelican-aruba.com) and **Vela Windsurf** (© **800/223-5443;** www.velawindsurf.com). Like any good college, Vela has prodigious course listings; its offerings include Intro to Harness Use—Da Cool Stance and Modern Science of Body Drags. Aruba Boardsailing Productions, Aruba Sailboard Vacations, and Vela are windsurf specialists—a good bet for novices.

3 Hitting the Links

Tierra del Sol Golf Course (© **297/586-0978;** www.tierradel sol.com), designed by Robert Trent Jones II, is Aruba's only championship course. With its desert terrain, ocean vistas, and challenging winds, it's an interesting one, located on the island's northwest tip near the California Lighthouse. Aruba's persistent winds are a factor during most approach shots, when club selection can be decisive, but gusts can affect putts, too. The arid links are flat for the most part, the Bermuda grass fairways are fairly wide for desert links, and the greens are accommodating. Although there are no hidden breaks, most putts are fast. Obstacles include sand bunkers, cacti, coral rock formations, and water hazards (referred to locally as salinas). The par-5, 534-yard 14th hole, with its crosswinds, narrow greens, and sand bunkers, may be the course's most challenging hole; play it cautiously. Views of the ocean and the California Lighthouse make hole 3 one of the most picturesque. For high-tech geeks, each golf cart is equipped with a GPS satellite dish and a color video screen that provides graphic hole and green overviews, and many other options. A morning tee time from December through March is $133; afternoon rounds drop to $98. During the summer, mornings are $88, afternoons $68. Packages are available.

Guests renting Tierra del Sol villas (see chapter 3) can opt for unlimited golfing privileges. The course also offers a 1½ hour "No Embarrassment" clinic for golfers of all levels. A pro shop, driving range, putting green, chipping green, locker rooms, spa, and restaurants are on site.

The **Aruba Golf Club,** Golfweg 82, near San Nicolas (© 297/ 584-2006), on the southeastern end of the island, offers a quirky, less pricey alternative. Although it has only 9 greens—the "greens" are actually oiled sand—the course allows play from different tees to simulate an 18-hole round. Twenty sand traps and five water traps add an extra challenge, but the course's most distinctive obstacles are gallivanting goats. Fees are $25 for 18 holes, $15 for 9 holes. The course is open daily from 7:30am to 5pm. Start before 1pm to complete 18 holes. Golf carts and clubs can be rented at the on-site pro shop, and caddies are available. An air-conditioned restaurant and bar as well as changing rooms with showers are on the premises.

If putt-putt's more your style, **Adventure Golf,** L. G. Smith Blvd., across from La Cabana (© 297/587-6625; www.blackhogsaloon. com/golf.htm), has two 18-hole miniature courses surrounded by a moat, where you can float in paddle or bumper boats. Video and table games, a batting cage, a go-cart racetrack, and a restaurant and saloon also provide diversion. During the week, the center's open from 5pm till 1am; on weekends the fun starts at noon. An 18-hole round is $7. Paddleboat rides are $5, bumper boats are $6.

Aruba Golf & Leisure, Sasakiweg, next to the Mill Resort (© 297/ 586-4590), has putting greens, a driving range, tee-off stations, chipping and sand-trap practice areas, a pro shop, and on-site pros. Kids can play at the batting cages, on the playground, and in the game room. Open daily from 7am till 11pm, the center offers private lessons starting at $50 per person per hour for a group of four; 1½-hour clinics for $45 per person; and a bucket of balls for $3. Clubs and shoes can be rented as well.

4 Other Active Pursuits

BICYCLING

Aruba is small—maybe too small for cyclists who think nothing of biking 60 miles a day. The exotic terrain is flat for the most part, but heading into the wind is a challenge, and the sun is intense at midday. You know to bring plenty of water, a hat, and sunscreen. The most scenic roads trace the northern coast. They're not paved, so think mountain bike. Bring a bandana, too, to cover your mouth against the dust. To rent a bike, call **Melchor Cycle Rental,** Bubali 106B (© **297/587-1787**), or **Pablito's Bike Rental,** L. G. Smith Blvd. 234 (© **297/5878655**). Prices start as low as $15 per day. **Rancho Notorious,** Borancana 8E, Noord (© **297/586-0508;** www.ranchonotorious.com), offers a couple of guided mountain bike tours that visit Alto Vista Chapel and the California Light-house. One's 2½ hours long ($35); the other tacks on a bit of snorkeling ($45, snorkeling gear included). Bikers must be at least 14 years old to take the tours.

BIRDING

Although no organized tours are offered, ardent birders have the opportunity to spy 170 different species in Aruba. In early winter, migratory birds swell the number to about 300. In the High-Rise area, the Bubali Bird Sanctuary's ponds and wetlands attract more than 80 species, including brown pelicans, black olivaceous cormorants, herons, and egrets. Arikok National Park, which makes up much of the island's north central region, is home to humming-birds (common emerald and ruby-topaz), rufous-collared sparrows, tropical mockingbirds, ospreys, yellow orioles, American kestrels, black-faced grassquits, yellow warblers, Caribbean parakeets, long-tongued bats, common ground doves, troupials, crested caracaras, and Aruban burrowing owls. For more information, see chapter 6, "Exploring the Island."

BOWLING

Eagle Bowling Palace, Pos Abao z/n, inland from the Low-Rise hotels (© **297/583-5038**), has 16 lanes, a cocktail lounge, and a snack bar. It's open daily from 10am to 2am, but children under 12 must clear out before 7pm. Depending on the time of day, lanes rent for $5.75 to $12 per hour. Shoes are another $1.20. Reserva-tions are recommended.

HIKING

The sun is hot, and shade is scarce, but if you bring water and a wide-brimmed hat, traipsing around Aruba's hills and coastline is full of rewards: otherworldly rock formations, bizarre cactus groves, fluorescent parakeets, and dewlapped lizards. Hiking boots are nice, but sneakers are fine. There are no organized tours; Arikok National Park has many clearly marked trails. Scale the island's highest hills, explore abandoned gold mines, tiptoe around plantation ruins, trek through caves, and comb sea bluffs for coral and bones. See chapter 6, "Exploring the Island."

HORSEBACK RIDING

Time to get back in the saddle? Several ranches offer morning and midday excursions, and, if you're hopelessly romantic, rides off into the sunset. Wear long pants or bring a large towel to protect yourself from the sun. Hats with chin straps, sunglasses, and sunblock are strongly recommended.

Based at a 17th-century coconut plantation on the northern coast, **Rancho Daimari,** Tanki Leendert 249 (℮ **297/587-5675;** www.visitaruba.com/ranchodaimari), offers 2-hour trips at 8:30am and 2pm daily. Trails lead through Arikok National Park and to the Natural Pool, where snorkeling and swimming in the restorative waters are encouraged. The price is $50, and for an extra $25 per person you can have a private honeymoon or sunset ride.

Rancho del Campo, Sombre 22E, Santa Cruz (℮ **297/585-0290;** www.ranchodelcampo.com), has two different tours. The Natural Pool ride crosses through Arikok National Park to the jagged north coastline and the Natural Pool for swimming and snorkeling. This 2½-hour trip starts at 9:30am and 3:30pm daily and costs $50. The 3-hour Natural Bridge excursion passes by the Ayo rock formations and makes a snorkeling stop at Andicuri Beach. This trip begins at 8:30am daily and costs $60. Private tours are available for $75 per person.

Rancho El Paso, Washington 44, Noord (℮ **297/587-3310**), boasts 25 years of experience and offers 2-hour rides through the countryside and along the beach. Daily trips start at 9am and 3pm and cost $50.

Rancho Notorious, Borancana 8E, Noord (℮ **297/586-0508;** www.ranchonotorious.com), offers several options. The 2-hour beach tour passes through the countryside on the way to Malmok Beach, with pick-up times of 8:30am and sunset ($50). Passing by Alto Vista Chapel and the small white-sand cove of Boca Pos di Noord, the 2½-hour tour follows trails through the countryside to the northeast coast (pick-up times at 8:30am and 4pm; $55). With pick-up at 8:30am and 3pm, the 3-hour tour covers more countryside, Tierra del Sol, the California Lighthouse, and Malmok and Arashi Beaches. The price is $65. Finally, the beach and snorkeling tour includes a trot along Malmok Beach and snorkeling at Malmok Reef. Departing at 8:30am and 3pm, this 2½-hour tour is $65.

PAINTBALL

Gotcha Paintball, Rancho Daimari, Tanki Leendert 249 (℮ **297/ 587-5675** or 297/586-0239; www.visitaruba.com/ranchodaimari), conducts referee-supervised paintball warfare daily. Every participant gets protective clothing and air guns that shoot gelatin capsules filled with water-soluble paint balls that explode on impact. The $35 fee includes round-trip transportation. Wear shorts, T-shirts, and sneakers, and make reservations several days in advance.

TENNIS

Most of the island's beachfront hotels have tennis courts, many of them lit for night play. Some also boast pros on hand to give clinics or individual instruction. Nonguests can make arrangements to play at hotel courts, but guests have priority. The island's best facilities are at the **Aruba Racket Club,** Rooi Santo 21, Palm Beach (© **297/ 586-0215**), which features eight lighted courts, an exhibition center court, pro shop, swimming pool, fitness center, and bar and restaurant. The club is open Monday through Saturday from 8am to 11pm and Sunday from 3 to 8pm. Rates are $10 per hour per court, and lessons are $20 for a half-hour or $40 per hour. The club is near the Tierra del Sol complex on the northwest coast.

6

Exploring the Island

Spend every day on the beach if you want—but you'll miss Aruba's wilder charms. With stark windswept hills, towering cacti, and rough and rocky coasts, the outback is completely different from the posh resort areas, and worthy of exploration. The island's small enough to cover in a day or two. For a complete adventure, rent a four-wheel-drive vehicle: The most picturesque routes are rubble-strewn dirt roads; ordinary cars will do, but rugged Jeeps are better. The circuit around the island's northern tip—to California Lighthouse, Alto Vista Chapel, Bushiribana Gold Smelter Ruins, and Ayo and Casibari rock formations—is the most popular. Although less frequented, Arikok National Park, with its flora, fauna, caves, dunes, and history, is just as worthwhile. If you're not the outdoorsy type, visit Oranjestad's small museums or drive down to San Nicolas on your way to Rodger's Beach or Boca Grandi.

1 Guided Tours

Major tour operators conduct guided tours through the outback or around Arikok National Park. Several incorporate sightseeing with swimming and snorkeling. **De Palm Tours** (*©* **297/582-4400;** www.depalm.com) dominates the field, with half-day and full-day excursions in air-conditioned motorcoaches, four-wheel-drive vehicles, or all-terrain buggies. On the four-wheel-drive trips, you drive your own Jeep as part of a caravan led by a guide who broadcasts commentary over the radio. Competitors include **ABC Aruba Tours** (*©* **297/582-5600**), **Pelican Adventures** (*©* **297/587-2302;** www. pelican-aruba.com), and **Wix Tours** (*©* **297/582-0347**). Half-day excursions start at $25; full-day trips with lunch, refreshments, and snorkeling climb to $55.

2 On Your Own

If you'd like to explore at your own pace, rent a Jeep. Prices for a roofless four-wheel-drive with standard transmission start at $40 per day. Air-conditioned automatics are $60 and up. Driving around on your own is fun, but be forewarned that road signs are often small, handmade, and unnoticeable. Ask for a map: Even if it's hopelessly inaccurate—it will be—a bad map's better than no map at all. If you plan to take a popular route, discreetly join a caravan or ask directions along the way. Even if you find yourself in the middle of nowhere, the island's too small to truly lose your bearings (the wind always blows from east to west). If you're more interested in sites along paved roads and don't feel like getting lost, hire a cab. The going rate is $35 per hour for a maximum of four people. See "Getting Around," in chapter 2.

3 What to See

ORANJESTAD

Aruba's capital attracts more shoppers than sightseers; it's also a popular cruise port. The town has a sunny Caribbean demeanor, with **Dutch colonial buildings** painted in vivid colors. The main thoroughfare, Lloyd G. Smith Boulevard, runs along the **waterfront** and abounds with marinas, shopping malls, restaurants, and bars. Caya G. F. Betico Croes, or Main Street, runs roughly parallel to the waterfront several blocks inland; it's another major shopping venue. The harbor is packed with fishing boats and schooners docked next to stalls, where vendors hawk fruits, vegetables, and fish. On the other side of the Seaport Marketplace shopping mall, **Queen Wilhelmina Park,** named after one of Holland's longest-reigning monarchs, features manicured lawns, views of colorful fishing boats, and luxuriant tropical vegetation. If you're looking for a little culture, Oranjestad has a handful of museums and houses of worship.

Archaeological Museum of Aruba 🟊🟊   Squeezed between St. Franciscus Roman Catholic Church and the parish rectory, this small museum highlights the island's Amerindian heritage. Pottery vessels, shell and stone tools, burial urns, and skulls and bones are among the artifacts on display. Pick up the museum's booklet *The Indians of Aruba* ($3) for a concise history of the island's original inhabitants. A must for archaeology and history buffs. The adjacent lab studies Aruba's archaeological treasures.

J. E. Irausquinplein 2A. Ⓒ **297/582-8979.** Free admission. Mon–Fri 8am–noon and 1–4pm.

Beth Israel Synagogue   Jews, mostly merchants, arrived in Aruba at the beginning of the 20th century, when the oil refinery drew people from the Caribbean and Europe. The Jewish population today is small, but this synagogue endures, with a membership of about 35 families. Most congregants at Friday night services are visitors on vacation. The temple is Conservative in style, with full participation of both men and women. The small gift shop has one-of-a-kind Aruban Judaica. If the temple's closed, knock next door at the cantor's home.

Adriaan Lacle Boulevard 2. ✆ **297/582-3272**. Fri service 8pm.

Cas di Cultura   This architectural melding of futuristic and Caribbean tropical elements is Aruba's cultural center. Programs include films, lectures, concerts, dance performances, folkloric shows, and art exhibits.

Vondellaan 2 (at the traffic circle off L. G. Smith Blvd. between the airport and downtown Oranjestad). ✆ **297/582-1010**. Free admission. Mon–Sat 10am–4pm; Sun 10am–2pm.

Fort Zoutman, Willem III Tower, and Museo Arubano 🅕 During the 18th century, pirates menaced Oranjestad's harbor, raiding horses and anything else of value. To defend the island, the Dutch erected Fort Zoutman in 1796. Aruba's oldest example of Dutch architecture, the bastion stands on what was once the shore (landfill construction in 1930 altered the coastline). In 1867, it gained Willem III Tower, named after the then-reigning Dutch monarch. Over the years, the site has served as an aloe garden, jail, courthouse, junk room, and tax office. The fort was restored in 1974, the tower in 1983. Since 1992, the complex has housed the modest Museo Arubano, which displays prehistoric Caiquetio artifacts and remnants from the Dutch colonial period. On Tuesday from 6:30 to 8:30pm, the museum hosts the Bon Bini Festival, a fair with local arts and crafts, food, music, and dance.

Zoutmanstraat z/n. ✆ **297/582-6099**. Admission $2. Mon–Fri 9am–noon and 1–4pm.

Numismatic Museum of Aruba   This small museum looks unpromising from the outside, but its meticulous, homemade exhibits tell the history of the world through coins. Dedicated numismatists can spend the better part of a morning perusing the 35,000 specimens from more than 400 countries, but anyone with a passing interest in coins or history will appreciate this labor of love. The amazing collection was the work of a single Aruban, who also researched and wrote the detailed historical notes for each item.

Zuidstraat 27 (a block northeast of Fort Zoutman). ✆ **297/582-8831**. Free admission; donations appreciated. Mon–Fri 7:30am–3:30pm.

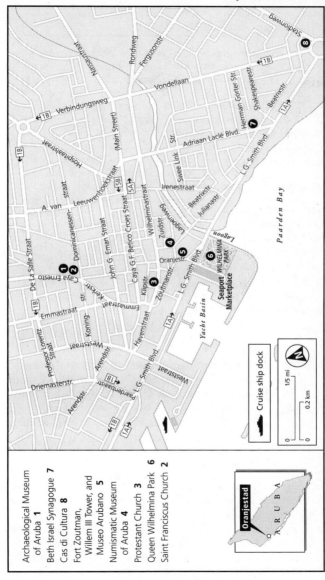

Archaeological Museum
of Aruba **1**

Beth Israel Synagogue **7**

Cas di Cultura **8**

Fort Zoutman,
Willem III Tower, and
Museo Arubano **5**

Numismatic Museum
of Aruba **4**

Protestant Church **3**

Queen Wilhelmina Park **6**

Saint Franciscus Church **2**

Cruise ship dock

1/5 mi

0.2 km

Paarden Bay

Lagoon

WILHELMINA
PARK

Seaport
Marketplace

Yacht Basin

Oranjestr.

Stadionweg

Shakespearestr.

Beatrixstr.

Herman Gorter Str.

Adriaan Laclé Blvd.

L. G. Smith Blvd.

Vondellaan

Swee Link
Str.

Irenestraat

Beatrixstr.

Julianastr.

Wilhelminastraat

Zuidstr.

Lagoenweg

Rondweg

Fergusonstr.

Verbindungsweg

Nassaustraat

Hospitaalstraat

(Main Street)

Leeuwenhoekstraat

A. van
straat

Dominicanessen-
straat

Caya G.F. Betico Croes Straat

John G. Eman Straat

Kerkstr.

Caya Ernesto

De La Salle Straat

Klipstr.

Zoutmanstr.

Emmastraat

Koning
str.

Emmastraat

Havenstraat

Weststraat

Arendstr.

L. G. Smith Blvd.

Professor Lorentz
Straat

Driemasterstr.

Arendstr.

Paardenbaai

L. G. Smith Blvd.

Weststraat

ARUBA

Oranjestad

111

⎛Fun Fact⎞ Aruban History 101

The first Arubans came from Venezuela by boat about 4,500 years ago. Living in small nomadic groups, they fished, hunted small animals, and collected fruit. They also fashioned crude tools from shells and stones and buried their dead in well-organized family groups. About 3,500 years later, the Caiquetios arrived, also from Venezuela and also by boat. Cultivating maize and manioc, this peaceful, more advanced group established villages near freshwater gullies.

In 1499, Alonso de Ojeda, a cohort of Christopher Columbus, became the first European to set foot on the island. Finding nothing of immediate value, the **Spanish** ignored Aruba until 1515, when they forcibly moved the entire Caiquetio population to Santo Domingo (now Haiti and the Dominican Republic) to work as slaves. Amerindians returned to Aruba in 1526, when Spain set up ranches on the island.

The Spanish left in 1636, when the **Dutch** gained control, but the first Dutch settlers arrived more than 100 years later, in 1754. For brief stints in the early 19th century, the English occupied the land, but Dutch sovereignty prevailed. Aruba remained a largely **ranch economy** with Amerindians and

Protestant Church   Built in 1846, Oranjestad's Protestant Church is Aruba's oldest house of worship. Looming above a terra cotta–tile roof, the square tower, decorated with stars, hearts, and wooden shutters, looks like something out of Pennsylvania Dutch country. The church is usually locked, but its tiny Bible Museum is open Monday through Friday from 10am till noon.

Wilhelminastraat 1 (behind the Renaissance). ℂ 297/582-1435. Mon–Fri 10am–noon. Services (in Dutch and English) Sun 10am.

Saint Franciscus Church   The largest Roman Catholic church in Aruba, modern Saint Franciscus boasts several architectural details that make it worth a visit. The barnlike ceiling soars heavenward, and a series of beautiful arches change shades of blue gradually to frame the altar, where the central crucifix stands in front of simple but elegant trompe l'oeil clouds and sky.

Irausquinplein 3, Oranjestad. ℂ 297/582-1434. Daily 24 hrs. Sun Mass (in Papiamento and English) 6:30am, 10am, and 7pm.

Dutch landowners herding horses and goats and cultivating millet, coconut, mango, and aloe.

In 1824 **gold** was discovered on the north coast, and a small gold rush ensued. Huge amounts of the metal were never mined, though, and the industry petered out as the first shots of World War I rang out. Production of phosphate waned at about the same time.

The island entered the modern era in 1924 when Standard Oil of New Jersey built an **oil refinery** at San Nicolas. To supplement Aruba's labor force, thousands of workers arrived from North America, Europe, and other islands of the Caribbean, bringing the first people of African descent to the island. In 1942, U.S. troops landed to protect the refinery. The complex closed in 1985, temporarily devastating the economy but prodding Aruba to develop its now successful tourism industry. (The refinery has since reopened.)

Although the island gained independence from the Netherlands Antilles in 1986, it remains an autonomous unit of the Kingdom of the Netherlands. Today, Aruba's multicultural population boasts more than 60 nationalities.

ALONG THE NORTHWEST COAST

If you can lift yourself from the sand, rent a four-wheel-drive vehicle and venture into the island's outback. Follow the dirt roads as they toil through alien landscapes of oddly balanced boulders, jagged cliffs, and furious seascapes. The terrain may seem harsh, but the cacti and divi divi trees love it. The tall organ-pipe cacti are known locally as *cadushi,* the prickly pear variety are called *tuna,* and the barrel species is *bushi.* Start from the resort area, head toward the California Lighthouse, then follow the dirt road as it traces the island's perimeter.

Ready for something completely surreal? At the south end of the High-Rise area, the tropical gardens of the **Butterfly Farm** *⟨★★*, J. E. Irausquin Blvd. z/n, across the street from the Divi Phoenix Beach Resort (© **297/586-3656**), dance with a thousand beautiful butterflies. The 46 species bred at the facility hail from every corner of the temperate world. It's easy to marvel at the colors of the ethereal flutterers, and guides provide amusing explanations of the short but sweet life of the average lepidopteran. Did you know that caterpillars double in size every 24 hours? That butterfly sex lasts for up to 48 hours? Visit as early in the day as possible—that's when the wing-flapping is maximal. Admission is $10. Open daily from 9am to 4:30pm.

Aruba's most distinctive landmark is the **Old Dutch Windmill,** J. E. Irausquin Blvd. 330, around the corner from the Butterfly Farm, near Palm Beach (*€* **297/586-2060**). It's an anomaly in the Caribbean, but it's authentic. Built in Friesland, Holland, in 1804, it originally drained water from low-lying land. Damaged by a storm in 1878, it was later rebuilt at another site in the Netherlands to mill grain. In 1929 another storm hit the windmill, which stood idle until 1960, when a Dutch merchant shipped it to Aruba. It reopened in 1974 to house a Dutch restaurant and late-night bar. Dutch antiques, Aruban farming implements, and a horse and carriage are the featured items of the simple, informal museum.

Although Aruba is as arid as the desert, the lush **Bubali Bird Sanctuary,** on J. E. Irausquin Boulevard, serves as a resting and breeding area for more than 80 species of local and migratory birds. Across the street from the Old Dutch Windmill, the sanctuary was once a salt pan. Today the two interconnected manmade lakes are flooded by overflow from a nearby water-treatment facility and surrounded by lush vegetation. The fish in the nutrient-rich ponds attract brown pelicans and black olivaceous cormorants. In the constantly undulating marsh grasses (like something out of a van Gogh painting), black-crowned night herons, Louisiana herons, great blue herons, common egrets, and snowy egrets abound. Gulls, skimmers, coots, and numerous species of ducks also make appearances. The observation tower gives birders a bird's-eye view of the oasis. Dawn and dusk, when the birds are most active, are the best times to visit. The sanctuary is always open; admission is free.

Go north from the bird sanctuary, past half of the High-Rise hotels, and turn right at the first traffic light. Proceed a mile or two to the next traffic light. Originally built in 1776 and last renovated in 1916, **Santa Anna Church** boasts a soaring ceiling and an intricately carved altar, communion rail, and pulpit. The neo-Gothic oak altar, carved in 1870 for a parish in the Dutch province of Noord-Brabent by Hendrik van der Geld, came to Aruba in 1928. The stained-glass windows, dating from 1932 and 1965, honor four former lay priests of Alto Vista Chapel (described in the next paragraph). The adjacent cemetery has no grass, but its hodgepodge of grave "houses" painted in tropical pastel colors is bright and meditative. The church is on

Caya F. D. Figueroa at the intersection of Palm Beach in Noord (© **297/586-1409**). Sunday Mass is celebrated at 7:30am and 6pm in Papiamento and English.

From the church, drive north for about 5 minutes. The **California Lighthouse** ⚲ sits on a hilltop perch at Aruba's northernmost tip, but its active days are over. Part of the adjacent restaurant once served as the lighthouse keeper's home. The beacon itself has been closed to the public for a number of years, ever since someone committed suicide by jumping from its summit. The surrounding area features some of the island's most spectacular scenery—gentle sand dunes, rocky coral shoreline, and turbulent waves. The picturesque structure gets its name from the *California,* a passenger ship that sank off the nearby coast before the lighthouse was completed in 1916.

Now it's time to leave paved roads behind. Turn right at the lighthouse and follow the dirt trail along the dramatic northern coast. The road's rough state precludes speeding, but within 15 minutes you'll reach another manmade attraction. Built in 1750 and renovated 200 years later, the picturesque **Alto Vista Chapel** ⚲ radiates serenity from its cactus-studded perch overlooking the sea. The chapel, Aruba's first, was built by Caiquetio Indians and Spanish settlers before the island had its own priest. The church's ancient Spanish cross is one of the oldest European artworks in the Dutch Caribbean, and the altar's statue has a devoted local following. Secluded near the island's northwestern corner, just off the rough dirt road hugging the northeast coast, the bright yellow structure, little more than a hut, rests at the end of a winding road lined with white crosses marking the stations of the cross.

Five minutes farther down the coast, you'll come to the **Bushiribana Ruins.** According to local legend, in 1824 a 12-year-old boy came across gold in one of the dry creek beds on Aruba's north coast. Naturally, the discovery set off a gold frenzy. For 30 years, Arubans were allowed to collect the precious metal, provided they sold it at a set price. In 1854, a gold-mining concession was granted to the Aruba Island Goldmining Company, which built this smelter on the north coast in 1872. Although the facility operated for only 10 years, its hulking ruins still dominate the area. Climb the multitiered interior for impressive sea views. Too bad the walls have been marred with artless graffiti.

From the ruins, you'll be able to see a line of cars heading for the next site, just minutes away. The island's most photographed attraction, the **Natural Bridge** ⚲⚲ rises 7.5m (25 ft.) above the sea and spans 30m (100 ft.) of rock-strewn waters. Centuries of relentless pounding by the surf carved the arch out of the limestone coast. One of the Caribbean's highest and most dramatic coral structures, it's a fitting crown for the tumultuous north coast. Because the bridge acts as a buffer between the sandy beach and open ocean, many people come here to swim and picnic. The nearby thirst-aid station supplies refreshments and souvenirs.

Retrace the dirt road back to the first intersection and turn left. The road soon becomes paved, and within 5 minutes, take a right. (Signage is nonexistent here, so don't be shy about asking for directions.) Looking like something out of "The Flintstones," the eerie **Ayo Rock Formations** served Aruba's early inhabitants as a dwelling or religious site. The reddish-brown petroglyphs on the boulders suggest magical significance, and the strange stones look as though they were stacked by giants. The site is open daily from 9am to 5pm, and admission is free.

If you like the Ayo rocks, continue on the main road to its end. Turn right, then take another right at the sign for the **Casibari Rock Formations.** These alien rocks rise from the cacti- and lizard-infested hills. Although the boulders weigh several tons each, they look freshly scattered by some cyclopean dice-roller. Look for the formations that resemble birds and dragons, or climb the trail to the top of the highest rock mound for a panorama of the area. Watch your head on the path to the top, though; the tunnels have low clearance. The rock garden is open daily from 9am to 5pm, with no admission charge. The nearby stands sell souvenirs, snacks, soft drinks, and beer.

ARIKOK NATIONAL PARK

Arikok National Park (© **297/582-8001**), Aruba's showcase ecological preserve, sprawls over roughly 20% of the island. Rock outcrops, boulders, and crevices create microclimates that support animal species found only in Aruba, including the Aruban rattlesnake, Aruban cat-eyed snake, Aruban whiptail lizard, Aruban burrowing owl, and Aruban parakeet. Iguanas and many species of migratory birds live in the park as well, and goats and donkeys graze on the hills. Examples of early Amerindian art, abandoned mines from Aruba's gold-rush past, and remains of early farms dot the park. Sand dunes and limestone cliffs ornament the coast. It's easy to explore the preserve, but bring water, sunscreen, and food, and wear a hat and comfortable walking shoes. Birds and animals are most active in the morning, so go as early in the day as you can.

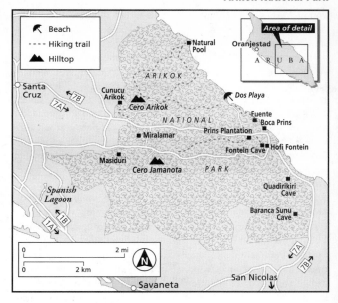

The government has plans to develop the area responsibly, but for now the sites can be reached by dirt road and hiking trail only. Routes are clearly marked, and signs are becoming more frequent and informative. If you're really into it, though, stop by the National Park office at Piedra Plat 42 in Paradera, on the main road between the Low-Rise area and Santa Cruz, to buy the excellent $15 guidebook. The office is open Monday through Friday from 7:30am till 3pm.

Miralamar, a complex of gold mines and trenches, was active during the first decade of the 20th century. The hills along the path here are overgrown with yellow poui and white gum trees, and derelict buildings at the site include an ore-testing lab, sleeping quarters, and a forge. Due to transportation problems and low-quality ore, the mines were abandoned in 1916, and many of the shafts collapsed. Century plants have now reclaimed the area.

Masiduri served as an experimental garden in the 1950s; the convergence of several creek beds makes the location reasonably moist. The eucalyptus trees and *cunucu* (farm) house date from the same era. The site now features an aloe-cultivation exhibit. In the early 1900s, Aruba was a major exporter of this plant known for its medicinal and healing properties. Today the sheltered location and comparatively moist conditions draw a variety of reptiles, including Aruban cat-eyed snakes. Feral donkeys, descendants of animals domesticated for transportation, come at night to rest.

The partially restored farm known as **Cunucu Arikok** ★ recalls Aruba's agricultural past. It takes 45 minutes to complete the circular hiking trail through boulders, vegetation, and wildlife; shaded benches provide relief along the way. Beans, corn, millet, peanuts, and cucumbers were once cultivated at the site, and to protect the crops from goats, sheep, and donkeys, cactus hedges and stone walls were built. The restored adobe farmhouse has typically small windows and a sloping roof. Cactus was used to make roof beams, and mud and grass formed the walls. A barn, threshing floor, pigpen, and outhouse surround the house. Before Europeans arrived, Amerindians left drawings of birds and marine animals on overhanging rocks just off the trail near the parking lot. At dawn and dusk, the area is alive with parakeets, doves, troupials, mockingbirds, hummingbirds, lizards, and cottontail rabbits.

Prins Plantation, a complex of abandoned adobe structures, witnessed the cultivation of hundreds of coconut trees as recently as the 1960s. Passing by an old farmhouse, well, aloe field, and crumbling stone walls, the 45-minute walk provides views of a nearby ocean cove. Wildlife attracted to the vegetation includes iguanas, cottontails, troupials, parakeets, mockingbirds, kestrels, and caracaras (huge vulturelike hawks).

At the seacoast, the terrain and vegetation change dramatically from hills covered with cacti and divi divi trees to sand dunes and limestone bluffs studded with sea grapes and sea lavender. Soldier crab and lizard trails crisscross the morning sand of **Boca Prins** ★, and in the early spring, baby sea turtles hatch and wobble frantically toward the sea. Steps from the parking lot, stairs descend to **Fuente** ★, a rocky cove pounded by the surf. On the limestone bluff across the sandy beach, salt spray infuses the air, and small salt pans form where trapped water has evaporated. Bleached coral and bones litter the sharp plateau, and ospreys and caracaras patrol the coast. A 20-minute walk farther west along the coast, **Dos Playa** ★ features two coves carved out of the limestone bluff. With its wide sandy beach, the first cove attracts sunbathers and is perfect for picnics, but its strong current makes swimming dangerous.

Tucked away on the coast northwest of Dos Playa, the **Natural Pool** ★ or *conchi* known as Cura di Tortuga is protected from the rough sea by surrounding rocks. It's said that the pool was once used to hold sea turtles before they were sold (*tortuga* means turtle in Papiamento). On quiet days, the pool is great for a swim, but bathing is risky when waves leap the rock barrier. It's a considerable hike to the pool from the parking lot at Boca Prins; take a horseback tour to the site on another day to fully enjoy the experience.

A 15-minute walk from Boca Prins, **Fontein Cave** ✤ is the most popular of several small limestone hollows along the north coast (you'll pass the park's only restaurant on the way to the cave). Brownish-red drawings left by Amerindians and graffiti etched by early European settlers ornament the walls and ceilings. Calcareous-rich water dripping through the limestone has caused stalagmites and stalactites to form, some in the shape of bison or human heads (park rangers stationed at the cave will point them out). The hole is an important roosting place for long-tongued bats. Early in the evening, the flying mammals leave the cave for nectar and pollen.

A Dutch family owned the patch of land south of Fontein Cave at the beginning of the 19th century. Known as **Hofi Fontein** (fountain garden), it's the only place along the north coast with a freshwater spring. In the early 20th century, Chinese immigrants grew vegetables here, which explains the area's other common name, Chinese Garden. The humble museum, with animal, plant, and colonial-life displays, is worth a look, and rangers are happy to answer your questions.

The **Quadirikiri Cave** features two large chambers with roof openings that allow sunlight in, making flashlights unnecessary. Hundreds of small bats use the 30m-long (100-ft.) tunnel as a passageway to their nests deeper in the cave. A tale associated with Quadirikiri is dubious: The fiercely independent daughter of an Indian chief was trapped in the cave with her "unsuitable" suitor and left to perish. Defiant even in death, the spirits of the star-crossed lovers burst through the cave's roof and up to heaven.

Also known as the Tunnel of Love because of its heart-shaped entrance, the **Baranca Sunu** cave requires a flashlight to explore. Helmets and lights can be rented from the stand at the entrance to the 90m-long (300-ft.) passageway for $6. Stories of pirates using the cave to hide treasure have circulated for generations, but there's no evidence to confirm the rumors. Rather than return to the park entrance, follow the road along the coast. It eventually becomes a paved route that leads to San Nicolas.

SAN NICOLAS & SAVANETA

Roughly 80% of Arubans are Roman Catholic, and parish churches dot the island. In Seroe Pretoe, near San Nicolas on the way from

Arikok National Park, the **Lourdes Grotto,** a shrine to Our Lady of Lourdes, was built in the limestone rocks in 1958 to celebrate the 150th anniversary of the Virgin Mary's purported appearance to a peasant girl, St. Bernadette, in the south of France. Another grotto lies directly across the road. Neither is particularly noteworthy, probably because the local parish prohibits anyone from leaving candles, statues, pictures, or testimonials. Chartreuse parakeets inhabit the area.

Farther along the same road, the outback suddenly gives way to Aruba's second-largest town, **San Nicolas.** A phosphate-exporting port from 1879 until 1915, this town landed Esso's Lago oil refinery in 1924. Once the world's largest, the refinery attracted workers from other Caribbean islands, South America, and Europe. In 1942, U.S. troops landed to protect the complex, which supplied much of the Allies' aircraft fuel during the war. By 1951, the town had a population of 20,000, far more than Oranjestad at the time. The refinery closed in 1985, devastating the town and the island. It reopened in 1990 with a new owner, Texas-based Coastal Oil. Now that tourism has replaced oil as the island's major business, San Nicolas has waned in importance. One remnant of the town's "port atmosphere" deserves mention: Prostitution is legal in San Nicolas.

The center of Aruba's fishing industry, **Savaneta** is the island's oldest town and original capital. During the early Dutch period, its harbor was the safest place for ships, and in the mid-1800s, the area was known for breeding cochineals, insects that were crushed to produce the dye carmine. Retaining its salty tang, the town boasts a couple of good restaurants and a beachside spa.

On your way back home, you'll pass **Hooiberg.** At 162m (541 ft.), it may not be Aruba's highest hill, but it's the island's favorite landmark. If you have the stamina, climb the hundreds of steps (15–20 min.) to the summit; on a clear day, you can see Venezuela.

7

Shopping

Although Aruba boasts plenty of shopping opportunities, don't expect cut-rate prices. The days of Caribbean bargains are waning. Nevertheless, the island's low 3.3% duty can make prices on certain items such as jewelry and fragrances attractive. What's more, there's no sales tax.

What should you keep your eye out for? Because the island's part of the Netherlands, Dutch goods like Delft porcelain, chocolate, and cheese are especially good buys. Items from Indonesia, another former Dutch colony, are reasonably priced, too. Although Aruban souvenirs tend toward cheesy *cunucu* (farm) houses or divi divi trees made from resin, the same items, when painted by hand and crafted from bisque or pottery, can hold their own in any folk art collection. Skin and hair care products made from locally produced aloe are also popular and practical. If you're looking for big-ticket items, Aruba offers the usual array of Swiss watches; German and Japanese cameras; gold and diamond jewelry; Cuban cigars; premium liquor; English and German china; Spanish porcelain; French, Swedish, and Danish crystal; and French and American fragrances. Before you bring out the credit card for a major purchase, though, do a little research at home: Know the difference between a steal and a mistake.

1 The Shopping Scene

Stores accept American dollars, credit cards, and traveler's checks. Because the island has no sales tax, the price marked or quoted is the total price you pay. Shopkeepers, like most Arubans, are pleasant. Haggling is considered rude, though, so don't push your luck.

Most stores are open Monday through Saturday from 9am to 6pm; some close for an hour at noon or 1pm. Stores in Oranjestad's major malls tend to open on Sunday as well, especially if cruise ships are in port.

Parking can be a hassle in downtown Oranjestad. If the lots along the waterfront are packed, there's usually a space behind the Seaport

Marketplace, past the Seaport Casino. Taking a cab or the bus is easier, though, unless you plan to do some heavy lifting.

2 Great Shopping Areas

Although the major resort hotels boast shopping arcades, Aruba's retail activity centers on Oranjestad. Half-mile-long **Caya G. F. Betico Croes,** better known as Main Street, is the city's major shopping venue, attracting tourists, young and fashionable Arubans, office workers, and families. Downtown also teems with contiguous shopping malls that stretch for several blocks along the harbor front. The gingerbread pastel-colored buildings are impossible to miss. **Seaport Mall** and **Seaport Marketplace** feature more than 130 stores, 2 casinos, 20 restaurants and cafes, and a movie theater. Just down the road, **Royal Plaza Mall** is chock-full of popular restaurants and generally upscale boutiques. **Port of Call Marketplace** is the first complex cruise-ship passengers encounter on their way to downtown. For late-night shopping or a temporary diversion from the slots, **Alhambra Moonlight Shopping Center,** adjacent to the Alhambra Casino in the Low-Rise area, features several souvenir shops, jewelry outlets, and cigar stores in an outdoor courtyard.

3 Shopping A to Z
ART/FOLK ART/CRAFTS

Art & Frames Unlimited   Provides custom framing and features a variety of accessories and posters. You may want to frame one of the works of local artists exhibited and sold on the premises. Kamerlingh Onnesstraat 34-A, Oranjestad. © 297/583-1322.

Art & Tradition   The most impressive items at this folk-art and handcrafts shop are mopa mopa boxes and figures made by the Quillasinga Indians of Colombia. Although the figures look handpainted, they're actually inlaid with layers of mopa mopa, a tree bud that's boiled until reduced to resin, stretched like gum, and cut into bits of color. Caya G. F. Betico Croes 30, Oranjestad. © 297/583-6534.

Artistic Boutique   Specializes in Spanish porcelain, Asian antiques, handmade dhurries and rugs, hand-embroidered linens, organdy tablecloths, and Indonesian woodcarvings. Caya G. F. Betico Croes 25, Oranjestad. © 297/582-3142. Branch at the Holiday Inn.

Casa Hannsi   Specializes in such Venezuelan crafts as Amazon baskets, carved vases, and cheery mobiles. Royal Plaza Mall, Oranjestad. © 297/588-9468.

Cuba's Cookin'   The works of art on display here are for the enjoyment of the restaurant's patrons, but if something strikes your fancy, you can probably work something out with the owner. Wilhelminastraat 27, Oranjestad. ✆ 297/588-0627.

Galería Eterno   Painting and sculpture by Aruba's premier artists. Open by appointment only. Emmastraat 92, Oranjestad. ✆ 297/583-9484.

Gasparito Restaurant and Art Gallery   This is one of the best places to buy paintings by local artists. Styles ranging from folk to abstract cover the restaurant's walls. Gasparito 3, Noord. ✆ 297/586-7044.

Mopa Mopa   This shop carries the island's largest selection of mopa mopa art (see listing for Art & Tradition, above), with prices starting at $10. Seaport Marketplace, Oranjestad. ✆ 297/583-7125.

Qué Pasa?   This restaurant and gallery displays and sells eclectic contemporary Aruban paintings. Wilhelminastraat 2, Oranjestad. ✆ 297/583-4888.

BOOKS
If reading on the beach is one of your favorite pastimes, bring books from home; the selection in Aruba is limited and the prices are steep.

Van Dorp Aruba   This shop stocks some English-language titles, including books on Aruban history, birds, and plants. Caya G. F. Betico Croes 77, Oranjestad. ✆ 297/582-3076.

CHINA, SILVER & GLASS
Champagne Linens & Gifts   Boasts Royal Albert bone china, Limoges Castel glassware, and Belleek china. Seaport Marketplace, Oranjestad. ✆ 297/583-8052.

Colombian Emeralds International   Carries Waterford crystal and Lenox china, not to mention emeralds. Seaport Mall, Oranjestad. ✆ 297/583-6238. Branch at the Marriott.

Gandelman Jewelers   Offers Lladró porcelain and Swarovski crystal. Royal Plaza Mall, Oranjestad. ✆ 297/588-6159. Branches at the Hyatt, Radisson, and Wyndham resorts, and at Seaport Mall.

Little Switzerland Jewelers   For china, crystal, and figurines from Baccarat, Waterford, Kosta Boda, Lalique, Orrefors, Swarovski, Rosenthal, Christofle, Lladró, and others. Caya G. F. Betico Croes 14, Oranjestad. ✆ 297/582-1192. Branches at the Holiday Inn, Allegro, Wyndham, and Tamarijn resorts, and in Royal Plaza Mall.

CIGARS

Cigar Emporium Features cigars from Cuba, the Dominican Republic, Brazil, and Sumatra. Labels include Cohiba, Montecristo, Romeo y Julieta, Partagas, H. Upmann, and Bolivar. Seaport Mall, Oranjestad. ✆ 297/582-5479.

La Bonbonnière Stocks Cuban, Dominican, and Canary Island cigars, as well as Spanish jewelry and replicas of Japanese and European swords. Holland Aruba Mall, Havenstraat 6, Oranjestad. ✆ 297/582-3112.

La Casa del Habano Here you'll find Cohibas, Romeo y Julietas, and Montecristos in walk-in humidors. Royal Plaza Mall, Oranjestad. ✆ 297/583-8509.

DEPARTMENT STORES

The Aruba Trading Company Offers one of the island's best moderately priced selections of fragrances, cosmetics, shoes, leather goods, clothing for men and women, liquor, and cigarettes. Caya G. F. Betico Croes 12, Oranjestad. ✆ 297/582-2602.

Boolchand's Sells jewelry, watches, cameras (Canon, Minolta, Nikon, Olympus, and Pentax), electronics (Bose, Braun, JVC, Kenwood, Nintendo, Sony, and Pioneer), sunglasses, and hand-embroidered linens. Seaport Mall, Oranjestad. ✆ 297/583-0147.

New Amsterdam Store Features an array of linens, napkins, place mats, and embroidered tablecloths. Caya G. F. Betico Croes 50, Oranjestad. ✆ 297/582-1152.

EYEWEAR

Optica Oduber & Kan In business for over 45 years, this shop features designer eyewear and contact lenses. Caya G. F. Betico Croes 44, Oranjestad. ✆ 297/582-4719.

FASHION

Active Boutique Carries sexy Brazilian women's swimwear. Dutch Crown Center, Havenstraat 27, Oranjestad. ✆ 297/583-7008.

Agatha Boutique Features the designs and fragrances of Agatha Brown, an American designer living in Aruba. Items include handbags, shoes, and apparel for women. The menswear boutique features Greg Norman sportswear, Gianni Versace ties, and Italian leather belts. Renaissance Resort Atrium, Oranjestad. ✆ 297/583-7965.

Azucar y Azuquita This store organizes its inventory by color and carries reasonably priced clothing for the entire family. Caya G. F. Betico Croes 49, Oranjestad. ✆ 297/588-9849.

Azul   This attractive two-story boutique features men's and women's clothing designed by Kenneth Cole, Tommy Hilfiger, Ralph Lauren, Lacoste, and Nautica. Caya G. F. Betico Croes 10, Oranjestad. ✆ 297/583-0131.

Benetton   This international chain store stocks fashionable men's and women's casual clothing, in addition to jewelry and electronics. Caya G. F. Betico Croes 2, Oranjestad. ✆ 297/582-5454.

Boolchand's   This department store boasts Adolfo leather goods, sunglasses, and clothing from Tommy Hilfiger, Nautica, Calvin Klein, Timberland, and Nike. Seaport Mall, Oranjestad. ✆ 297/583-0147.

Bula   This surf store stocks Brazilian bikinis, surf shorts, surfboards, accessories, sunglasses, T-shirts, and found-glass jewelry. Royal Plaza Mall, Oranjestad. No phone.

Caperucita Roja   The name means "Little Red Riding Hood" in Spanish, and the store sells baby and children's clothes and shoes. Wilhelminastraat 17, Oranjestad. ✆ 297/583-6166.

Confetti on the Beach   Has a wide selection of European and American beachwear for women, including swimsuits, cover-ups, and hats. Seaport Mall, Oranjestad. ✆ 297/583-8614.

Extreme Sports   Generation X tourists come here for rollerblades, boogie boards, backpacks, swimming trunks, and athletic shoes. L. G. Smith Boulevard z/n, Oranjestad. ✆ 297/583-7105.

Hugo Boss   Men's and women's fashion by Germany's premier designer. Caya Betico Croes 16, Oranjestad. ✆ 297/588-5406.

La Langosta   This shop's Venezuelan-born owner designs one-of-a-kind bikinis that incorporate rhinestones, leather straps, shells, ribbons, and lace inlays. Beach wraps, beaded sandals, bejeweled bags, and accessories are also available. Pelican Pier, Palm Beach. No phone.

La Venezolana   Supplies dress separates and suits, jeans, shoes, belts, underwear, and socks for women. Brands include Givenchy, Lee, and Van Heusen. Steenweg 12, Oranjestad. ✆ 297/582-1444.

Mango   Part of an international chain of more than 500 stores, Mango offers casual but fashionable women's clothing. Caya G. F. Betico Croes 9, Oranjestad. ✆ 297/582-9700.

Nautica   Upscale casual clothing. Royal Plaza Mall, Oranjestad. ✆ 297/583-7791.

Pinko   Chic, fashion-forward designs for women. Strada Mall III (near Caya G. F. Betico Croes and Plaza Daniel Leo), Oranjestad. ✆ 297/588-3680.

Polo Ralph Lauren   Mr. Lauren's Polo line of clothing and accessories. Seaport Mall, Oranjestad. ✆ **297/582-3674.**

Red Sail Sports Port of Call   Stocks European, South American, and U.S. sportswear, scuba and snorkeling equipment, souvenirs, suncare products, and beachwear. Port of Call Marketplace, Oranjestad. ✆ **297/582-4038.**

Secrets of Aruba   Supplying lingerie, massage oils, and lotions, Secrets caters to those looking to add a little spice to their life. Seaport Mall, Oranjestad. ✆ **297/583-0897.**

Sun & Sand   Sells T-shirts, sweatshirts, cover-ups, and polo shirts. Dutch Crown Center, L. G. Smith Blvd. 150, Oranjestad. ✆ **297/583-8812.**

Tommy Hilfiger Boutique   Stocks fashionable casual wear for the style-conscious man, woman, and child. Royal Plaza Mall, Oranjestad. ✆ **297/583-8548.**

Wulfsen & Wulfsen   Offers European men's and women's clothing, both classic and casual. Operating in the Netherlands Antilles for 30 years and in Holland for more than a century, the store features designs by Betty Barclay, Bianca, Verse, Cerruti, and Zegna. Caya G. F. Betico Croes 52, Oranjestad. ✆ **297/582-3823.**

GIFTS & SOUVENIRS

City Towel   Come here for one-of-a-kind Aruban-flag beach towels. Royal Plaza Mall, Oranjestad. ✆ **297/583-0137.**

Coconut Trading Co.   A good selection of gifts and handcrafted jewelry. In the Marriott Ocean Club, L. G. Smith Blvd. 99, Palm Beach. ✆ **297/586-3696.**

Creative Hands   Sells miniature pottery and ceramic *cunucu* (farm) houses and divi divi trees, as well as Japanese dolls. Socotorolaan 5, Oranjestad. ✆ **297/583-5665.**

Ecco   An eclectic inventory of tablecloths, Delft blue porcelain, handcrafts, T-shirts, beachwear, and men's sportswear. Caya G. F. Betico Croes 22, Oranjestad. ✆ **297/582-4726.**

Juggling Fish   Owned and operated by a transplanted New Englander, these shops supply beachwear, casual clothing, and quirky souvenirs. J. E. Irausquin Blvd. 330, Palm Beach (next to the Mill Resort). ✆ **297/586-3204.** Branches at the Aruba Beach Club and the Playa Linda.

Kwa Kwa   Sells wind chimes, pottery, and souvenir tchotchkes. Port of Call Marketplace, Oranjestad. ✆ **297/583-9471.**

La Bottega di Regalo   Specializes in gifts made in Italy, including picture frames, silver figurines, Murano glass, lamps, clocks, and pottery. In the Playa Linda Beach Resort, J. E. Irausquin Boulevard 87, Palm Beach. ℭ 297/586-2666.

Vibes   Local art; hand-carved knives and pipes; Cuban cigars; jewelry; Caribbean pewter frames; and Dutch Delft ceramics. Royal Plaza Mall, Oranjestad. ℭ 297/583-7949.

HOUSEWARES

Décor Home Fashions   Sells sheets, towels, and place mats from Italy, Germany, Holland, Portugal, and the United States. Steenweg 14, Oranjestad. ℭ 297/582-6620.

New Amsterdam Store   This department store also offers a good collection of linens, napkins, and embroidered tablecloths. Caya G. F. Betico Croes 50, Oranjestad. ℭ 297/582-1152.

JEWELRY & WATCHES

Boolchand's   Boasts jewelry and watches from Movado, Concord, Swatch, Seiko, Citizen, ESQ, Fossil, and Swiss Army. Seaport Mall, Oranjestad. ℭ 297/583-0147.

Cartier Boutique   Carries the venerable French house's jewelry and timepieces. Seaport Mall, Oranjestad. ℭ 297/588-6717.

Colombian Emeralds International   Stocks emeralds, diamonds, sapphires, and semiprecious jewelry, as well as watches by Breitling, Baume & Mercier, Jaeger, and Seiko. Seaport Mall, Oranjestad. ℭ 297/583-6238. Branch at the Marriott.

Diamonds International   Features 60 showcases of jewelry and watches. Choose loose diamonds and mountings to custom design your own piece. Port of Call Marketplace, Oranjestad. ℭ 297/588-0443.

The Effy Collection   Boasts a selection of diamond, emerald, ruby, and sapphire earrings, pins, rings, bracelets, and necklaces. L. G. Smith Boulevard 90–92, Oranjestad. ℭ 297/588-9812.

Gandelman Jewelers   Offers an extensive collection of diamond, gemstone, and fine gold jewelry, as well as timepieces and writing instruments. Brands include David Yurman, Gucci, Rolex, Montblanc, Tag Heuer, Raymond Weil, and Cartier. Royal Plaza Mall, Oranjestad. ℭ 297/588-6159. Branches at the Hyatt, Radisson, and Wyndham resorts, and at Seaport Mall.

Gold Mine   This store has been selling diamonds, watches, and jewelry since 1928. Watch brands include Vacheron Constantin,

Bregeut, Hublot, Audemars Piguet, and Baume & Mercier. Caya G. F. Betico Croes 7, Oranjestad. ✆ **297/582-1542.**

Gold Palace   Deals in 14-karat gold jewelry set with diamonds, emeralds, sapphires, and rubies. The store also carries Seiko and Citizen watches and Mallorca pearls. Caya G. F. Betico Croes 5A, Oranjestad. ✆ **297/583-3599.**

Jeweler's Warehouse   Stocks a complete line of jewelry with diamonds, rubies, emeralds, sapphires, and pearls. Watches from Seiko, Swatch, Fossil, Catamaran, Citizen, and Lucien Picard abound. Seaport Mall, Oranjestad. ✆ **297/583-6045.**

Kenro Jewelers   Features Mikimoto pearls, gemstones, gold, and watches. Seaport Mall, Oranjestad. ✆ **297/583-4847.** Branches at the Casa del Mar, La Cabana, Allegro, and Playa Linda resorts.

Little Switzerland   Offers 14- and 18-karat gold jewelry and watches. Brands include Mikimoto, Honora, Antonini, Tag Heuer, Breitling, Raymond Weil, Omega, Rado, Concord, Swiss Army, and Baume & Mercier. Caya G. F. Betico Croes 14, Oranjestad. ✆ **297/582-1192.** Branches at the Holiday Inn, Allegro, Wyndham, and Tamarijn resorts, and in Royal Plaza Mall.

Noble Jewelers   Sells yellow and white diamonds, emeralds, rubies, sapphires, and platinum jewelry. Watch brands include Christian Bernard and Festina. Dutch Crown Center, Havenstraat 27, Oranjestad. ✆ **297/583-9662.**

PearlGems   Create your own strand from an extensive collection of unstrung pearls, including black specimens from Tahiti. Pre-strung strands are also available. L. G. Smith Blvd. 90-92, Oranjestad. ✆ **297/588-4927.**

Rage   Specializes in sterling silver with a Southwestern U.S. theme; carries Danish, German, Greek, and Italian designs as well. Seaport Marketplace, Oranjestad. ✆ **297/588-6262.**

Shiva's Gold and Gems   Boasts a large loose diamond inventory and a collection of emerald, tanzanite, ruby, and sapphire jewelry. Watch brands include Franck Muller, Wittnauer, Audemars Piguet, Bucherer, Seiko, Citizen, Zenith, and Girard-Perregaux. Royal Plaza Mall, Oranjestad. ✆ **297/583-4077.**

Touch of Gold   Platinum and gold jewelry set with diamonds, tanzanite, emeralds, rubies, and sapphires. 32-D Havenstraat, Oranjestad. ✆ **297/588-9587.**

MARKETS

Merchandise stands clutter Oranjestad's waterfront. Catering to cruise-ship passengers who pass by on their way to the more varied shopping in town, most sell garden-variety T-shirts and souvenirs. Fruit and vegetables brought daily by boat from Venezuela add color to the hubbub.

MUSEUM-TYPE STORES

The Butterfly Farm   The farm's gift shop has a large, quality collection of note cards, postcards, books, and gifts focused on butterflies. J. E. Irausquin Blvd. z/n, Palm Beach. ✆ 297/586-3656.

Congregation Beth Israel   The temple's small gift shop sells Judaica with an Aruban accent. If the temple's closed, knock at the cantor's house next door. Adriaan Lacle Blvd. 2, Oranjestad. ✆ 297/582-3272.

MUSIC

Non Stop CD Shop   A good place to start or add to your collection of soca, salsa, merengue, reggae, calypso, bachata, and vallenato music. Ask for help if you're new to Antillean genres. Caya G. F. Betico Croes 66, Oranjestad. ✆ 297/582-8484.

PERFUMES & COSMETICS

Many of the island's jewelry stores also carry fragrances and cosmetics from the United States and France.

Aruba Aloe Balm   Direct from the factory, moisturizer, sunscreen, and shampoo made from Aruba's famous aloe. Pitastraat 115, Oranjestad. ✆ 297/588-6881.

Tips Hello, Aloe. So Long, Sunburn.

Aruba has cultivated aloe for more than 150 years. Well-known as a moisturizer and sunburn healer, the plant— pronounced *ah*-loh-weh locally—also aids digestion and, when applied topically, serves as a kind of folk-medicine minoxidil. Aruba Aloe, a local company, manufactures a wide assortment of shampoos, facial masks, creams, and gels that soothe after a day in the sun. The products are cheapest at a pharmacy or supermarket, but you can also get them at souvenir stands and the factory itself (don't waste the $5 for the factory tour, though; you'll be sorely disappointed).

Aruba Trading Company Offers a good, reasonably priced selection of perfumes and cosmetics. Caya G. F. Betico Croes 12, Oranjestad. ✆ 297/582-2602.

Penha & Sons Boasts a large selection of top-name perfumes and cosmetics, including brands like Boucheron, Dior, Cartier, and Givenchy. Caya G. F. Betico Croes 11, Oranjestad. ✆ **297/582-4160.**

Weitnauer This Swiss retailer stocks a variety of fragrances and cosmetics. Caya G. F. Betico Croes 29, Oranjestad. ✆ **297/582-2790.** Branches at the airport and in the Royal Plaza, Aventura, and Seaport Malls.

SHOES & ACCESSORIES

The Athlete's Foot This chain store is your best bet in Aruba for Nike, Adidas, New Balance, and Asics. Caya G. F. Betico Croes 50, Oranjestad. ✆ **297/582-9035.** Also at Seaport Plaza.

Extravaganza Accessories Italian, Spanish, and French leather handbags, shoes, and accessories. Seaport Mall, Oranjestad. ✆ **297/583-6688.**

Fendi Italian luxury leather items. Emmastraat 1, Oranjestad. ✆ **297/583-7828.**

Gucci Boasts everything you expect from the Italian luxury store, including handbags, luggage, wallets, shoes, watches, belts, and ties. Don't expect bargains unless there's a sale going on. Seaport Mall, Oranjestad. ✆ **297/583-3952.**

Land Collection At the beginning of Main Street, this leather goods store features handbags, travel accessories, shoes, belts, and casual clothing for men and women. Plaza Daniel Leo, Oranjestad. ✆ **297/588-3610.**

Neo Scarpa Offers a sophisticated, high-end collection of women's and men's shoes and accessories. Anne Klein, Via Spiga, Paloma, and Charles Jourdan are among the labels. Seaport Mall, Oranjestad. ✆ **297/8-80104.**

The Nike Shop Stocks a range of Nike merchandise, including shoes, clothes, watches, and sunglasses. Seaport Mall, Oranjestad. ✆ **297/8-80103.**

Salvatore Ferragamo Shoes and handbags from the fabled Italian designer. Emmastraat 1 (Plaza Daniel Leo), Oranjestad. ✆ **297/582-8218.**

SUPERMARKETS

Kong Hing Supermarket A massive, modern, American suburban-style supermarket with wide aisles. In addition to familiar items such as Oreos and Coca-Cola, the store stocks Dutch cheeses, South American fruits and vegetables, liquor, fresh-baked breads, and over-the-counter pharmacy items. L. G. Smith Blvd. 152, Oranjestad. © 297/8-25545.

Ling & Sons Supermarket & Bakery   This island institution's new superstore carries a large assortment of American and European foods as well as a wide selection of South American and Asian items. Also here are a deli, a liquor department, a bakery, and over-the-counter drugs and personal care items. Ling & Sons takes grocery orders online for delivery to your hotel the day you arrive. Italiestraat 26, Oranjestad (behind Kong Hing Supermarket). © 297/583-2370. www.ling andsons.com.

WINE & LIQUOR

The supermarkets on the road connecting Oranjestad with the Low-Rise area—Kong Hing Supermarket and Ling & Sons Supermarket, listed above—boast sizable liquor departments and the best prices in town.

Aruba Trading Company   Carries an array of liquors and wines and operates a duty-free shop at Queen Beatrix International Airport. A variety of fragrances, cosmetics, watches, cigars, and chocolates is also available. Caya G. F. Betico Croes 12, Oranjestad. © 297/582-2602.

Weitnauer   This store's branch at the airport stocks your favorite scotch or vodka, as well as chocolate, cheese, and tobacco. Caya G. F. Betico Croes 29, Oranjestad. © 297/582-2790.

8

Aruba After Dark

Another "busy" day on the beach, another great dinner. What's next? Revived by nourishment and a couple of drinks, maybe you're ready for some gambling, some dancing, a little carousing. Or what about a show or a movie?

Aruba's casinos are a sure-fire after-dinner diversion, attracting both serious players and dabblers who've saved up a few dollars for the slot machines. Even if risk makes you nervous, the sensory overload is an irresistible spectacle—bells ringing, lights flashing, people groaning and screaming. Better yet, watching's free.

Striving to keep you and your wallet in the neighborhood, many casinos have theaters with Las Vegas–style shows, most of them professional and entertaining. "Let's Go Latin!" is especially recommended. Book the hottest tickets in advance—at least a day or two—especially during the high season, or you may miss out. Ask your hotel's concierge or activities desk for help.

For something less dazzling, the bar and club scene is surprisingly robust. You can start early with a beachside bar happy hour, move on to dinner and cocktails, then progress to a little jazz and cigars, or maybe board a booze cruise for some shenanigans at sea. Expect live entertainment or a DJ at most bars. If you're still not sated, head for one of the high-energy dance clubs, but don't show up before midnight or 1am—that's when the party really starts. To find out what's happening, check any of the free local magazines: *Aruba Nights, Island Temptations, Aruba Experience, Menu, Aruba Events, Destination Aruba,* and *Aruba Food & Wine*. For daily and weekly entertainment listings, consult the three English-language dailies—*Aruba Today, Aruba Daily,* and *The News*—and the weekly pamphlet *K-Pasa*. All of these publications are free and available at hotels and restaurants. Check with your hotel's activities and tour desks, too. The free flyers that you'll find on every public countertop are also a good source of information; many have coupons for discounts or freebies like free drinks and casino chips.

The dress code in Aruba is clean and casual, but a touch of elegance or trendiness never hurts.

1 Casinos

For many years after Aruba's first casino opened in 1959, gambling was the island's major attraction (next to the beaches, of course). Today, Aruba boasts 11 gambling venues, most of them casually elegant. Table games like baccarat, blackjack, poker, roulette, and craps usually start in the afternoon or early evening; slot machines can be played at 10am. Bingo, another diversion, starts in the afternoon at some places, in the evening at others. The action goes on as long as there's a crowd, usually till 2, 3, or 4am. The Crystal Casino in downtown Oranjestad is open 24 hours a day, 7 days a week.

ORANJESTAD

Located in downtown Oranjestad at the Renaissance Aruba Beach Resort, the **Crystal Casino,** L. G. Smith Blvd. 82 (*© **297/583-6000**), is Aruba's only 24-hour casino. More elegant than most gaming venues on the island, the Crystal boasts Austrian crystal chandeliers, gold-leaf columns, ornate moldings, Spanish mirrors, and Italian marble and brass. The 4,500 sq. m (15,000-sq.-ft.) parlor features 355 slot machines, bingo, and tables for roulette, craps, baccarat, blackjack, Caribbean stud poker, and Let It Ride. In a sequestered area, the race and sports book boasts a satellite link-up and wagering based on Las Vegas odds. Most major sporting events are covered. The salon privé gives high rollers a room of their own. There's live entertainment nightly in the main hall, and the adjacent Crystal Theatre is home to Aruba's hottest show, "Let's Go Latin!", an extravaganza with impressive performers, costumes, and choreography.

The **Seaport Casino,** L. G. Smith Blvd. 9 (*© **297/583-5027**), also part of the Renaissance in downtown Oranjestad, is Aruba's only waterfront casino. The casual 2,400 sq. m (8,000-sq.-ft.) emporium fits in well with the surrounding shopping mall; you might think it's just another store. Besides 240 slot machines, the casino features tables for blackjack, roulette, Let It Ride, and Caribbean stud poker. The Tuesday and Sunday bingo games are especially popular. Slot machines are available from 10am to 4am; tables are open from 2pm to 4am. Live bands entertain on Friday and Saturday evenings, but the harbor views never stop.

LOW-RISE AREA

The **Alhambra Casino & Aladdin Theatre,** J. E. Irausquin Blvd. 47, Manchebo Beach (*© **297/583-5000**), is a busy complex in the Low-Rise area near the Divi and the Casa del Mar. The theme at this

17-year-old facility is pure Kismet. Dressed like a jovial genie, the doorman greets every guest with a robust handshake (at last count, he's shaken more than 3.5 million hands). Inside, the casino's leaded glass, serpentine mahogany columns, arches, and domes have a pronounced Moorish flavor. The atmosphere is casual. The 3,000 sq. m (10,000-sq.-ft.) casino features 300 slots and tables for Caribbean stud poker, three-card poker, craps, blackjack, Let It Ride, and roulette, with a range of wagering minimums. Slots open at 10am; tables start business at noon during the high season, at 6pm during the low season. Year-round, you can play till the early morning, usually 3am. Bingo starts at 1pm on Sunday, Monday, Wednesday, and Friday. Take a break at one of the bars, the restaurant, or the deli. The 2,400 sq. m (8,000-sq.-ft.) Aladdin Theatre's eclectic program features a singer, impersonators, dancers, and gymnasts. Several shops lining the open-air courtyards in the back sell souvenirs, leather goods, jewelry, and beachwear until midnight.

The **Royal Cabana Casino,** at the La Cabana All Suite Beach Resort & Casino, J. E. Irausquin Blvd. 250, Eagle Beach (© **297/ 587-9000**), is known for its multitheme three-in-one restaurant and its 600-seat showcase cabaret theater and nightclub. The largest casino in Aruba, the Royal Cabana offers 33 tables (blackjack, Caribbean stud poker, roulette, craps, and Let It Ride), plus almost 400 slot machines. Slots open daily at 11am; table games are ready at 4pm and remain active until 3am. Bingo's another alternative on Wednesday, Friday, Saturday, and Sunday. On-site shopping includes jewelry and cigar stores. For many years, the theater featured a highly entertaining revue of female impersonators, but over the past couple of years, various acts have come and gone. The restaurant serves dinner nightly.

HIGH-RISE AREA

Casablanca Casino, at the Wyndham, J. E. Irausquin Blvd. 77, Palm Beach (© **297/586-2283**), is buzzing with action in the evening, especially after the hotel's Havana Tropical show lets out. The 3,600 sq. m (12,000-sq.-ft.) facility features 300 slot machines, and tables for blackjack, roulette, craps, Caribbean stud poker, and baccarat. The theme has something of a Bogart twist, and there's a bar and live entertainment. The room in back caters to higher rollers. At the adjacent bar, hookah pipes and exotic cocktails are on hand. Open daily from noon till 4am.

The **Casino** at the Radisson, J. E. Irausquin Blvd. 81, Palm Beach (© **297/586-4045;** www.thecasinoaruba.com) is Aruba's newest casino. On the hotel's lower-level lobby, its domed ceiling twinkles with thousands of lights and looms over 4,200 sq. m (14,000 sq. ft.) of space. The 235 slots open at noon; while tables for blackjack, roulette, Caribbean stud poker, three-card poker, mini-baccarat, craps, and Let It Ride open at 2pm in the high season, at 6pm otherwise. The action lasts till 3am daily. The bar features big-screen TVs tuned to sporting events, and there's live music Wednesday through Saturday.

A casual, relatively low-key operation, the **Casino Merengue** is in the Aruba Grand Resort, J. E. Irausquin Boulevard 79, Palm Beach (© **297/586-3900**). You can choose from slots, blackjack, computerized roulette, baccarat, craps, and poker. Slots open at 10am; table games are ready for action at 6pm and shut down between 2 and 3am. The wildly colorful Carnival-voodoo decor will make you smile.

The Hyatt's **Copacabana Casino,** J. E. Irausquin Blvd. 85, Palm Beach (© **297/586-1234,** ext. 2021), has a "Carnival in Rio" theme and works to evoke the glamour of Monaco. With the many columns, murals, and stone walls, it's certainly one of Aruba's more elegant gambling venues. The 23 tables feature craps, roulette, blackjack, baccarat, and Caribbean stud poker. The 3,600 sq. m (12,000-sq.-ft.) facility also has more than 300 slot machines. Live bands play Latin or popular American music every evening. Slots open at noon; tables open 4 hours later. The action lasts till 4am.

Completely renovated in 1998, the Holiday Inn's busy **Excelsior Casino,** J. E. Irausquin Blvd. 230, Palm Beach (© **297/586-7777;** www.excelsiorcasino.com), has plenty of slots plus tables for blackjack, craps, roulette, Let it Ride, and Caribbean stud poker (this popular game originated at the Excelsior in 1988). It's the only Aruban casino besides the Crystal to offer a race and sports book with live simulcasting; in this case, thoroughbred, harness, and dog racing. Slots are available at 8am, and sports book and tables are ready for play at noon till 3 or 4am. Monday through Friday bingo games fill the house at 3:30pm. There's an ATM next to the cashier, a bar, and live entertainment.

The **Allegro Casino** at the Allegro, J. E. Irausquin Blvd. 83, Palm Beach (© **297/586-9039**), opens daily at noon for slot action; table games are available after 7pm. As long as folks are making wagers, the casino stays open till 4am. You can feed one of the 250 slot machines (with as little as a penny) or play baccarat, craps, blackjack, roulette, poker, or Caribbean stud poker at the tables. Bingo takes center stage at 10:30pm every night. There's live entertainment most nights.

The **Stellaris Casino,** at the Marriott, L. G. Smith Blvd. 101, Palm Beach (© **297/586-9000**), hums with the sound of slot machines from noon, but the real buzz begins after 4pm, when the tables open and the crowd thickens. Slots range from a nickel to $50. Games include blackjack, super seven, craps, Caribbean stud poker, roulette, Wild Aruba Stud, Let It Ride, and mini-baccarat. The live band can be heard throughout the 3,200 sq. m (10,700-sq.-ft.) casino in spite of the groans of disgust and squeals of delight.

2 Entertainment

At least a couple of Aruba's stages offer first-rate entertainment, and the others are nothing to sneeze at. You don't have to be a resort guest to see shows at the hotels, but you should make a reservation. Seats for the hottest spectacles are likely to book up early in the day, especially during the high season.

ORANJESTAD

One of the island's current sensations, "Let's Go Latin!" at the Renaissance's **Crystal Theatre,** L. G. Smith Blvd. 82, Oranjestad (© **297/583-6000**), features 26 performers and more than 180 costumes. Combining Latin rhythm, Las Vegas spectacle, and New York sophistication, the show boasts dazzling choreography and riveting vocalists. Most of the talented dancers hail from one of Cuba's elite ballet companies, but their moves are more Bob Fosse than Bolshoi. Perhaps the production's greatest asset is its modern sensibility: Fresh and well paced, it's sexy, slightly cheeky, and never stale. Several futuristic, modern gymnastic-acrobatic interludes require herculean strength and would make Cirque du Soleil proud. (The whole show isn't futuristic—just the interludes are.) Showtime is 9pm, Monday through Saturday, and tickets at the first-class, 430-seat theater are $39 (children under 12, $19). An even better deal is the dinner and show package: For $68 you get the show and a three-course dinner at L'Escale (see chapter 4).

LOW-RISE AREA

New curtains and enhanced sound and lighting have transformed the **Aladdin Theatre** at the Alhambra Casino, J. E. Irausquin Blvd. 47 (© **297/583-5000**), into a more up-to-date showcase for its live show, "Las Vegas Fantasy." Fifteen performers crowd the stage, including a singer, female impersonators, dancers, and two gymnasts.

The show lasts a little over an hour and runs Monday through Saturday at 9pm. The price is $25.

For many years, the **Tropicana Showroom** at the Royal Cabana Casino, J. E. Irausquin Blvd. 250 (© **297/587-7000**), showcased a top-notch female-impersonator extravaganza that featured drag divas such as Barbra Streisand, Madonna, Bette Midler, and Tina Turner. Since the show closed in 2002, none of the acts the room has booked—magicians, dance revues, and so forth—has approached the success of the drag show, and rumor has it that the theater is desperately seeking another class act of female impersonators. Check to see if it's succeeded. The show must go on, in any event, and whatever's on the stage while you're there starts at 9pm on Monday, Tuesday, Thursday, and Saturday, at 10pm on Wednesday and Friday. Depending on the act, tickets should cost $20 to $35.

HIGH-RISE AREA

The **Cabaret Royal Showroom** at the Wyndham, J. E. Irausquin Blvd. 77, Palm Beach (© **297/586-4466**), offers "Havana Tropical Revue," a fiesta featuring the rhythms and salsa of Cuba. Most of the singers, dancers, and musicians are from Havana. The gorgeous, high-energy dancers change costumes with every new musical number. The comfortable dinner theater serves the meal from 7pm to 9pm, followed by the 1½-hour show. Dinner and show is $46.

The Allegro's **Las Palmas Showroom,** J. E. Irausquin Blvd. 83, Palm Beach (© **297/586-4500**), boasts the largest stage in Aruba and an early-1980s aesthetic. When they're not tending bar, working in the office, or orchestrating guest activities at the hotel, the theater's multinational performers present six different spectacles each week. The shows include "Frenesi" (a celebration of Latin rhythms), "Grease" (an interpretation of the Hollywood movie), "Broadway" (a revue of the Great White Way's best), "Moulin Rouge" (based on the Nicole Kidman film), "Las Vegas" (with costumes and themes not confined to Nevada), and "One Step into the Future" (a trippy alien fantasy with outlandish characters, acrobatic dancers, and bizarre costumes—this one's really a hoot!). The all-you-can-eat dinner buffet starts at 6:30pm, followed by the show at 8:30pm. The package is $53; the 45-minute shows alone are $20. Skip the food, but make a point of seeing one of the productions.

3 Clubs & Bars

Many hotel bars are cozy and conversation-friendly, and most offer live entertainment—a jazz combo, a piano soloist, maybe a chanteuse. If you want higher decibel and energy levels, the trendiest and busiest bars and clubs are in Oranjestad. The strip along L. G. Smith Boulevard on the harborfront abounds with spots, making a bar crawl as easy as saying "bottoms up." Crowds tend to be mixed: Aruban/tourist, gay/straight, young/young-at-heart. Although most bars open at noon, they generally don't get started until 10 or 11pm and stay open until 2am. Clubs open at 10pm, are empty until midnight or 1am, and peak around 2am.

ORANJESTAD

Café Bahia   Located on the capital's busiest strip, across from the Royal Plaza Mall, Café Bahia features a tropical ambience, a fishing-boat bar, and hand-painted murals. The kitchen is open until 11pm so you can snack on Caribbean conch fritters as you drink. After 10pm, the place starts hopping, especially on weekends and holidays, when there's disco dancing. Popular libations include the Chocolate City and Barnamint Bailey (ask about their sweet, calorie-laden ingredients). You can drink and dance until 2 or 3 in the morning. Weststraat 7. ✆ **297/588-9982.**

Carlos 'n Charlie's   Party-bus tours bring lots of fun-loving vacationers to this chain establishment for retro music, Mexican food, and drinks. Twenty-somethings can be seen drinking frozen margaritas to excess just about every night of the week. Weststraat 3A. ✆ **297/582-0355.**

Castaway's   Once the home of a fisherman, this simple bar-restaurant serves cold beer and juicy, all-you-can-eat ribs. It's off the beaten path a bit, on a corner behind the Royal Plaza Mall. Schelpsraat 43. ✆ **297/583-3619.**

The Cellar   An Oranjestad favorite for years, the club boasts a fairly even mix of tourists and locals. Upstairs, known as "Sky," features dance music ranging from disco to house to merengue. Downstairs, the raucous cellar is the place to sit, chat, and people-watch. It's noisy and crowded on weekends, but still appealing and friendly. It's open until 4am. Klipstraat 2. ✆ **297/582-8567.**

Cheerios   One of Oranjestad's newest late-night dance venues, this upstairs space packs them in. The music's eclectic, and the open-air design allows breezes to cool off nonstop revelers. The party goes on till 4am. Plaza Daniel Leo, at the beginning of Main St. No phone. Cover free to $10.

Choose-A-Name   A perennial favorite, this friendly bar moved from Main Street to new digs behind the Royal Plaza Mall in early

2002. Karaoke makes it a popular first stop on the bar-crawl circuit, but you can avoid off-key singers by retreating to the terrace. There are also big-screen TVs and live music 4 nights a week. Havenstraat. ✆ 297/588-6200.

Club 2000 Nobody cool shows up here until after midnight, but the bar starts serving drinks at 10pm. A young crowd turns out for a diverse mix of disco, merengue, and hip-hop, with hip-hop winning out most nights. The music is *loud*. Top of the Royal Plaza Mall, L. G. Smith Blvd. 94. ✆ 297/588-9450. $5 cover.

Cuba's Cookin' This restaurant offers late-night live music with a Latin beat. The cozy, intimate atmosphere draws everyone to the dance floor for salsa and merengue moves. Try the house mojito, a Cuban rum and mint refresher. Wilhelminastraat 27. ✆ 297/588-0627.

E Zone If you hit only one club while you're in Aruba, make it this futuristic establishment. Dazzling lights, a stainless-steel dance floor, and talented DJs spinning the latest music bring out the island's hip and beautiful, gay and straight. The door opens at 9:30pm, but things don't heat up until 1am. Wednesday is Ladies' Night (free admission and free drinks 10–11:30pm); on Friday and Saturday there's nonstop dancing until 5am ($2 drinks 10pm–midnight). Weststraat 5. ✆ 297/588-7474. $5 cover.

Garufa This clubby, smoky room is a favorite place for jazz- and bolero-loving cigar smokers. It features a premium bar and a humidor for Montecristos and Cohibas. Sip a single malt or port from the comfort of your cigar-motif chair. The food comes from El Gaucho, the Argentine steakhouse across the street. Live music includes a jazz saxophonist and an Argentine guitarist who plays tangos and boleros. Open from 6pm until about 2am, Monday through Saturday. Wilhelminastraat 63. ✆ 297/582-3677.

Iguana Joe's Across the street from Café Bahia, this place emphasizes all things reptilian and cranks out big, bold, boozy drinks like the Lethal Lizard. It attracts a mix of Arubans and tourists; the crowd gets younger as the night progresses. Royal Plaza Mall, L. G. Smith Blvd. 94. ✆ 297/583-9373.

Jimmy's Place Friday happy hours at this Dutch bar attract cigar-smoking power brokers who like American rock 'n' roll. After midnight (and until the roosters crow) the restaurant-bar serves hearty soups and sandwiches to a mixed straight and gay crowd of entertainers and insomniacs. Kruisweg 15 (1 block off Caya Betico Croes or Main St.). ✆ 297/582-2550.

La Fiesta The main space of this trendy spot (on the second floor of the Benetton building, just behind the Renaissance) has a wrap-around outdoor terrace, a long bar, mahogany stools, red velvet sofas, and dramatic lighting. A wooden bridge connects the room with a cozy bar and lounge across the road. Two DJs play an eclectic dance mix. A two-for-one happy hour runs from 10 to 11pm every night. The club opens at 9pm, and the party lasts until 3 or 4am. Aventura Mall, Plaza Daniel Leo. ℂ 297/583-5896. $5 cover.

Mambo Jambo Mambo Jambo is sultry and relaxing early in the evening and starts hopping after 9pm. Expect a cosmopolitan blend of Dutch and Latino visitors, and lots of Latin-Caribbean rhythms. There's an array of specialty drinks, served in coconut shells, with colorful straws and chunks of fruit. Royal Plaza Mall, L. G. Smith Blvd. 94. ℂ 297/583-3632.

The Paddock This is Aruba's most popular hangout for Dutch residents and vacationers. The blond, hip staff serves cocktails, tea and coffee, snacks, and full-fledged meals. Happy hours change frequently but always attract a festive crowd. The cow-themed bistro is open until 2am on weekdays, until 3am on weekends. L. G. Smith Blvd. 13. ℂ 297/583-2334. www.paddock-aruba.com.

HIGH-RISE AREA

Kokoa Beach Bar This thatch-roofed, tropically colored perch is popular with sunbathers who want to do a little socializing before showering off the sunscreen. And why not? Happy hour lasts from 3 until 5pm. Open from 8am until 10pm, the place has lots of blond-haired, blue-eyed Dutch employees. De Palm pier, Palm Beach. ℂ 297/586-2050.

Moomba Beach This casual, fun spot is essentially a couple of giant *palapas* on the beach with a party every day and night. "No shirts, no shoes, no problem" is the slogan here. At night, live bands play beneath a giant Heineken beer chandelier. Happy hour is from 5 to 7pm daily; the bartenders pour drinks from 10am until very late. Try the Tropical Treasure (melon and banana liqueurs, coconut cream, and pineapple juice). Food is served until 11pm. This may be the only bar on the island that has showers and beach chairs, so don't worry about the tanning lotion and sand. Between the Holiday Inn and Marriott, Palm Beach. ℂ 297/592-6584.

Salt 'n Pepper A mostly tourist crowd comes here for sangria and cocktails, live entertainment in an outdoor courtyard (after 8pm), and a variety of Spanish tapas, sandwiches, and soups. The kitchen closes just before midnight, but the bar's open until 1am every night. J. E. Irausquin Blvd. 368A (across from the Allegro), Palm Beach. © 297/586-3280. www.visitaruba.com/saltandpepper.

Sirocco This elegant open-air venue in the Wyndham features a live jazz combo every Thursday, Friday, and Saturday from 9pm to midnight. Arabian hookah pipes and Moroccan chairs create a hallucinatory casbah ambience. At the Wyndham Aruba Beach Resort & Casino, J. E. Irausquin Blvd. 77, Palm Beach. © 297/586-4466.

4 Party & Dinner Cruises

Tattoo Party Cruises (© 297/586-2010; www.arubaadventures. com/tattoo) follow the coastline nightly, offering views of the island's lights. The triple-decked catamaran features a full-service bar (with $1 and $2 drinks) and a dinner buffet (barbecue or Italian). The first floor boasts the island's largest floating dance floor, a DJ, and a live band; the second deck is dedicated to imbibing, and the top floor opens to views of the moon's reflection in the water. You're encouraged to don your bathing suit and swing on a rope into the Caribbean. The crew puts on a show, and guests are invited to join various contests. The crowd is foolish and young (chronologically or at heart), but no one's under 18. The party takes place Tuesday through Saturday from 8pm till midnight. The ship departs from the De Palm pier on Palm Beach at the Aruba Grand. The damage is $49 per person.

Jolly Pirates (© 297/583-7355; www.jollypirates.com) boards at the Moomba pier, between the Holiday Inn and Marriott, and offers two very casual evening sea cruises. The buccaneer theme can only mean walking the plank and singing "Yo, ho, ho, and a bottle of rum." The sunset sail features an open bar and rope swing (Mon and Fri, 5–7pm, $26 per person). After a brief sail, the starlight dinner cruise drops anchor in a cove, where rabblerousers dine, dance to live entertainment, and take a moonlight rope swing into the sea (evenings vary by season, 8:30–11:30pm, $55 per person).

Le Dôme on the Ocean, offered by De Palm Tours (© 297/ 582-4400), is a more elegant cruise, featuring dinner prepared by the culinary team of the eponymous French/Belgian restaurant (see chapter 4). Once aboard the catamaran, guests receive flutes of champagne at tables dressed with linen, china, and silver. Hors d'oeuvres circulate during the leisurely cruise along the coast; the route allows views of California Lighthouse and the sunset. Once the ship's anchored, guests are served a smoked salmon appetizer, a main course of grouper in lobster sauce or lamb in wine sauce, and Bavarian custard drizzled with wild berry sauce, followed by coffee or tea. Upscale open-air dining on the sea is hard to carry off: The breezes can be blustery, and the food is prepared beforehand for logistical purposes. Frankly, you'd do better to savor a meal at Le Dôme's terra firma address. The 3-hour tour departs from the De Palm pier on Palm Beach at 6pm every Thursday. The $90 price includes the cruise, dinner, and unlimited drinks. Reservations are required.

5 Other Diversions

PARTY BUSES

Kukoo Kunuku (✆ 297/586-2010; www.arubaadventures.com/kukookunuku) invites you to party on a colorfully painted '57 Chevy bus. A bar crawl on wheels, it's like getting drunk with the Partridge Family. The coach has no glass in its windows—the fresh air will do you good—and every reveler gets maracas. Prepare to sing a solo and do the macarena. The carousing attracts a mixed crowd with a surprisingly large number of folks over 40; the minimum age is 18. The price of $55 per person includes champagne at sunset, an Aruban dinner under the stars, and the first drink at each of three watering holes. The carousing begins at 6pm and lasts until about midnight, Monday through Saturday. Pick-up and drop-off is at your hotel.

In the same vein but without dinner, the **Banana Bus** (✆ 297/593-0757) rolls Tuesday through Friday from 8pm till midnight. After your guide and driver rounds up the gang, you zoom away to three local bars. For $37, you get five drinks (three on the bus), and door-to-door transportation.

Chiva Paranda (✆ 297/582-0347), a wooden, open-air '47 Ford bus, is also colorfully hand-painted and features the same kind of bar-hopping with a dinner pit stop. The carousing starts at 6:30pm and lasts till 12:30am on Wednesday and Thursday only. The $53 price tag includes dinner and the first drink at each of three Aruban hangouts.

THEME NIGHTS

Just about every hotel in Aruba offers theme nights with buffet dinner, live entertainment, and dancing. Everyone's invited, not just hotel guests. The price depends primarily on the cuisine: A lobster fest might set you back $40 to $45 per person; more modest fare can be had for about $25 (half that for kids). You can choose from at least 15 events every night of the week. They may include the

Aruban folkloric show (Allegro), **Caribbean dance and food festival** (La Cabana, Wyndham, Renaissance), **Carnival extravaganza** (Casa del Mar, Costa Linda, Divi, Holiday Inn, La Cabana, Marriott, Playa Linda, Renaissance, Tamarijn, Wyndham), **Fajitas and Margaritas** (Hyatt), **Harley-Davidson rides around the pool** (Holiday Inn), **Havana night** (Wyndham), **Italian night** (Allegro, Bucuti Beach, Casa del Mar, Costa Linda, Holiday Inn, La Cabana, Marriott, Renaissance), **karaoke** (La Cabana, Tamarijn), **magic show** (Divi), **Mexican fiesta** (Divi, Holiday Inn, Marriott, Wyndham), **pirates' seafood cookout** (Bucuti Beach), **steel-band and limbo barbecue** (Allegro, Divi, Tamarijn), **water ballet** (Holiday Inn, Tamarijn), and **Western night** (Holiday Inn).

MOVIES

Aruba's only indoor movie theaters are at the **Seaport Cinema** in the Seaport Marketplace shopping mall in downtown Oranjestad, L. G. Smith Blvd. 82 (✆ **297/583-0318;** www.seaportcinemas.com). The six-screen complex shows first-run films, mostly Hollywood blockbusters, in English. Midnight flicks are popular on Friday and Saturday. Tickets range from $3 to $7.

A real throwback to a simpler time, the **E. De Veer Drive-In Theatre,** Kibaima z/n, across from the Balashi Brewery on the road to Savaneta and San Nicolas (✆ **297/585-8355;** www.seaport cinemas.com), is a rare treat. The chance to watch a film (usually American) in a vast field under the stars? In Aruba? That's exotic. Admission is about $4, but Sunday and Wednesday are "car crash" nights—less than $6 admits a whole carload. Expect tons of Aruban teens, sweethearts, and families with kids in tow. Scheduling information is available online.

9

A Side Trip to Curaçao

Just 35 miles north of Venezuela and a 30-minute flight from Aruba, Curaçao, the "C" of the Dutch ABC islands, is the most populous and sophisticated of the Netherlands Antilles. Its beaches and resorts are no match for those of Aruba, but its distinctive cultural offerings are superior, and it too boasts warm people, shopping, casinos, and watersports.

Columbus's Spanish lieutenants first spotted Curaçao in 1499. The Spaniards killed most of the island's peaceful Caiquetio Indians, only to be ousted in 1634 by the Dutch, who later fought off French and English assaults.

The Dutch made the island a Caribbean Gibraltar, bristling with forts and commercial activity, including slave trading. Ramparts guarded the harbor's narrow entrance, while hilltop forts protected coastal approaches. In 1915 the Royal Dutch/Shell Company built one of the world's largest refineries here to process crude oil from Venezuela. The influx of workers from 50 countries transformed Curaçao into a multicultural, cosmopolitan community.

Just 37 miles long and 7 miles wide, the island features many centuries-old Dutch buildings, including classic Dutch-style windmills. Outside the capital, **Willemstad,** the desertlike countryside evokes the American Southwest, with cacti, spiny-leafed aloe, and divi divi trees studding the arid landscape.

Bonaire, St. Eustatius, St. Maarten, Saba, and Curaçao make up the Netherlands Antilles, an autonomous part of the Kingdom of the Netherlands. Curaçaons are Dutch nationals and carry European Union passports. The island's 171,000 people have roots in more than 50 countries around the world.

1 Essentials

VISITOR INFORMATION

The **Curaçao Tourist Board** has an office at 19495 Biscayne Blvd., Suite 804, Aventuna, FL 33180 (© **800/328-7222**). You can also get information online at **www.curacao-tourism.com**. Once you're

Avila Beach Hotel **5**
Breezes Curaçao **6**
Curaçao Marriott Beach Resort
& Emerald Casino **2**
Hilton Curaçao Resort **3**
Kurá Hulanda Hotel and Casino **4**
Landhuis Daniel Inn **1**
Porto Paseo Hotel & Casino **7**

✈ Airport
🏝 Beach
⚓ Cruise Ship Dock
▲ Mountain

on the island, visit the **Curaçao Tourist Board,** Pietermaai 19, Willemstad (℃ **599/9-434-8200**).

GETTING THERE

Curaçao's national carrier, **Dutch Caribbean Airlines** (℃ **800/ 327-7230;** 297/583-8080 in Aruba; www.flydca.net), **Avia Air** (℃ **297/583-4600**), and **Royal Aruban Airlines** (℃ **297/588- 3300;** www.royalarubanairlines.com) provide 25-minute shuttle service between Aruba and **Curaçao International Airport,** Plaza Margareth Abraham (℃ **599/9-888-0101**). Flights from North America are often linked to Aruba; **American Airlines** (℃ **800/ 433-7300;** www.aa.com) offers daily nonstop flights to Curaçao from Miami.

GETTING AROUND

BY RENTAL CAR   Driving in Curaçao is easy. Valid U.S., British, and Canadian licenses are honored, driving is on the right side, and road signs use international symbols. **Avis** (© **800/331-2112;** www.avis.com), **Budget** (© **800/472-3325;** www.budgetrentacar. com), and **Hertz** (© **800/654-3001** in the U.S., or 599/9-868-1182 on Curaçao; www.hertz.com) have offices. Compact cars with manual transmission start at about $35 per day.

BY TAXI   Taxis are unmetered, but drivers carry an official rate sheet. Fares rise 25% after 11pm, and drivers appreciate a 10% tip. The $18 trip from the airport to Willemstad can be split among four passengers. Each piece of oversized luggage is an extra $1. In town, taxis are easiest to get on the Otrabanda side of the floating bridge. You can also call © **599/9-869-0752.** Taxi island tours are $30 per hour for up to four passengers.

BY BUS   Some hotels operate a free shuttle to Willemstad's shopping districts, but public transportation is limited. Large yellow buses cover the most traveled urban routes, and bus terminals are outside the post office on the Waaigat inlet in Punda and next to the underpass in Otrabanda. Fares in town and east of Willemstad are NAf1; it's NAf1.50 to the western end of the island. Buses run most city routes hourly, every 2 hours for points west, and less frequently on Sunday.

 FAST FACTS: Curaçao

Banking Hours   Bank hours are Monday to Friday from 8:30am to noon and 1:30 to 4:30pm. Willemstad has several banks and ATMs.

Currency   U.S. dollars and credit cards are accepted almost everywhere. The official currency, the Netherlands Antillean florin (NAf), also called a **guilder,** is divided into 100 NA (Netherlands Antillean) cents. The stable exchange rate is US$1 to 1.77 NAf (1 NAf = US56¢).

Documents   To enter Curaçao, U.S. and Canadian citizens need either a passport or an original birth certificate and photo ID, along with an onward or return ticket. Other nationals need a passport.

Electricity Electricity is 110–130 volts/50 cycles, similar but not identical to the U.S. standard. Most U.S. electrical appliances will function.

Hospital St. Elisabeth Hospital, Breedestraat 193 (℗ 599/ 9-462-4900), near Otrabanda in Willemstad, is one of the Caribbean's most up-to-date facilities.

Language As in Aruba, Dutch, Spanish, and English are spoken, along with Papiamento. Most people in the tourism industry speak English.

Police The police emergency number is ℗ 911.

Safety Curaçao isn't plagued with crime, but safeguard your valuables.

Taxes Curaçao levies a room tax of 7% on accommodations. The departure tax for international and Aruban flights is US$20; to other islands in the Netherlands Antilles, it's US$10.

Telephone To call Curaçao from the United States, dial **011** (the international access code), then **599** (the country code), and then **9** (the area code) and the local number. In Curaçao, to call another number on the island, dial the local number only; to make off-island calls, dial **021** and then the area code and number. The direct-dial access number for AT&T is ℗ **001-800/225-5288,** and for MCI it's ℗ **001-800/888-8000.** Sprint's access number throughout the Caribbean is ℗ **001-800/877-8000.**

Time Curaçao is on Atlantic Standard time year-round, 1 hour ahead of Eastern Standard time and the same as Eastern daylight saving time.

Water Water comes from a modern desalination plant and is perfectly safe.

Weather Curaçao's average temperature is 81°F (27°C), and trade winds make the island fairly pleasant. Annual rainfall averages a meager 22 inches.

2 Where to Stay

Hotels cluster in Willemstad and the suburbs 10 to 15 minutes away. The bigger hotels have free shuttle buses into town, and most have beaches and pools. Ask if the quoted price includes the 7% room tax and 12% service charge. Expect to pay a $3 daily energy tax.

EXPENSIVE

Breezes Curaçao 𝓡𝓡 *Kids*   The old and fading Princess Beach Resort has reincarnated itself as Curaçao's first major all-inclusive resort. Adjacent to both the Undersea National Park and Sea Aquarium, this large complex opens onto one of Curaçao's most beautiful beaches. This high-energy complex has one of the longest beaches on the island, with good snorkeling offshore. Catering to both couples and singles, the resort also welcomes families. For those who like to gamble, it boasts the largest casino in Curaçao. The most desirable rooms overlook the ocean; others front the hotel's gardens. Bathrooms have either a shower or a shower/tub combination, and all open onto private patios or balconies. The food won't make gourmets swoon, but there's plenty of it. The resort's active entertainment program includes guest and staff talent shows.

Dr. Martin Luther King Blvd., Willemstad, Curaçao, N.A. 𝓒 **599/9-736-7888.** Fax 599/9-461-7205. www.breezes.com. 339 units. Winter $600 double, from $1,040 suite; off season $570 double, from $990 suite. Rates are all-inclusive. AE, MC, V. **Amenities:** 4 restaurants; 3 bars; casino; 3 pools; 2 tennis courts; fitness center; spa; children's program; playground; limited room service; babysitting; laundry; deep-sea fishing; windsurfing; dive shop; snorkeling; kids snack bar. *In room:* A/C, TV, minibar, fridge (on request), coffeemaker, hair dryer, iron, safe, CD player.

Curaçao Marriott Beach Resort & Emerald Casino 𝓡𝓡   The most glamorous and prominent hotel on the island, this resort borders Curaçao's largest and most popular beach. The hotel's three-story ochre buildings reflect traditional Dutch colonial architecture, and the open lobby boasts views of the beach and the property's many fountains. Scattered throughout, unusual, often monumental, artworks by local and international artists, and comfortable, overstuffed chairs add a touch of elegance. Each colorful room offers an ocean view, one king or two queen beds, and a spacious bathroom.

Piscadera Bay (P.O. Box 6003), Willemstad, Curaçao, N.A. 𝓒 **800/223-6388** in the U.S., or 599/9-736-8800. Fax 599/9-462-7502. www.marriott.com. 257 units. Winter $259–$309 double, from $339 suite; off season $159–$189 double, from $219 suite. AE, MC, V. **Amenities:** 3 restaurants (Caribbean, Continental, Northern Italian); 2 bars; casino; outdoor pool with swim-up bar; 2 tennis courts lit for night play; health club; 2 open-air Jacuzzis; sauna; watersports; children's program; concierge; tour/activities desk; car-rental desk; business center; shopping arcade; salon; limited room service; babysitting; laundry service; dry cleaning; theme nights. *In room:* A/C, TV, dataport, minibar, hair dryer, iron, safe.

Hilton Curaçao Resort 𝓡   Originally built in 1965, this former Sheraton is often credited with launching Curaçao's tourism boom. After 30 years of wear and tear, the hotel was radically renovated in

1999. Today, it rises five floors above rocky bluffs that open onto a narrow but sandy beach. The large freeform pool and a location convenient to the center of town offset the lack of a wide swath of beach. Glass-enclosed elevators cling to the outside walls, offering a panoramic view as they whisk you to your room; each accommodation overlooks either the ocean or the garden. Outfitted in bold tropical colors, each unit features traditional furnishings, comfortable mattresses, private balconies, and generously proportioned bathrooms.

Piscadera Bay, John F. Kennedy Blvd. (P.O. Box 2133), Willemstad, Curaçao, N.A. © **800/HILTONS** in the U.S. and Canada, or 599/9-462-5000. Fax 599/9-462-5846. www.hiltoncaribbean.com. 196 units. Winter $190–$210 double, $220–$280 suite; off season $140–$160 double, $180–$240 suite. AE, MC, V. **Amenities:** 2 restaurants (Caribbean, Italian); 2 bars; casino; outdoor freeform pool; 18-hole mini-golf course; 2 tennis courts lit for night play; health club; extensive watersports; bike rental; children's program; playground; shopping arcade; limited room service; babysitting; laundry service; dry cleaning; nonsmoking rooms; executive-level rooms; wheelchair-accessible rooms; free shuttle bus service to Willemstad. *In room:* A/C, TV, fax, coffeemaker, hair dryer, iron, safe.

Kurá Hulanda Hotel and Casino ★★

Curaçao's most imaginative and unusual hotel opens onto St. Anna Bay in central Willemstad near the Queen Emma Bridge. In the heart of the city's Dutch colonial historic district, the property is part of the Kurá Hulanda Museum complex (see "Exploring the Island," later in this chapter), and the hotel's Dutch colonial architecture dates from the 18th and 19th centuries. The gorgeous rooms feature hand-woven linens from India and hand-carved mahogany and teak furniture. Delicately woven mosquito netting drapes the four-poster beds, and each room boasts one-of-a-kind hand-painted walls decorated by local artisans. The Indian marble bathrooms have tub and shower. Some accommodations also have kitchenettes. It's not on a beach, but this hotel offers the Dutch Caribbean's best West Indian character.

Longestraat 8, Willemstad, Curaçao, N.A. © **599/9-434-7700.** Fax 599/9-434-7701. www.kurahulanda.com. 100 units. Winter $275 double, $450 suite; off season $250 double, $425 suite. AE, DC, MC, V. **Amenities:** Restaurant; bar; small casino; 2 pools; fitness center; limited room service; babysitting; dry cleaning. *In room:* A/C, ceiling fans, TV, minifridge, hair dryer, safe, CD player, robes.

MODERATE

Avila Beach Hotel ★★

The only beachfront hotel in Willemstad proper, the charming Avila presides over its own sandy beach. It features three separate structures: a beautifully restored 200-year-old mansion (built by the English governor of Curaçao), a large extension of deluxe rooms called La Belle Alliance, and the Blues wing, an all-wood complex of deluxe rooms, each with a private terrace or balcony. Converted into a hotel in 1949, the colonial house today occasionally entertains the royals of the Netherlands. The basic rooms in the original mansion are charming but small, bathrooms have showers only, and hot-water use is restricted to daylight hours only. Each Blues wing room has a full bathroom, kitchenette, and a balcony or terrace with an ocean view. Similarly, La Belle Alliance units have a full bathroom and balcony; some have a kitchenette.

Penstraat 130 (P.O. Box 791), Willemstad, Curaçao, N.A. (C) **800/747-8162** or 599/9-4614377. Fax 599/9-4611493. www.avilahotel.com. 108 units. Winter $125–$242 double, $325 suite; off season $115–$190 double, $260 suite. Meal plans available. AE, MC, V. **Amenities:** 3 restaurants (breakfast cafe, international, seafood); 2 bars; tennis court; business service; babysitting; laundry service. *In room:* A/C, TV, coffeemaker, hair dryer.

INEXPENSIVE

Landhuis Daniel Inn *(Value* South of Westpunt, near the island's westernmost point, this mustard-colored plantation house is a 7- to 10-minute drive from the beach, but it offers the best value in Curaçao. Very simple but comfortable guest rooms are tidily maintained and have small private bathrooms with showers. Only two rooms are air-conditioned, but all units have ceiling fans—or you can rely on the trade winds to stay cool. Ask for a room in the main house: The converted slave quarters are small but charming. The basic rooms and communal TV room give this simple country inn the aura of a youth hostel; guests also play billiards and darts.

Wegnaar, Westpunt, Curaçao, N.A. (C)/fax **599/9-864-8400**. www.landhuisdaniel. com. 8 units. $45–$60 double. AE, DC, MC, V. **Amenities:** Restaurant; bar; pool; babysitting; laundry; dive shop. *In room:* A/C, safe, no phone.

3 Where to Dine

All restaurants, unless noted, are in Willemstad.

EXPENSIVE

Bistro Le Clochard *(★* FRENCH/SWISS This restaurant fits into the grim ramparts of Fort Rif, at the gateway to the harbor. Its canopied entrance leads to a series of rooms under the vaulting of the 19th-century Dutch fort. Several tables have a view of the Caribbean, but the outdoor terrace features a panorama of the town lights. Start with the fresh local fish soup. Alpine specialties include raclette (Swiss cheese melted over boiled potatoes, onions, and pickles) and a fondue bourguignonne (good, though heavy for the tropics). Many main courses—tournedos, sirloin, T-bone, chicken breast, and fresh fish—are cooked on a stone heated in the oven and brought to your table. Heavy or light, the food is reliable and good, although pricey.

Riffort, on the Otrabanda side of the pontoon bridge. ⓒ **599/9-462-5666.** Reservations recommended. Main courses $25–$35. AE, DISC, MC, V. Mon–Fri noon–2pm; Mon–Sat 6:30–10:45pm. Harborside Terrace Mon–Sat 2–11pm.

La Pergola ⓖ ITALIAN   Nestled in the weather-beaten core of the island's oldest fort, this trattoria has thrived for more than a decade. The eatery's centerpiece is a Renaissance-style pergola, or arbor. The kitchen and one of the three dining rooms are in the cellar; two others overlook the seafront. The menu changes daily but might include chicken gnocchi and fettuccine with ham, cream, and mushrooms. Some dishes have a touch of island panache, such as seafood-stuffed ravioli and red snapper in olive-tomato sauce.

In the Waterfront Arches, Waterfort Straat. ⓒ **599/9-461-3482.** Reservations recommended. Main courses $20–$33. AE, MC, V. Mon–Sat noon–11pm; Sun 6–11pm.

Wine Cellar ⓖ CONTINENTAL   Opposite the cathedral in the center of town, this restaurant boasts an extensive wine list and old-fashioned Dutch ambience. The kitchen turns out excellent lobster salad and sole meunière in butter-and-herb sauce. Other good choices include veal in red wine and pine-nut sauce, poached Norwegian salmon, and U.S. beef tenderloin with goat cheese sauce. Game dishes, imported throughout the year from Holland, include venison roasted with mushrooms.

Ooststraat/Concordiastraat. ⓒ **599/9-461-2178.** Reservations required. Main courses $23–$38. AE, MC, V. Mon–Fri noon–2:30pm and 7–10pm; Sat 7–11pm.

MODERATE

Belle Terrace ⓖ INTERNATIONAL   This open-air restaurant in a 200-year-old mansion overlooking the sea offers satisfying food in a relaxed atmosphere. Sheltered by an arbor of flamboyant branches, the restaurant features Scandinavian, Continental, and local cuisine with specialties such as pickled herring and smoked salmon. Local dishes include *keshi yena* (baked Gouda cheese with a spicy meat filling). The fish is always fresh, and the chef prepares a seafood platter to perfection: grilled, poached, or meunière.

In the Avila Beach Hotel, Penstraat 130. ⓒ **599/9-461-4377.** Reservations required. Main courses $15–$27; *menu dégustation* $27 for 2 courses, $32 for 3 courses. AE MC, V. Daily noon–2:30pm and 7–10pm.

Blues SEAFOOD/INTERNATIONAL   Perched over lapping water on a jutting pier, this restaurant features platters of fresh seafood that challenge even the heartiest appetite. The sapphire and aqua tile interior is accented with oversized blues and jazz album covers, echoing the live entertainment. Blue mussels are cooked in wine sauce with shallots and herbs; dorado comes with mustard-flavored beurre blanc (white butter). The "seafood challenge" of fresh seafood caught that day may include tuna, salmon, squid, langoustine, and scallops. Dessert lovers can forego a main course and plunge into the "Jam Session," a hefty sampling of every dessert on the menu.

In the Avila Beach Hotel, Penstraat 130. ✆ 599/9-461-4377. Reservations recommended. Main courses $16–$31; 2-course menu $30; 3-course menu $35. AE, MC, V. Daily 5–11pm.

Rijsttafel Restaurant Indonesia ✦ *Value* INDONESIAN   This is the best place in Curaçao to sample Indonesian rijsttafel, the traditional rice table with various zesty appetizer-size dishes. At lunchtime, the selection is comparatively modest, but for dinner, Javanese cooks prepare rijsttafel with 16, 20, or 25 dishes. There's even an all-vegetarian option. Season your plate with peppers rated hot, very hot, or palate-melting, and share the cornucopia with a group of friends. The spicy feast is a good change of pace after a week of seafood and steak.

Mercuriusstraat 13, Salinja. ✆ 599/9-461-2606. Reservations recommended. Main courses $16–$25; *rijsttafel* $22 for 16 dishes, $27 for 20 dishes, $43 for 25 dishes; vegetarian $23 for 16 dishes. AE, MC, V. Mon–Sat noon–2pm; daily 6–9:30pm.

INEXPENSIVE

Golden Star CREOLE   With the air of a Caribbean roadside diner, this restaurant is simple, but its Antillean dishes are tasty. Choose from *carco stoba* (conch stew), *bestia chiki* (goat meat stew), *bakijauw* (salted cod), and *concomber stoba* (stewed meat and spiny cucumbers). Everything comes with a side order of *funchi*, a cornmeal polenta. Diners are locals for the most part, with an occasional tourist.

Socratesstraat 2 (at Dr. Hugenholtzweg and Dr. Maalweg, southeast of Willemstad). ✆ 599/9-465-4795. Main courses $10–$30. AE, MC, V. Daily noon–1am.

4 Hitting the Beaches & Active Pursuits

BEACHES

Although Curaçao's beaches are inferior to Aruba's, there are nearly 40 of them, ranging from hotel sands to secluded coves. The northwest coast's rugged waters make swimming difficult, but the more tranquil waters of the west coast have sheltered bays that are good for swimming and snorkeling. The best beaches are along the southern coast, west of Willemstad.

Man-made **Seaquarium Beach,** just east of central Willemstad, charges $2.50 for beach-chair rental, changing facilities, and showers. Two bars, two restaurants, and a watersports shop are on site. The calm waters are ideal for swimming.

Northwest of Willemstad, **Blauwbaai** is the island's largest and most popular beach. Along with showers and changing facilities, there's plenty of shade. Head toward Juliandorp, then bear left for Blauwbaai and San Michiel.

Farther up the west coast, about 30 minutes from Willemstad in the Willibrordus area, **Daaibooi** draws crowds of locals on Sunday. Wooden umbrellas provide shade, but there are no showers or changing rooms. Rainbow-hued fish and coral attract snorkelers.

Family-friendly **Playa Lagun,** in the fishing village of Lagun, hides in a narrow cove and boasts tranquil, shallow water excellent for swimming. Snorkelers appreciate the plentiful marine life. Concrete huts provide shelter, and the snack bar opens on weekends.

Knip Bay, north of Playa Lagun, has white sand, rocky sides, and turquoise waters, making it suitable for snorkeling, swimming, and sunbathing. The beach is crowded on weekends, often with locals.

Playa Abao, or Playa Grandi, at the northern tip of the island, is one of Curaçao's most popular strands. Thatched shade umbrellas provide some protection, and there's a snack bar in the parking lot.

On the northwestern tip of the island, **Westpunt** is known for the Sunday divers who jump from its cliffs into the ocean—an amazing sight. Colorful boats and fishermen's nets adorn the area, which has no facilities or shade trees. The calm waters are great for swimming.

South of Willemsted, **Santa Barbara Beach** is owned by a mining company and near Table Mountain, an old phosphate mine. The beach has pure-white sand and calm water. Facilities include restrooms, changing rooms, a snack bar, and a terrace; water bicycles and small motorboats are available for rent.

OUTDOOR PURSUITS

CRUISES Taber Tours, Dokweg (© **599/9-737-6637**), offers a 5-hour sunset and snorkeling trip for $30 per person, $15 for children under 10 (Mon and Wed–Fri). A 2-hour sunset cruise, with wine and cheese, leaves at dusk on Friday; it's $32 for adults, $20 for children under 12. *Insulinde,* Handelskade (© **599/9-560-1340;** www.insulinde.com), a 36m (120-ft.) traditionally rigged clipper, offers afternoon, sunset, and dinner cruises, as well as longer excursions to Bonaire and Venezuela. Most trips include snorkeling, snacks, and beverages. Prices start at $43 per person (half price for kids) for a 4-hour afternoon snorkeling cruise.

WATERSPORTS   Seascape Dive and Watersports, at the Four Points Resort Curaçao (© **599/9-462-5905**), offers the most complete facilities. Snorkeling excursions are $25 per person, and jet-ski rentals are $40 per half-hour. Introductory scuba lessons go for $45, and four-dive packages are $110. If demand warrants it, Seascape also offers a $75 day trip to Little Curaçao—an uninhabited island just off the main island's eastern tip—for fishing, snorkeling, and sunbathing. Deep-sea fishing is $336 for a half-day tour (6-person maximum), $560 for a full-day tour, drinks and equipment included.

Curaçao is no match for Bonaire when it comes to marine environments, but scuba divers and snorkelers can still enjoy healthy reefs and good visibility. Stretching along 20km (12½ miles) of Curaçao's southern coastline, the **Curaçao Underwater Park** ⊛ features steep walls, shallow wrecks, gardens of soft coral, and more than 30 species of hard coral. A snorkel trail with underwater interpretive markers is laid out just east of the Princess Beach Resort & Casino and is accessible from shore.

WINDSURFING   Top Watersports Curaçao (© **599/9-461-7343**), at Seaquarium Beach, is the island's best windsurfing center. Equipment is $15 per hour, plus a refundable $60 deposit. Lessons are available.

5 Exploring the Island

Venture out into the countryside and explore the towering cacti and rolling hills topped by *landhuizen* (plantation houses) built more than 3 centuries ago. There's more to Curaçao than Willemstad, but our tour starts there.

WILLEMSTAD

Originally founded as Santa Ana by the Spanish in the 1500s, Willemstad was renamed in the 17th century by Dutch traders, who found the natural harbor a perfect hideaway along the Spanish Main. Willemstad's historic pastel-colored, red-roofed town houses and natural harbor are on UNESCO's World Heritage List.

Hemmed in by the sea, a tiny canal, and an inlet, the narrow streets are crosshatched by still narrower alleyways.

Take the 75-minute **trolley tour,** which visits the city's highlights. The open-sided cars, pulled by a silent "locomotive," make several trips each week. The tours are offered between 8:30am and 4pm and begin at Fort Amsterdam near the Queen Emma Pontoon Bridge. The cost is $10 for adults, $5 for children ages 2 to 12. Call © 599/9-462-8833 for information.

The city grew up on both sides of the canal. **Punda** has Old World Dutch ambience and the best shopping; **Otrabanda** ("the other side") is more modern. **Queen Emma Pontoon Bridge** connects the two districts. The **statue of Pedro Luis Brion** dominates the square known as Brionplein, at the Otrabanda end of the pontoon bridge. Born in Curaçao in 1782, Brion became the island's favorite son and best-known war hero. Under Simón Bolívar, he was an admiral and fought for the independence of Venezuela and Colombia.

Fort Amsterdam, site of the Governor's Palace and the 1769 Dutch Reformed church, guards the waterfront. The church still has a British cannonball embedded in it, and the arches leading to the fort were tunneled under the official residence of the governor.

A few minutes' walk from the pontoon bridge, at the north end of Handelskade, the **Floating Market** features scores of schooners tied up alongside the canal. Boats arrive here from Venezuela and Colombia, and from other West Indian islands, to sell tropical fruits and vegetables, as well as handcrafts.

Near Fort Amsterdam, at the corner of Columbusstraat and Hanchi di Snoa, the **Mikve Israel-Emanuel Synagogue** ⊛ (© 599/9-461-1067) dates from 1651 and is the New World's oldest Jewish congregation. Joaño d'Illan led the first Jewish settlers to the island in 1651, almost half a century after their expulsion from Portugal by the Inquisition. Next door, the **Jewish Cultural Historical Museum,** Kuiperstraat 26–28 (© 599/9-461-1633), occupies two buildings dating from 1728. On display are ritual and cultural objects, many dating from the 17th and 18th centuries but still used by the congregation. The synagogue and museum are open Monday through Friday from 9 to 11:45am and 2:30 to 4:45pm. Services are Friday at 6:30pm and Saturday at 10am. Museum admission is $2.

Museum Kurá Hulanda ⊛, Kipstraat 9 (© 599/9-434-7765), is one of the most unusual and largest museums in the Caribbean. Housed in once-dilapidated 19th-century buildings, the exhibits here reflect the passion of Dr. Jacob Gelt Dekker, who's spent much of his life roaming Africa in search of cultural artifacts. His collection includes a life-size reconstruction of a slave ship that once sailed from the Ivory Coast, fossils, wood masks, fertility dolls, stone sculptures, and musical instruments. Hours are Monday to Saturday 10am to 5pm, and the entrance fee is $6 for adults, $3 for children.

WEST OF WILLEMSTAD

You can walk from the Queen Emma pontoon bridge to the **Curaçao Museum,** Van Leeuwenhoekstraat (© **599/9-462-3873**). Built in 1853 by the Royal Dutch Army Corps of Engineers as a military quarantine hospital, the building has been restored and now houses paintings, art objects, and antique furniture. There's also a large collection of indigenous Amerindian artifacts. It's open Monday to Friday from 8:30am to 4:30pm, Sunday from 10am to 4pm. Admission is $3 for adults, $1.75 for children under 14.

The **Maritime Museum,** Van De Brandhof Straat 7 (© **599/ 9-465-2327**), in the historic Scharloo district, just off the old harbor of St. Anna Bay, boasts 40 permanent displays that trace Curaçao's history. Admission is $6 for adults, $4 for children 12 to 16, free for children under 12. Hours are Tuesday to Saturday from 10am to 5pm.

On Schottegatweg West, northwest of Willemstad, **Beth Haim Cemetery** is the oldest European burial site still in use in the Western hemisphere. Consecrated before 1659, the 3-acre site has 2,500 graves, some with exceptional tombstones.

Toward the western tip of Curaçao, a 45-minute drive from Willemstad, 4,500-acre **Christoffel National Park** 𝕮𝕮 in Savonet (© **599/9-864-0363**) features cacti, bromeliads, and orchids, as well as the Dutch Leewards' highest point, St. Christoffelberg (369m/1,230 ft.). Donkeys, wild goats, iguanas, Curaçao deer, and many species of birds thrive in the arid countryside, and Arawak paintings adorn a coral cliff near two caves. The 32km (20 miles) of one-way trail-like roads pass the highlights, but the rough terrain makes even the shortest trail (8km/5 miles) a 40-minute drive. Hiking trails include a 1½-hour climb to the summit of **St. Christoffelberg.** The park is open Monday to Saturday from 7:30am to 4pm, Sunday from 6am to 3pm, but go early, before it gets too hot. The $10 entrance fee includes admission to the museum.

NORTH & EAST OF WILLEMSTAD

Just northeast of the capital, **Fort Nassau** was completed in 1797 and christened Fort Republic. Built high on a hill overlooking the harbor entrance to the south and St. Anna Bay to the north, it was fortified as a second line of defense in case the waterfront gave way.

The **Curaçao Liqueur Distillery,** Landhuis Chobolobo, Saliña Arriba (② 599/9-461-3526), operates in a 17th-century *landhuis* where Curaçao's famous liqueur is made. Distilled from dried Curaçaon orange peel, the cordial is spiced with several herbs. The tour, offered Monday to Friday from 8am to noon and 1 to 5pm, ends with a free snifter of the liqueur.

Curaçao Seaquarium, off Dr. Martin Luther King Boulevard at Bapor Kibrá (② 599/9-461-6666), displays more than 400 species of fish, crabs, anemones, sponges, and coral. Located a few minutes' walk along the rocky coast from the Breezes Curaçao Resort, the Seaquarium is open daily from 8:30am to 4:30pm. Admission is $13 for adults, $7.25 for children under 15. Divers, snorkelers, and experienced swimmers can feed, film, and photograph sharks through a large window with feeding holes and swim with stingrays, lobsters, tarpons, and parrotfish in a separate controlled environment. The experience is $58 for divers, $30 for snorkelers. The Seaquarium also boasts Curaçao's only full-facility, palm-shaded, white-sand beach.

Guides at the **Hato Caves** ⨀, F. D. Rooseveltweg (② 599/9-868-0379), take visitors through the stalagmites and stalactites of Curaçao's highest limestone terrace. Featuring an underground lake, large rooms, and ancient Indian petroglyphic drawings, the caves are open daily from 10am to 4pm; admission is $6.50 for adults, $5 for children ages 4 to 11.

6 Shopping

Willemstad's shops concentrate along Heerenstraat and Breedestraat in the **Punda** shopping district. Most stores are open Monday through Saturday from 8am to noon and 2 to 6pm (some stay open at midday). When cruise ships are in port, many shops open for a few hours on Sunday and holidays as well.

Good buys include French perfumes, Dutch Delft blue china, Italian silks, Japanese and German cameras, jewelry, watches, linens, leather goods, and liquor, especially Curaçao liqueur. The island is famous for its 5-pound wheels of Gouda and Edam cheeses, and you'll also see wooden shoes, lacework, woodcarvings, and paintings from Haiti and the Dominican Republic.

Curaçao Creations, Schrijnwerkerstraat 14, off Breedestraat (② 599/9-462-4516), showcases authentic handcrafts that are made at the on-site workshop.

Every garment at **Bamali,** Breedestraat 2 (© **599/9-461-2258**), is designed and, in many cases, crafted by the store owners. Based on Indonesian patterns, the airy women's clothing includes V-neck cotton pullovers and linen shifts.

Gandelman Jewelers, Breedestraat 35, Punda (© **599/9-461-1854**), is the island's best and most reliable source for diamonds, rubies, emeralds, sapphires, and other gemstones. You'll also find watches and leather goods.

Penha & Sons, Heerenstraat 1 (© **599/9-461-2266**), is known for perfumes, cosmetics, and designer clothing for men and women.

7 Curaçao After Dark

Most of the action spins around the island's **casinos.** The fun usually starts at 2pm, and some places remain open until 4am. The casino at the **Breezes Curaçao Resort,** Dr. Martin Luther King Blvd. 8 (© **599/9-736-7888**), is the liveliest on the island. The **Emerald Casino** at the Curaçao Marriott Beach Resort, Piscadera Bay (© **599/9-736-8800**), features slot machines, roulette wheels, and tables for blackjack, Caribbean stud poker, craps, baccarat, and minibaccarat. Other casinos are at the **Holiday Beach Hotel & Casino,** Pater Euwensweg 31, Otrabanda (© **599/9-462-5400**), and the **Plaza Hotel & Casino,** Plaza Piar, Willemstad (© **599/9-461-2500**).

The **Salinja** district is the heart of Curaçao nightlife. One of its best venues, **Blues,** a restaurant and bar (see "Where to Dine," earlier in this chapter) in the Avila Beach Hotel, Penstraat 130 (© **599/9-461-4377**), is packed every night except Monday. Live jazz plays Thursday from 7pm to midnight and Saturday from 9pm to 1:30am. There's no cover charge.

Façade, Lindbergh 32 (© **599/9-461-4640**), a popular disco with several levels, has a huge bar, three dance floors, and live music. It's open Wednesday to Sunday from 8pm to 3am. The cover is $5 to $10.

10

A Side Trip to Bonaire

There's no better place to find out what's going on under the Caribbean's azure waters than Bonaire—"Diver's Paradise," as the island's license plate claims. Bonaire has none of Aruba's glitzy diversions, but avid divers have flocked to this unspoiled treasure for years. With its pristine waters, stunning coral reefs, and vibrant marine life, Bonaire is one of the best places in the Caribbean for both diving and snorkeling. Reefs encircle the island just feet from shore, making this one of the easiest places on the planet to dive 24 hours a day.

Fifty miles north of Venezuela and 86 miles east of Aruba, Bonaire is the "B" of the ABC Dutch islands. Its small-scale tourism industry revolves around underwater activities, but the island also offers hiking, mountain biking, kayaking, and first-rate windsurfing. Bonaire's coral-strewn beaches can't compare with Aruba's, but they're intimate and uncrowded.

Shaped like a boomerang, Bonaire is slightly larger than Aruba, just 39km (24 miles) long and 5km to 11km (3 miles–7 miles) wide. Iguanas, parrots, lizards, donkeys, and flamingos populate the parched countryside, where cacti and permanently windswept divi divi trees vie for water.

Traveling from Venezuela by boat a thousand years ago, Amerindians (known as Caiquetios) were Bonaire's first human inhabitants. Amerigo Vespucci, the first European, arrived in the name of Spain in 1499. The Spanish enslaved the indigenous people and moved them to other Caribbean islands. Later, the Europeans used the island to raise cows, goats, horses, and donkeys. The Dutch gained control in the 1630s, and, on the back of African slave labor, Bonaire became an important salt producer. Tourism, the island's major industry today, developed after World War II, when self-rule was granted (the island remains a Dutch protectorate). The 14,000 people of Bonaire claim Dutch, South American, and African roots.

1 Essentials

VISITOR INFORMATION

Before you go, contact the **Bonaire Government Tourist Office,** Adams Unlimited, 10 Rockefeller Plaza, Suite 900, New York, NY 10020 (© **800/BONAIRE** or 212/956-5912; fax 212/956-5913). The **Tourism Corporation Bonaire'**s informative website (**www. infobonaire.com**) has links to other helpful sites. On the island, the **Tourism Corporation Bonaire** is at Kaya Grandi 2 in Kralendijk (*crawl*-en-dike), the capital and major town (© **599/717-8322**).

GETTING THERE

Three airlines now connect Aruba and Bonaire: **Dutch Caribbean Airlines** (© **800/327-7230;** 297/583-8080 in Aruba; www.flydca. net), **Avia Air** (© **297/583-4600**), and **Royal Aruban Airlines** (© **297/588-3300;** www.royalarubanairlines.com). Most flights stop in Curaçao on the way, but there are nonstops as well. Flights leave several times a day. Nonstops take 35 minutes; flights stopping in Curaçao take 1 hour and 10 minutes. From the United States, Dutch Caribbean Airlines offers daily flights from Miami. Through its American Eagle subsidiary, **American Airlines** (© **800/433-7300;** www.aa.com) has nonstop service from San Juan, Puerto Rico, on Tuesday, Thursday, and Saturday. Flights from numerous U.S. cities feed into **Air Jamaica'**s (© **800/523-5585;** www.air jamaica.com) nonstop flight from Montego Bay on Wednesday, Saturday, and Sunday.

GETTING AROUND

BY RENTAL CAR   Bonaire is flat, and the roads are fine, except the rocky trails in the outback. Highway signs are in Dutch and sometimes English, with easy-to-understand international symbols. Driving is on the right, and a valid driver's license is all that's needed to rent and drive a car. Car-rental agencies include **Avis** (© **800/230-4898** in the U.S., or 599/717-5795; www.avis.com); **Budget** (© **800/527-0700** in the U.S., or 599/717-4700; www.budgetrent acar.com); **Hertz** (© **800/654-3001** in the U.S., or **599/717-7221;** www.hertz.com); and **National** (© **800/CAR-RENT** in the U.S., or 599/717-7940; www.nationalcar.com). Rates start at $40 per day, $60 to $70 for a four-wheel-drive vehicle.

BY TAXI   Taxis are unmetered, but drivers charge uniform, government-authorized rates. The fare from the airport to most hotels is $7 to $18. Fares increase by 20% between 7pm and midnight, by 50% from midnight to 7am. Most drivers give tours of the island

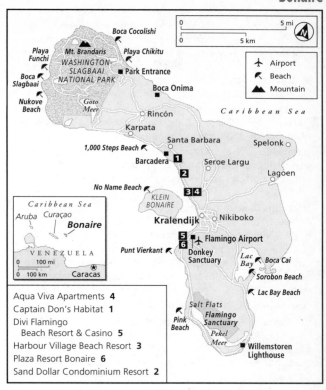

Bonaire

0	5 mi
0	5 km

✈ Airport
ㅅ Beach
▲ Mountain

Boca Cocolishi
Playa Funchi
Mt. Brandaris
WASHINGTON-SLAGBAAI NATIONAL PARK
Playa Chikitu
Boca Slagbaai
■ Park Entrance
Nukove Beach
Boca Onima ■
Goto Meer
○ Rincón
Caribbean Sea
Karpata
1,000 Steps Beach
Santa Barbara
Spelonk ○
Barcadera **1**
Seroe Largu ○
Lagoen ○
2
No Name Beach
KLEIN BONAIRE
3 **4**
Kralendijk
○ Nikiboko
Caribbean Sea
Aruba Curaçao
Bonaire
VENEZUELA
0   100 mi
0   100 km
Caracas
5
6 ✈ Flamingo Airport
Punt Vierkant
Donkey Sanctuary
Lac Bay
Boca Cai
Sorobon Beach
Lac Bay Beach

Aqua Viva Apartments **4**
Captain Don's Habitat **1**
Divi Flamingo
 Beach Resort & Casino **5**
Harbour Village Beach Resort **3**
Plaza Resort Bonaire **6**
Sand Dollar Condominium Resort **2**

Salt Flats
Flamingo Sanctuary
Pink Beach
Pekel Meer
Willemstoren Lighthouse

for $25 per hour. For more information, call **Taxi Central Dispatch**
(✆ **599/717-8100**).

BY SCOOTER OR MOPED   If you're not venturing too far,
scooters and mopeds are practical alternatives. You can rent one
from **Hot Shot Scooters,** Kaya Bonaire 4C (✆ **599/717-7166**).
Mopeds are $18 a day; two-seat scooters are $38.

 FAST FACTS: Bonaire

Banks Banks are open Monday through Friday from 8 or
8:30am until 3:30 or 4pm. ATMs are along Kaya Grandi in Kralendijk and at the airport.

Currency Bonaire's official currency is the Netherlands Antillean florin (NAf). Don't waste time exchanging money, though—the U.S. dollar is as widely accepted as the local currency. The exchange rate is 1.78 florins to US$1 (NAf 1 = 56¢). Most stores and businesses convert at 1.75 florins to the dollar. Traveler's checks and credit cards are widely accepted.

Customs Besides articles for personal use, visitors can bring in 400 cigarettes, 50 cigars, 250 grams of tobacco, 2 liters of distilled alcohol, and 2 liters of wine.

Documents U.S. and Canadian citizens need a valid passport or a birth certificate with a picture ID; British subjects need a valid passport. All visitors must produce a return or ongoing ticket as well.

Electricity Bonaire's electricity (127 volts/50 cycles) is slightly different from North America's (110 volts/60 cycles). Some North American appliances function without a transformer but may run warm or burn out if left plugged in for a long time. Although many laptop computers have universal power supplies, power surges and brownouts occur; use a surge protector.

Emergencies Call ☎ **133** for the police or an ambulance.

Hospital **San Francisco Hospital,** Kaya Soeur Bartola 2, Kralendijk (☎ **599/717-8900**), handles most emergencies and has a hyperbaric recompression chamber for divers suffering from the bends. An evacuation plane takes seriously ill patients to Curaçao.

Language English is widely spoken, but you'll hear Dutch (the official language), Spanish, and Papiamento (the tongue spoken in Aruba and Curaçao, with local spelling and pronunciation variations).

Safety Bonaire is safe, but keep an eye on your valuables and use your hotel's safe.

Taxes Virtually all goods and services are subject to a 5% tax. A room tax of $6.50 per person per day is also charged. The international and Aruban departure tax is $20 per person; for flights to Curaçao, it's $5.75.

Telephone To call Bonaire from the United States, dial **011** (the international access code), **599** (the country code), **717** (the area code), and then the four-digit local number. On Bonaire, dial the four-digit local number only. You can reach

AT&T Direct by dialing ✆ **001-800/872-2881**. It's often difficult to make international calls from hotel rooms, and lines aren't always clear. If you're having a problem, contact **TELBO** (✆ **599/717-7000**), the central phone company on Kaya Libertador Simón Bolívar.

Time Bonaire is on Atlantic Standard time year-round, 1 hour ahead of Eastern Standard time and the same as Eastern daylight saving time.

Tipping Tipping is much the same as in the U.S., with some restaurants adding a 10% to 15% service charge automatically. Taxi drivers and dive masters expect a 10% tip.

Water Drinking water is distilled seawater and perfectly safe.

Weather The year-round temperature averages 82°F (28°C), and annual rainfall is only 22 inches. Trade winds make evenings pleasant, and the island is outside the hurricane belt.

2 Where to Stay

VERY EXPENSIVE

Harbour Village Beach Resort 🕊🕊   Easily Bonaire's most luxurious resort, Harbour Village caters to an ultra-upscale clientele. The cluster of Dutch Caribbean–style one- and two-bedroom suites rests in lush tropical gardens bordered by a sandy beach and picturesque marina. Most guests come from the U.S., many to dive but a good number to pamper themselves at the spa, which boasts the island's most comprehensive array of massages and other treatments. Each suite has a spacious balcony or terrace (with hammock) and beach or marina views. The stylish rooms, completely renovated in 2001, boast teak furniture and four-poster beds. Other features include commodious closets, large glass-enclosed showers, separate claw-foot tubs, and fully equipped kitchens with state-of-the-art appliances.

Kaya Gobernador N. Debrot 72, Bonaire, N.A. ✆ **800/424-0004** in the U.S. and Canada, or 599/717-7500. Fax 599/717-7507. www.harbourvillage.com. 46 units. Dec 20–Jan 2 $520–$595 1-bedroom suite, $830 2-bedroom suite; Jan 3–Mar $470–$545 1-bedroom suite, $780 2-bedroom suite; Apr–Dec 20 $370–$445 1-bedroom suite, $625 2-bedroom suite. Children under 12 stay free in parent's room. Packages available. AE, MC, V. **Amenities:** 2 restaurants (international, casual waterfront); 2 bars; 3 outdoor pools; Bonaire's best tennis facilities (4 courts lit for night play, resident pro); health club and spa; watersports; bike rental; children's program during high season; game room; concierge; tour/activities desk; car-rental desk; courtesy car; shopping arcade; salon; limited room service; babysitting; laundry service; dry cleaning; nonsmoking rooms; wheelchair-accessible rooms. *In room:* A/C, TV, kitchen, hair dryer, iron, safe.

EXPENSIVE

Captain Don's Habitat ⊀ Built on a coral bluff overlooking the sea just north of Kralendijk, this informal, congenial dive resort was created by Captain Don Stewart, Caribbean legend, former Californian, and the godfather of Bonaire's passionate protection of its marine environment. More than 90% of guests come on vacation-length dive packages, so side-trip stays of 1 or 2 nights are hard to arrange. The accommodations, which include cottages and one- and two-bedroom villas, are bright and airy. All have a balcony or patio, many feature fully equipped kitchens, and some have phones. All rooms except the cottage living rooms have air-conditioning; some units hold ceiling fans. Primarily from the U.S., guests are avid divers more concerned about what's going on underwater than what's happening topside. The resort's tiny beach is good for snorkeling.

Kaya Gobernador N. Debrot 103, Bonaire, N.A. © **800/327-6709** in the U.S. and Canada, or 599/717-8290. Fax 599/717-8240. www.habitatdiveresorts.com. 82 units. Rates for 4-night stays: Jan–Mar $615–$800 per person; Apr–Dec $500–$660 per person. Rates based on double occupancy and include breakfast, airport transfers, tax, service, equipment, 4 boat dives, and unlimited shore dives. Children under 12 stay free in parent's room. AE, DISC, MC, V. **Amenities:** Restaurant; pizza bar; outdoor bar; outdoor pool; bike rental; children's program; tour/activities desk; car-rental desk; courtesy car; babysitting; laundry service; dry cleaning; wheelchair-accessible rooms. *In room:* TV, dataport, hair dryer (on request), iron (on request), safe.

Plaza Resort Bonaire ⊀⊀ Bonaire's only large-scale, full-service, Aruba-style luxury resort, the Plaza sprawls over 12 acres of tropical grounds bordered by a saltwater lagoon and a long stretch of natural beach. The nine two-story buildings have white walls and terra-cotta roofs, creating a sunny village connected by a pair of bridges that cross the lagoon, the site of a full-service dive and boat shop. Guests are a mix of Americans and Europeans, divers and nondivers. In the rooms, terra cotta–tile floors, slatted-wood ceilings, rattan furniture, and spacious balconies or terraces emphasize the tropical locale. Although the units referred to as "suites" have no room dividers, they boast 180 sq. m to 210 sq. m (600 sq. ft.–700 sq. ft.) of space. Suites feature fridges, and the larger one- and two-bedroom villas boast kitchenettes. All units have grand bathrooms.

J. A. Abraham Blvd. 80, Bonaire, N.A. (*) **800/766-6016** in the U.S. and Canada, or 599/717-2500. Fax 599/717-7133. www.plazaresortbonaire.com. 174 units. Dec–Apr $205–$245 double, $270–$290 1-bedroom villa, $340–$370 2-bedroom villa; May–Nov $155–$195 double, $210–$230 1-bedroom villa, $280–$310 2-bed-room villa. Children under 13 stay free in parent's room. Packages available. AE, MC, V. **Amenities:** 3 restaurants (international, oceanside, tropical); 3 bars; casino; large outdoor pool; children's pool; 4 tennis courts lit for night play; exercise room; spa; extensive watersports; scooter and bike rental; children's program; concierge; tour/activities desk; car-rental desk; salon; limited room service; babysitting; laundry service; dry cleaning; wheelchair-accessible rooms. *In room:* A/C, TV, kitchenette in some units, fridge, hair dryer, iron (on request), safe.

MODERATE

Divi Flamingo Beach Resort & Casino (*)   Having risen from the ashes of neglect, the cheery, comfortable Divi Flamingo might more appropriately be called the Divi Phoenix. Dark and dank before major renovations in 2001, this unpretentious hotel boasts bright, colorful rooms with white-tile floors, attractive floral prints, and good-size bathrooms. Every unit features a balcony or terrace that overlooks the sea or tropical gardens, and the pink, ochre, and cobalt-blue exterior walls maintain the upbeat tone. The Divi Flamingo also offers a small but sandy beach, a sunbathing pier, a "barefoot" casino, and a full-service dive shop (the only one on the island that's wheelchair accessible). In addition to standard rooms, the hotel has 40 studios with kitchenettes.

J. A. Abraham Blvd. 40, Bonaire, N.A. (*) **800/367-3484** in the U.S. and Canada, or 599/717-8285. Fax 599/717-8238. www.diviresorts.com. 129 units. Dec–Apr $130–$170 double, $190 studio; May–Nov $110–$120 double, $140 studio. Children under 16 stay free in parent's room. Packages available. AE, DISC, MC, V. **Amenities:** 2 restaurants (seaside terrace, breakfast); 3 bars; casino; 2 outdoor pools; car-rental desk; salon; massage; babysitting; laundry service; dry cleaning; wheelchair-accessible rooms. *In room:* A/C, TV, dataport, safe.

Sand Dollar Condominium Resort (*) (Kids)   The comfortable, casual Sand Dollar is a favorite with repeat visitors. Almost all guests are from the U.S., and the hotel's extensive children's programs attract families. Decor varies in each of the individually owned studios and one-, two-, and three-bedroom apartments. All units feature a terrace or balcony, full kitchen, and good-size bedrooms, but no phones. The huge bathrooms have showers and tubs. At high tide, water engulfs the tiny beach, but most people are here to dive, and the resort's dive shop is one of the island's best. The on-site tour operator offers an array of island adventures.

Kaya Gobernador N. Debrot 79, Bonaire, N.A. (*) **800/288-4773** in the U.S. and Canada, or 599/717-8738. Fax 599/717-8760. www.sanddollarbonaire.com.

86 units. Dec–Apr $160–$176 double, $195–$215 1-bedroom, $220–$242 2-bedroom, $330–$363 3-bedroom; May–Nov $150 double, $175 1-bedroom, $210 2-bedroom, $315 3-bedroom. Children under 12 stay free in parent's room. Packages available. AE, DISC, MC, V. **Amenities:** Restaurant; 2 bars; outdoor pool; 2 tennis courts lit for night play; extensive watersports; bike rental; excellent children's program; extensive adventure-tour operator; babysitting; laundry service; dry cleaning. *In room:* A/C in bedrooms only, ceiling fans, TV, kitchen, iron on request, safe.

INEXPENSIVE

Aqua Viva Apartments   Although this no-frills apartment complex has few amenities, it offers attractive dive, windsurfing, and adventure packages that include a rental car. The best deals are for stays of at least a week, but non-package rates are almost as good. The large rooms feature bold colors, rattan furniture, and high ceilings. All apartments boast front porches and full kitchens, and have air-conditioning in the bedrooms only. There are no phones, and the simple bathrooms have showers only. Beaches, a marina, tennis courts, dive operators, a minimart, a bank, and several restaurants are a 5-minute walk away.

Kaya Gobernador N. Debrot 60, Bonaire, N.A. ℂ **599/717-5945.** Fax 599/717-7273. www.aquavivabonaire.com. 10 apts. Dec–Apr $70 1-bedroom, $100 2-bedroom; May–Nov $55 1-bedroom, $85 2-bedroom. Rates are per night per apartment and based on 1-week stay. Packages available. AE, DISC, MC, V. **Amenities:** Access to nearby pool; babysitting; laundry service; dry cleaning. *In room:* Ceiling fans, TV, kitchen, no phones.

3 Where to Dine

MODERATE

Capriccio 🅰🅰 NORTHERN ITALIAN   One of Bonaire's most popular restaurants, Capriccio has served impeccably fresh Northern Italian cuisine on the harborfront for almost a decade. Originally from Padua and Milan, the restaurateurs offer savory salads, homemade pastas, straight-from-the-oven focaccia, and thin-crust pizzas for lighter appetites. More substantial fare includes flavorful mahimahi braised in onion, olives, and sun-dried tomatoes, and braised duck in port-wine sauce. The 8,000-bottle wine cellar holds Italian, Californian, and French vintages, and the grappa and brandy list, although not as extensive, is formidable. Savoring the chocolate mousse is like mainlining sugar. Dining areas include an alfresco terrace, a cozy air-conditioned interior bathed in flickering candlelight, and raised, dimly lit alcoves inside for special occasions.

Kaya Isla Riba 1, Kralendijk. ℂ 599/717-7230. Reservations recommended. Pizzas and pastas $9–$21; main courses $20–$23. AE, MC, V. Mon and Wed–Sat noon–2pm; Wed–Mon 6:30–10:30pm.

Den Laman Restaurant *(Kids* SEAFOOD   Located next to the Sand Dollar Condominium Resort, Den Laman serves some of the best seafood in Bonaire and features the island's only lobster tank. The conch marinated in coconut-cilantro vinaigrette with salsa picante on the side is a good start. Follow with red snapper meunière, or pick a lobster from the tank. Other dishes include grouper Creole and New York sirloin steak. Refreshing key lime pie ends the meal on a tangy note. Tables hover over the sea on a breezy terrace. The long-in-the-tooth aquarium, seashells, and kids' menu are popular with tykes and tots.

Kaya Gobernador N. Debrot 77, Kralendijk. 🕐 **599/717-8955.** Main courses $16–$45. AE, MC, V. Wed–Mon 5–11pm. Closed Sept 1–22.

Le Wok *(★(★* INDIAN/THAI/FRENCH   In a beautiful 200-year-old colonial mansion across the street from the sea, Le Wok serves expertly seasoned French, Indian, and Thai dishes lovingly prepared by Lucille Martijn, one of the island's trailblazing restaurateur-chefs. Despite the stark, modern beauty of the interior dining room, most guests opt to dine on one of three tranquil garden terraces, where fairy lights glow and breezes cool. "Treasures of the sea" soup combines fish, scallops, squid, shrimp, and crabs with onions, leeks, white wine, coconut milk, and curry. Thai curry or Indian biryani sauce seasons fish, chicken, shrimp, lamb, and vegetables; French specialties include sautéed duck breast with orange and Grand Marnier sauce. A favorite dessert is crepes with cherries flambé.

Kaya C. E. B. Hellmund 19, Kralendijk. 🕐 **599/717-7884.** Reservations recommended. Main courses $10–$27. AE, MC, V. Wed–Mon 6–11pm.

Rendez-Vous *(★* INTERNATIONAL/SEAFOOD   This intimate, casually elegant bistro specializes in seafood with both tropical and Northern European accents. For starters, try smoked marlin in coconut dressing or escargots with mild sauerkraut, garlic, and cheese. Seafood lovers should sample rainbow runner in lemon and butter sauce, or puff pastry wahoo in a creamy white wine sauce. Oven-baked beef tenderloin topped with brie gets rave reviews from carnivores. Save room for superb flan, cheesecake, or chocolate mousse. Dine in the airy, rustic interior or on the breeze-cooled terrace.

Kaya L. D. Gerharts 3, Kralendijk. 🕐 **599/717-8454.** Reservations recommended. Main courses $16–$23. AE, MC, V. Mon–Fri noon–2pm; Mon–Sat 6–10:30pm.

INEXPENSIVE

Kon Tiki *(★ (Finds* INTERNATIONAL   If you're headed to Lac Bay to windsurf, make a point of stopping at this charming oasis in

Bonaire's outback. Kon Tiki offers casual dining at its best: beach-bum cheerful decor, pleasant ambience, stunning vistas, cool breezes, and scrumptious food. Creamy lemon soup and a smoked salmon sandwich washed down with a mango shake are perfect on a hot day and, at under $15, reasonably priced. The expanded dinner menu features Bonairean stews, vegetarian pastas, Argentine steak, and a variety of fresh seafood. Sugar addicts relish the dessert sampler—a little bit of apple pie, pumpkin fritters, cheesecake, and tiramisu for you alone. There's a special menu for the little ones, and on the first Sunday of each month, jazz, salsa, and bossa nova combos play on the outdoor patio.

Kaminda Sorobon 64, Sorobon. © 599/717-5369. Dinner reservations recommended. Dinner main courses $14–$18. MC, V. Tues–Sun noon–3pm and 6–10pm.

4 Diving & Other Outdoor Pursuits
DIVING & SNORKELING

Bonaire has 80 dive sites and a rich marine ecosystem that includes brain, elkhorn, staghorn, mountainous star, gorgonian, and black coral; anemones, sea cucumbers, and sea sponges; parrotfish, surgeonfish, angelfish, groupers, blennies, frogfish, and yellowtails; and morays and sea snakes. Created in 1980 to protect the island's coral-reef ecosystem, **Bonaire Marine Park** ℛ incorporates the entire coastlines of both Bonaire and Klein Bonaire, the small uninhabited island opposite Kralendijk. Collecting shells or coral is prohibited, as are spearfishing and anchoring (boats use permanent moorings).

Dive shops are numerous and highly professional. Expect to pay $35 to $50 for a one-tank dive (equipment extra) and $100 for an introductory resort course (equipment included). Every operation offers multiple dive packages.

Great Adventures at Harbour Village, Kaya Gobernador N. Debrot 72 (© **800/868-7477** in the U.S. and Canada, or 599/717-7500), is the island's poshest operation. It's upscale but unpretentious and friendly. In addition to two of the island's most beautiful boats, it boasts a first-class photo shop that rents underwater still and video cameras.

Sand Dollar Dive & Photo, Kaya Gobernador N. Debrot 77 (© **599/717-5433**), is popular with return visitors and offers comparable services. The San Dollar Condominium Resort's "Sand Penny" children's program is a godsend for parents who want to dive without worrying about the kids.

Habitat Dive Center, Kaya Gobernador N. Debrot 103 (© **800/ 327-6709** in the U.S., or 599/717-8290), attracts diving fanatics, including disciples of Captain Don Stewart, an island icon and the driving force behind the Marine Park. The full-service shop includes a photo shop and lab and equipment repair.

Thanks to shallow-water coral reefs, snorkelers can enjoy Bonaire's awesome marine environment, too. The island's **Guided Snorkeling Program** includes a slide-show introduction to reef fishes, corals, and sponges, an in-water demonstration of snorkeling skills, and a guided tour of one of several sites. The cost is $25 per person. Equipment rental is about $10 more. You can arrange a tour through any of the dive shops listed above or through **Buddy Dive Resort,** Kaya Gobernador N. Debrot 85 (© **800/934-DIVE** in the U.S., or 599/717-5080); **Bon Bini Divers,** at the Lions Dive Hotel Bonaire, Kaya Gobernador N. Debrot 90 (© **800/327-5424** in the U.S., or 599/717-5425); **Carib Inn,** J. A. Abraham Boulevard (© **599/717-8819**); or **Dive Inn,** Kaya C. E. B. Hellmund 27 (© **599/717-8761**). The more adventurous can purchase a map that marks all the dive sites on Bonaire, most of which are excellent for snorkeling (as well as diving) and can be reached by wading into the water.

BEACHES

Bonaire's beaches are narrow and full of coral, but they're clean, intimate, and uncrowded. Swimming on the tranquil leeward coast is never a problem, but the east coast is rough and dangerous.

Pink Beach 𝒦, south of Kralendijk, is the island's best strand. Aptly named, the sand turns pink as the sun sets. No refreshment stands or equipment rentals mar the panoramic setting, so bring a cooler and towels. Bring sun protection, too: The few palm trees offer little shade. The southern end has less exposed rock. Crowded with Bonaireans on weekends, it's yours alone during the week. The strong steady winds make it an excellent locale for kite-flying.

North of Kralendijk, stairs descend a limestone cliff to the white sand of **1,000 Steps Beach,** which offers good snorkeling and diving, and nearly perfect solitude. The picturesque coves, craggy coastline, and tropical waters of changing hues don't get much better, but there are no facilities.

Farther north, Washington-Slagbaai National Park boasts a number of beaches. **Boca Slagbaai,** once a plantation harbor, draws snorkelers and picnickers. A 19th-century building houses toilets, showers, and a snack bar. Be careful venturing into the water bare-foot, though: The coral bottom can be sharp. The island's north-ernmost beach, **Boca Cocolishi,** is a perfect spot to picnic; the calm, shallow basin is good for snorkeling, but stay close to shore. Algae make the water purplish, and the sand, formed by coral and mollusk shells, is black. The water's treacherous at **Playa Chikitu,** but the cove, sand dunes, and crashing waves are secluded and beautiful.

The water at **Lac Bay Beach** is only .6m (2 ft.) deep, making it popular with families and windsurfers. In a protected area of Bonaire's southeast coast, it boasts windsurfing concessions and snack bars. Trees provide shade.

Klein Bonaire ⋒, less than a mile west of Kralendijk, boasts **No Name Beach,** which features a 273m (300-yd.) white-sand strip. Parrotfish and yellowtail snappers patrol the finger, brain, and mus-tard hill corals, attracting snorkelers and divers. There are no facili-ties or shade.

OTHER OUTDOOR PURSUITS

BIRDING   Bonaire is home to 190 bird species, including lora parrots and flamingos. **Sand Dollar Dive & Photo,** Kaya Gober-nador N. Debrot 77 (© **599/717-5433**), offers trips to Washing-ton-Slagbaai National Park's bird havens for $45.

FISHING   Accessibility, calm waters, and abundant fish make Bonaire an attractive fishing destination. The catch varies by season but includes marlin, sailfish, dorado, wahoo, amberjack, yellowfin, and bonito. **Big Game Sportfishing,** Kaya Warawara 3 (© **599/717-6500**), **Piscatur Fishing,** Kaya J. Pop 3 (© **599/717-8774**), and **Multifish Charters,** Kaya Pikuditu 8 (© **599/717-7033**), offer deep-sea, reef, and bonefishing options. A half-day charter with up to six people runs between $250 and $350; a full day is $425 to $500.

HIKING   **Washington-Slagbaai National Park**'s terrain is inter-esting and varied. Climbs up the steepest hills are rewarded with panoramic views, while cliffside beaches with crashing waves make ideal picnic sites.

KAYAKING   While kayaking through the mangroves of Lac Bay, take time to observe the baby fish and bizarrely shaped tree roots. Bring protection from the sun and the ravenous mosquitoes. Guided trips and kayak rentals are available from **Discover Bonaire,** Kaya Gobernador N. Debrot 79 (© **599/717-5252**), and, in Sorobon, from **Jibe City** (© **599/717-5233**). A half-day guided tour through the mangroves is $45. Half-day kayak rental alone is $20, $25 for a two-seater.

MOUNTAIN BIKING   Explore Bonaire's scenery on its 290km (180 miles) of trails and dirt roads. **Cycle Bonaire,** Kaya L. D. Gerharts 11D (© **599/717-7558**), rents 21-speed mountain bikes ($15–$20) and arranges half- ($40) and full-day ($55) excursions.

TENNIS   Several hotels have courts lit for night play, but the best facilities are at **Harbour Village Bonaire,** Kaya Gobernador N. Debrot (© **599/717-7500**), which offers clinics, custom racquet services, and a resident pro. Courts are $15 an hour; a 1-hour private lesson is $50.

WINDSURFING   Shallow waters, steady breezes, and protection from choppy waters make Lac Bay perfect for beginners and pros. Sorobon has two equipment-rental centers: **Jibe City** (© **599/717-5233**) and **Bonaire Windsurf Place** (© **599/717-2288**). Boards and sails are $45 for half a day, $60 for a full day. Beginner lessons are $45, including equipment.

5 Exploring the Island

Bonaire has several large, full-service tour operators, including **Discover Bonaire,** Kaya Gobernador N. Debrot 79 (© **599/717-5252**), **Baranka Tours,** Kaya Gobernador N. Debrot 79A (© **599/717-2200**), and **Bonaire Tours,** Kaya L. D. Gerharts 22 (© **599/717-8778**). In addition to island tours, each conducts snorkeling, fishing, kayaking, mountain-biking, sailing, nature, and windsurfing excursions. Options vary from day to day.

KRALENDIJK

You can walk the length of sleepy Kralendijk in less than half an hour. Because Bonaire has always been off the beaten track, highlights are modest and few. Stroll along the seafront, with its views and restaurants, and along Kaya Grandi, the major shopping district. Just south of the dock, tiny Fort Oranje boasts a cannon dating from the time of Napoléon. The town has some charming Dutch Caribbean architecture—gabled roofs painted ochre and terra cotta. If you're up early, visit the waterfront food market.

NORTH OF KRALENDIJK

The coastal road north of Kralendijk is one of the most beautiful in the Antilles. Turquoise, azure, and cobalt waters stretch to the horizon on the left, while pink and black coral cliffs loom on the right. Towering cacti, intimate coastal coves, strange rock formations, and panoramic vistas add to the beauty.

Just north of Kralendijk, **Barcadera** is an old cave once used to trap goats. Take the stone steps down to the cave and examine the stalactites. Farther north, just past the Radio Nederland towers, **1,000 Steps Beach** offers picturesque coves, craggy coastline, and tropical waters of changing hues.

Turn right on Kaya Karpata for **Rincon,** the island's original Spanish settlement. Today, the quiet village is home to Bonaire's oldest church—a handsome ochre-and-white structure—and **Prisca's,** on Kaya Komkomber, the island's best ice cream shop.

On the way back to Kralendijk, take the road along the northeast coast to **Onima,** the site of 500-year-old Caiquetio Indian petroglyphs.

Make your last stop at the home of **Sherman Gibbs,** Kaminda Tras di Montaña, the road back to Kralendijk. Sherman combines old detergent bottles, boat motors, buoys, car seats, and just about anything else to create an outsider-art fantasyland.

WASHINGTON-SLAGBAAI NATIONAL PARK

Washington-Slagbaai National Park ✦ (✆ 599/717-8444) occupies the island's northern tip. Formerly aloe plantations, the 13,500-acre reserve showcases Bonaire's geology, animals, and vegetation. Residents include 190 bird species, thousands of organ-pipe and prickly-pear cacti, wild goats, donkeys, flamingos, and lizards. The scenery includes stark hills, quiet beaches, and wave-battered cliffs. Take either the 24km (15-mile) or the 35km (22-mile) track around the park. Admission is $10 for adults, $2 for children under 15. The park is open from 8am to 5pm daily except for major holidays; enter before 3pm. Guide booklets, maps, and a small museum are at the gate. The unpaved roads are well marked and safe, but rugged; Jeeps trump small cars.

Just past the gate, the **Salina Mathijs** salt flat attracts flamingos during the rainy season. Beyond the salt flat on the road to the right, **Boca Chikitu**'s cove, sand dunes, and crashing waves provide a splendid seascape. A few miles farther up the coast, **Boca Cocolishi,** a black-sand beach, is perfect for a private picnic, and the calm, shallow basin is perfect for close-to-shore snorkeling.

Back along the main road, **Boca Bartol**'s bay is full of elkhorn coral, sea fans, and reef fish. Nearby **Poosdi Mangel,** a popular watering hole, is good for twilight birding, while the remote reef of

Wajaca harbors sea turtles, octopuses, and triggerfish. Immediately inland, 235m (784-ft.) **Mount Brandaris** is Bonaire's highest peak. At its foot, **Bronswinkel Well** attracts pigeons and parakeets.

SOUTH OF KRALENDIJK

Just south of town, dazzlingly bright **salt pyramids** dominate the horizon. Looking more like snowdrifts than sodium mounds, they're the product of the nearby salt pans.

Farther from the road, saltworks serve as a **flamingo sanctuary.** Bonaire is one of the world's few nesting places for pink flamingos, and the island's spring flamingo population swells to 10,000. Because the birds are wary of humans, the sanctuary is off-limits, but from the road you can see the birds feeding in the briny pink and purple waters.

At the island's southern tip, restored **slave huts** recall the island's slave past. Each hut, no bigger than a large doghouse, provided nighttime shelter for African slaves brought over by the Dutch West Indies Company.

Near the island's southern tip, **Willemstoren Lighthouse** was built in 1837. It's fully automated today and closed to visitors, but is classically picturesque.

A few minutes up the east coast, **Lac Bay**'s shallow water and steady breezes are ideal for windsurfing. Deep inside the lagoon, mangrove trees with dramatic roots lunge from the water.

6 Shopping

Aruba has more stores and better prices than Bonaire, but dive-related items such as dive watches, underwater cameras, and marine-themed jewelry are abundant. Most shops are on Kaya Grandi.

For Tag-Heuer dive watches, Cuban cigars, porcelain, and crystal, try **Littman Jewelers,** Kaya Grandi 33 (© 599/717-8160). **Atlantis,** across the street at Kaya Grandi 32B (© 599/717-7730), has a similar selection of jewelry and watches. In **Harborside Mall, Little Holland** (© 599/717-5670) has silk neckties, menswear, blue Delft porcelain, and Cuban cigars. **Sparky's** (© 599/717-5288), in the same mall, carries perfume and other cosmetics.

Benetton, Kaya Grandi 49 (© 599/717-5107), has smart men's and women's casual wear. For batik shirts, pareos, bathing suits, or souvenir T-shirts, try **Boutique Vita,** Kaya Grandi 16 (© 599/717-8438), or **Bye-Bye Bonaire,** Harborside Mall (© 599/717-7578). The best place for dressier women's clothing is **The Shop at Harbour Village,** Kaya Gobernador N. Debrot 72 (© 599/717-7500).

Cultimara Supermarket, Kaya L. D. Gerharts 13 (℃ **599/717-8278**), stocks Dutch cheeses and chocolates, fresh baked goods, and products from the Caribbean, Europe, South America, and the United States.

7 Bonaire After Dark

The **Divi Flamingo Beach Resort & Casino,** J. A. Abraham Boulevard 40 (℃ **599/7-8285**), offers blackjack, roulette, poker, wheel of fortune, video games, and slot machines, Monday to Saturday from 8pm to 2am. The larger and more animated **Plaza Resort Bonaire Casino,** J. A. Abraham Blvd. 80 (℃ **599/717-2500**), is open daily from 8pm to 4am.

Karel's Beach Bar, on the waterfront (℃ **599/717-8434**), features high ceilings and sea breezes. Sit at the long bar with the island's dive professionals, or take a table overlooking the surf. Local bands entertain on weekends.

City Cafe, Kaya Isla Riba 3 (no phone), the island's funkiest bar, is painted electric blue, magenta, and banana. This popular hangout has a no-holds-barred vibe.

Slide shows of Bonaire's underwater treasures provide entertainment for both divers and nondivers. The best shows are at **Captain Don's Habitat** (℃ **599/717-8290;** see "Diving & Snorkeling," earlier in this chapter) on Thursday from 7 to 8:30pm.

Index

See also Accommodations and Restaurant indexes below.

Restaurants

FROMMER'S® COMPLETE TRAVEL GUIDES

Alaska
Alaska Cruises & Ports of Call
Amsterdam
Argentina & Chile
Arizona
Atlanta
Australia
Austria
Bahamas
Barcelona, Madrid & Seville
Beijing
Belgium, Holland & Luxembourg
Bermuda
Boston
Brazil
British Columbia & the Canadian Rockies
Brussels & Bruges
Budapest & the Best of Hungary
California
Canada
Cancún, Cozumel & the Yucatán
Cape Cod, Nantucket & Martha's Vineyard
Caribbean
Caribbean Cruises & Ports of Call
Caribbean Ports of Call
Carolinas & Georgia
Chicago
China
Colorado
Costa Rica
Cuba
Denmark
Denver, Boulder & Colorado Springs
England
Europe
European Cruises & Ports of Call

Florida
France
Germany
Great Britain
Greece
Greek Islands
Hawaii
Hong Kong
Honolulu, Waikiki & Oahu
Ireland
Israel
Italy
Jamaica
Japan
Las Vegas
London
Los Angeles
Maryland & Delaware
Maui
Mexico
Montana & Wyoming
Montréal & Québec City
Munich & the Bavarian Alps
Nashville & Memphis
New England
New Mexico
New Orleans
New York City
New Zealand
Northern Italy
Norway
Nova Scotia, New Brunswick & Prince Edward Island
Oregon
Paris
Peru
Philadelphia & the Amish Country
Portugal

Prague & the Best of the Czech Republic
Provence & the Riviera
Puerto Rico
Rome
San Antonio & Austin
San Diego
San Francisco
Santa Fe, Taos & Albuquerque
Scandinavia
Scotland
Seattle & Portland
Shanghai
Sicily
Singapore & Malaysia
South Africa
South America
South Florida
South Pacific
Southeast Asia
Spain
Sweden
Switzerland
Texas
Thailand
Tokyo
Toronto
Tuscany & Umbria
USA
Utah
Vancouver & Victoria
Vermont, New Hampshire & Maine
Vienna & the Danube Valley
Virgin Islands
Virginia
Walt Disney World® & Orlando
Washington, D.C.
Washington State

FROMMER'S® DOLLAR-A-DAY GUIDES

Australia from $50 a Day
California from $70 a Day
England from $75 a Day
Europe from $70 a Day
Florida from $70 a Day
Hawaii from $80 a Day

Ireland from $60 a Day
Italy from $70 a Day
London from $85 a Day
New York from $90 a Day
Paris from $80 a Day

San Francisco from $70 a Day
Washington, D.C. from $80 a Day
Portable London from $85 a Day
Portable New York City from $90 a Day

FROMMER'S® PORTABLE GUIDES

Acapulco, Ixtapa & Zihuatanejo
Amsterdam
Aruba
Australia's Great Barrier Reef
Bahamas
Berlin
Big Island of Hawaii
Boston
California Wine Country
Cancún
Cayman Islands
Charleston
Chicago
Disneyland®
Dublin
Florence

Frankfurt
Hong Kong
Houston
Las Vegas
Las Vegas for Non-Gamblers
London
Los Angeles
Los Cabos & Baja
Maine Coast
Maui
Miami
Nantucket & Martha's Vineyard
New Orleans
New York City
Paris
Phoenix & Scottsdale

Portland
Puerto Rico
Puerto Vallarta, Manzanillo & Guadalajara
Rio de Janeiro
San Diego
San Francisco
Savannah
Seattle
Sydney
Tampa & St. Petersburg
Vancouver
Venice
Virgin Islands
Washington, D.C.

FROMMER'S® NATIONAL PARK GUIDES

Banff & Jasper
Family Vacations in the National Parks

Grand Canyon
National Parks of the American West
Rocky Mountain

Yellowstone & Grand Teton
Yosemite & Sequoia/Kings Canyon
Zion & Bryce Canyon

FROMMER'S® MEMORABLE WALKS

Chicago
London

New York
Paris

San Francisco

FROMMER'S® WITH KIDS GUIDES

Chicago
Las Vegas
New York City

Ottawa
San Francisco
Toronto

Vancouver
Washington, D.C.

SUZY GERSHMAN'S BORN TO SHOP GUIDES

Born to Shop: France
Born to Shop: Hong Kong,
  Shanghai & Beijing

Born to Shop: Italy
Born to Shop: London

Born to Shop: New York
Born to Shop: Paris

FROMMER'S® IRREVERENT GUIDES

Amsterdam
Boston
Chicago
Las Vegas
London

Los Angeles
Manhattan
New Orleans
Paris
Rome

San Francisco
Seattle & Portland
Vancouver
Walt Disney World®
Washington, D.C.

FROMMER'S® BEST-LOVED DRIVING TOURS

Britain
California
Florida
France

Germany
Ireland
Italy
New England

Northern Italy
Scotland
Spain
Tuscany & Umbria

HANGING OUT™ GUIDES

Hanging Out in England
Hanging Out in Europe

Hanging Out in France
Hanging Out in Ireland

Hanging Out in Italy
Hanging Out in Spain

THE UNOFFICIAL GUIDES®

Bed & Breakfasts and Country
  Inns in:
  California
  Great Lakes States
  Mid-Atlantic
  New England
  Northwest
  Rockies
  Southeast
  Southwest
Best RV & Tent Campgrounds in:
  California & the West
  Florida & the Southeast
  Great Lakes States
  Mid-Atlantic
  Northeast
  Northwest & Central Plains

Southwest & South Central
  Plains
  U.S.A.
Beyond Disney
Branson, Missouri
California with Kids
Central Italy
Chicago
Cruises
Disneyland®
Florida with Kids
Golf Vacations in the Eastern U.S.
Great Smoky & Blue Ridge Region
Inside Disney
Hawaii
Las Vegas
London
Maui

Mexio's Best Beach Resorts
Mid-Atlantic with Kids
Mini Las Vegas
Mini-Mickey
New England & New York with
  Kids
New Orleans
New York City
Paris
San Francisco
Skiing & Snowboarding in the West
Southeast with Kids
Walt Disney World®
Walt Disney World® for
  Grown-ups
Walt Disney World® with Kids
Washington, D.C.
World's Best Diving Vacations

SPECIAL-INTEREST TITLES

Frommer's Adventure Guide to Australia &
  New Zealand
Frommer's Adventure Guide to Central America
Frommer's Adventure Guide to India & Pakistan
Frommer's Adventure Guide to South America
Frommer's Adventure Guide to Southeast Asia
Frommer's Adventure Guide to Southern Africa
Frommer's Britain's Best Bed & Breakfasts and
  Country Inns
Frommer's Caribbean Hideaways
Frommer's Exploring America by RV
Frommer's Fly Safe, Fly Smart

Frommer's France's Best Bed & Breakfasts and
  Country Inns
Frommer's Gay & Lesbian Europe
Frommer's Italy's Best Bed & Breakfasts and
  Country Inns
Frommer's Road Atlas Britain
Frommer's Road Atlas Europe
Frommer's Road Atlas France
The New York Times' Guide to Unforgettable
  Weekends
Places Rated Almanac
Retirement Places Rated
Rome Past & Present